A HAIR PAST A FRECKLE

A LARRIKIN LIFE IN FOLKLORE, MUSIC & MAYHEM

WARREN FAHEY

BODGIE PRODUCTIONS

Copyright © 2024 by Warren Fahey - Bodgie Productions

All rights reserved.

No part of this book may be reproduced in any form or by any electronic or mechanical means, including information storage and retrieval systems, without written permission from the author, except for the use of brief quotations in a book review.

Contact bodgieproductions@gmail.com

Cover art: richard@seriousbusiness.com.au

Warren Fahey's website of Australian history, folklore & music

www.warrenfahey.com.au

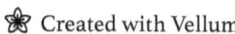 Created with Vellum

1

THE 'YIDS' AND THE 'TYKES'

I feel like I haven't 'grown up' yet. Surely, I am far too young to write a memoir, and despite getting close to knocking on the door of eighty, I feel like I am in my midlife. Is this a crisis? Possibly. Yet, if I don't write the darned thing now, I fear it will be too late, much too late, to tackle in my eighties when I hope I will feel like I am in my fifties with fewer brain cells. Anyway, the brain is a liar, a big fat fibber; it makes us believe what we want to believe, and that, my friends, can be very selective. It's time, and the time is a hair past a freckle!

Age often brings regrets, and I regret not keeping a diary. I have kept calendars, passports and boxes of documents relating to travel, projects, contracts and other aspects of my life. Fortunately, I have a good memory - the diary we all carry. My head is crammed with knowledge, probably useless unless you want to know about curious Australian history, music trivia, song words, recipes, travel stories, long-forgotten traditions and a bagatelle of other nonsense. So, with some trepidation, I am setting out on a personal adventure to tell some of my life stories.

I am very much my father's son. I inherited his stoicism. In the mid-nineteen-sixties, I tape-recorded my father, George Fahey, and asked him about his time in WW2. I knew he had been a sergeant major in the Australian Army and that he marched every ANZAC Day, but by then, I was in my twenties, a radical thinker and defiantly anti-war. I recorded some of his family songs, but he was reluctant to speak about his war service. George was a thinker and a sensitive soul with a soft rolling Australian voice that refused to give up his Irish family heritage. He was first generation Irish-Australian, but like many of his generation, his accent was influenced by family and friends, unlike today, where it is influenced by popular entertainment. Those early forms of Australian speech have essentially disappeared to make our present homogenous language. Dad was never open about his wartime experience other than to say I was conceived near the war's end in 1945. I just scraped in as a 'baby boomer' by a few days, having appeared on the 3rd of January 1946.

George served in Papua New Guinea and was involved in what was then called the Army's 'physical education program'. He was part of the medical unit and often told me about the kindness of the 'fuzzy-wuzzy angels', the volunteer local indigenous people who carried the wounded and assisted in so many other everyday areas of an ugly war on our northern doorstep.

Dad also told me about conscientious objectors, those who refused to go to war and, as targets of public anger, intended to humiliate them, were given white feathers that appeared anonymously by mail or dropped in the letterbox. I assume that's where the term 'chicken' originated, implying cowardice. Dad didn't like war and instilled in me the notion of pacifism. I liked how post-WW2 pacifists, myself included, reinterpreted the white feather as a peace symbol.

Many years later, as the first publisher of Eric Bogle's song catalogue, particularly 'And The Band Played Waltzing Matilda' and 'No Man's Land', the futility of war became a familiar reminder.

Dad (far right) and his PNG mates WW2

Like many returned soldiers, Dad had a tin box containing his various medals, official service and discharge cards and a few yellowing photographs. He carried a much deeper reminder on his body, vicious skin cancers that resulted in years of treatment at Concord Repatriation Hospital. Many soldiers believed that irritating tropical ulcers, caused mainly by mosquito bites, could be cured by applying methylated spirits to the sore and then letting it dry in the tropical sun. It was an open invitation for melanomas. Dad had fair Irish skin, including light reddish hair, placing him in the number one candidate zone. I remember the hundreds of visits to Concord - my mother always solid - although she was no doubt struggling with fear - as we hoped for good news and Dad's all-clear release. Dad was stoic, ever the optimist on the outside, but no doubt harboured fears. The Repat treatments continued for most of his life, including one horrific spell where the hospital used a new 'treatment' of cobalt ray to burn resistant cancer. Unfortunately, treating a spot on the bridge of his nose, they also burned out his tear ducts, which advanced his glaucoma, a condition I have inherited. In the end, in his early sixties, certainly much younger than I am as I write this, he was forced to retire and become homebound. He remained stoic.

In 2010, I filmed my uncle, Mossy Phillips, my mother's eldest brother, at the Montefiore Home at Hunters Hill. Mossy was 93 and had lost both legs, but not his infectious joy for life and love for family. I had done a concert at the home a few months earlier where I had sung some of the songs and ditties I had learnt off Mossy and returned in early 2011 with my older sister Zandra, always Mossy's favourite niece, and a small camera team. I wanted to record some of his memories, old family songs, and his playing the piano and ukulele. I thought I knew a fair bit about my family history, but you could have knocked me over with a feather when Mossy told us that my father had been a conscientious objector. He refused to be placed in any situation where he would have to kill another man; however, he said, "I'll do anything else to serve, including latrine duty." He was sent to the training camp at Goulburn, and despite having no medical experience, he was positioned in the medical unit. Not long in Papua New Guinea, he was promoted to Medical Quartermaster.

Sgt Major Fahey, PNG, WW2

Mossy had been very close to George and held him in awe as the one who morally led the family. Maybe it was because Dad loved my mother and, unusual for the time, had been determined to marry Mossy's eldest sister and into a poor Jewish family. Dad always said the 'tykes', a peculiarly unflattering Australian reference to Irish Catholics, and 'yids', an equally offensive nickname from the Jewish Yiddish, were the ideal family combo. He also said religion, government and busybodies had no place in love. It was a lifelong union.

I cannot consider my own life without telling the stories of my parent's lives. I am very much a proud product of both their families and, I suspect, the fact that my father, George Patrick, was the eldest son of 16 children to Mary and John Fahey, and my mother, Deborah, the eldest of 9 children from Polly and Sid Phillips, they were always seen as the family leaders. My parents were the quasi patriarch and matriarch - the sensible guardians of both families prepared for what would inevitably be 'thick and thin'.

George and Deborah 'Debbie' Fahey dressed to the nines!

The Fahey and Phillips families had one thing in common: they didn't have a cracker between them. The Fahey's, good Irish catholic breeders, never had enough to satisfy hunger but always enough for Granny Marie and eldest daughter, Kathleen, to drop a few coins onto the church's plate every Sunday. My memories of Grandma Fahey were of a frail, tiny woman with a life of hardship stamped on her brow. She smelled of lavender and sunlight soap. My father, ever the dutiful son, visited every week and always presented me with her gift of a holy picture card or yet another brown scapular to tie around my neck.

Grandfather John 'Jack' Fahey was born in Balmain in 1875, and granny Marie Moore was born in the small NSW town of Dalton in 1878. Her father was a teacher in nearby Gunning. Jack and Marie were married in 1898. Marie was twenty. Dad always said his mother went to Mass every single day of her life. I wish I had spent more time with her, but my visits to their little house on Balmain Road,

Leichhardt, were almost exclusively reserved for time in Granddad's shed. It was a wonderland, and I can still see, smell and hear it as I write these notes. John Fahey, a wire worker by trade, was a short man with a fire in his belly. His beard was brown from Champion ready-rubbed tobacco and strong china tea. He had what I later recognised as a stain known as 'Jack the Painter', a permanent brown tea stain around the face. Jack also liked a drink and, more often than not, too much at the local Bald Faced Stag Hotel at the end of the street on Parramatta Road. I liked hanging around the footpath waiting for him because the pub was next door to the Leichhardt Stadium - one of the old-time wrestling and boxing stadiums. The stadium screamed memories and still had old, tattered posters on the wall, and if I was lucky, I could sneak in and watch training sessions. In the thirties, forties and fifties, competitive fighting was a massive sport with its own legal and illegal gambling support system. Years later, the great carrier of Australian folk songs, Sally Sloane, told me how she wrestled at the Leichhardt Stadium during the Great Depression. "I was a good fighter, and after a fight, the audience would throw coins, five and sixpenny pieces, up on the ring. We could make good money." The stadium eventually became a ten-pin bowling alley.

Marie & John 'Jack' Fahey

John Fahey's shed was at the rear of the tiny duplex cottage. It seemed very big to me, and my favourite fun was turning the slow grindstone, which produced a continual modulated hum. Jack was a Jack-of-all-trades; he would have had to have been and had tools to repair just about anything. He had shoe lasts, chimney sweeping apparatus, all manner of hammers, tiles, bits of wood, rubber and old tobacco tins of tacks, nails, rubber seals and whatever. Pop Fahey had what he called "a lot of dooverlackies' which he stored along with his 'whatchamacallit' and the 'thingamajig'. He seemed to be constantly rolling his cigarettes and to have a fag end in his mouth. As he worked, he inevitably sang some old ditty. If that wasn't enough, the radio was always broadcasting parliament. Above the hammering, grinding, radio and singing came the occasional curse - "Bugger that Pig Iron Bob". "Black Jack McEwen - bah! wouldn't know what work is!" he would declare. He disliked the conservative and divisive catholic commentator B. A. Santamaria, who he despised as a 'toady scab' for his part in splitting the Labor Party ranks, which eventually led to the formation of the Democratic Labor Party. He maintained an even longer and louder hatred for Labor renegade socialist and unionist turned conservative William 'Billy' Hughes. My father, George, sang one ditty he had from his father, referring to Billy Hughes door-knocking in their electorate.

Knock, Knock,
Who's that knocking on the door?
If it's Billy Hughes and his wife,
We will chase them with a knife,
And they won't come knocking any more.

I liked playing with the shoe last, rubber strips and glue pots in the shed. Three lasts of different sizes were used to mend the family shoes (when the kids had shoes!). The Fahey's were too poor to be able to afford new shoes or the luxury of a bootmaker. Dad inherited the last, which he used to mend *our* shoes. Considering Grandad's smoking and drinking and Granny's seemingly never-ending pregnancies, it is somewhat surprising they both lived long lives. Marie Fahey died in 1967 at 89, and John (Jack) Fahey a year later at 93.

Fahey family gathering circa 1949 at Nancy and Alfred Fahey's wedding. (I'm the wee lad in the bottom right-hand corner with dad's hand across my chest. Mom is on the far right with the embroidery top.

My father voted ALP all his life, and my mother, unusually defiant, never revealed her vote. She would always say it was her hard-earned prerogative and a secret vote. For all we knew, she could have scribbled 'bananas' or something on the voting forms. I quite enjoyed the mystery of not knowing and the surprising fact that my father never made a fuss about it.

Dad's Labor beliefs certainly passed to me, and we would have healthy political discussions whenever possible. The more we talked, the more he revealed. He had been a socialist in his youth, even flirting with communism, but, like many, abandoned those ideals when the Russian Bear invaded its neighbours. He was a big supporter of Arthur Caldwell, leader of the ALP. Still, he referred to him as 'Cocky Caldwell,' referencing the man's unfortunate facial features and manner of speech, "A good man, but Cocky will never be prime minister with a moosh like that." Like his father, Dad despised Prime Minister Robert Menzies, berating his continual 'Reds under the beds' campaigning and never forgetting his 'Pig Iron Bob' legacy during the build-up to WW2. In 1989, I wrote The Balls of Bob

Menzies, a book that tracked the history and parodies of twentieth-century political and social change. I dedicated the book to my father and quoted one of his most boisterous songs, the book's title.

> The balls of Bob Menzies are wrinkled and crinkled,
>
> Curvaceous and spacious as the dome of St. Paul's,
>
> The crowds they all muster to gaze at that cluster;
>
> They stand and stare at that wondrous pair
>
> Of Bob Menzies' balls -
>
> Balls, balls, balls, balls
>
> Balls, balls, balls, balls,
>
> Bob Menzies' balls.

The book was a decent seller; however, my publisher, Angus & Robertson, reported having a few problems with booksellers - some elderly female customers were embarrassed to approach the sales desk to ask, "Where can I find 'The Balls of Bob Menzies?". I can imagine the snide response, "You'll probably have to ask Dame Patti." The revised edition adding the 'greedy nineties', edited by Katharine Brisbane and published by Currency Press in 2000, was titled *Ratbags & Rabblerousers*. Its publication was given an appropriately rowdy launch. We took over the corner of Hyde Park where Liverpool and Elizabeth Streets meet, turned it into Speaker's Corner, and celebrated the book with two feisty writers worthy of the book's title - Bob Ellis and Piers Ackerman. John Dengate, the legendary satirist, sang some of his biting political parodies.

In 2011, interviewing Mossy, I was floored when he related that my grandfather, John Fahey, was a full-time union organiser for the Seaman's Union. This would have been in the first decade of the twentieth century when bitter struggles were commonplace in the maritime industry. I suspect this also meant John had been a socialist, as the Seamen's Union held very close ties to the emerging Left. Socialism at this stage was not necessarily a dirty word. It was akin to the ideals of worker rights of early international socialism, the emerging International Workers of the World (IWW), and its cry of

One Big Union. Socialist dreams were idealistic from necessity. He could not have been a communist, as the Communist Party of Australia wasn't established until 1920. I still can't imagine how Granny, Pop Fahey, their sixteen children, and dad's sister Kathleen's son, Colin, all lived in the one tiny duplex house. Dad, the eldest, was born there in 1910, and Mary and John died there in their late nineties. Pop Fahey smoked like a chimney, drank like a fish, bred like a rabbit and lived until 93. My father recalled his siblings going to Leichhardt Public School, a rather draconian institution, and going through the garbage bins at lunchtime to find food scraps.

In 1967, Dad scribbled out a note with the names and ages of each of his siblings as of that year: Eileen Ann, 69, Mabel deceased; Madeline Ann, 65, Thomas deceased; Kathleen Mary, 62, John deceased, Veronica 60, Winifred Mary 59, George Francis 57, Mary Patricia 55, William Joseph 52, Alfred Francis 52, Francis deceased, Minnie Joanna 48, Leslie deceased.

MY MOTHER WAS BORN in London's east end. Her parents, my grandparents, were Mary 'Polly' Solomons and Sidney 'Sid' Phillips. Both families originally came from Holland in the nineteenth century. Sid had been a cook in the British Army, and Polly's family were 'travellers' and costermongers near Bow Bells. Like many Jews, they skedaddled out of Europe after WWI. Sid, Polly, my mother Deborah, and her brother, Moses 'Mossy', arrived in Sydney in 1920. Mom was eight. They had no money and no contacts. They weren't religious Jews, so no support was forthcoming from the Jewish aid organisations. I asked Mossy, the eldest son, where the family had lived in the eastern suburbs. He reckoned they had lived in "over one hundred different places, always one step in front of the landlord". He recalled my mother, as the eldest daughter and himself being told to "collect the babies" as the family did their familiar midnight flit to avoid the rent collectors.

Sid and Polly Phillips.

To say they were dirt poor would be an understatement, but they managed to survive. Eventually, their east-ender history proved helpful, and they were given one of the first sanctioned street vendor barrow licenses in Sydney. Sid's cart was situated on Liverpool Street in front of the fashionable Mark Foy's department store, and they sold fruit and flowers. Mossy told of how the eldest Phillips kids were despatched every morning at 4 am to walk from 122 Hastings Parade, Bondi, to the wealthy suburbs of Double Bay, Bellevue Hill, Rose Bay and Darling Point to 'harvest' flowers. These stolen flowers were then fashioned into posies and comprised most of the 'stock' sold from the barrow.

122 Hastings Parade, Bondi, home to 16 people.

My sister, Zandra, eight years older than me, remembers our newly married parents living in a rented semi-detached house in Spring Street, Abbotsford. She was born there, where the family lived before Dad went to war.

Before being sent to the Goulburn Training Camp, George was employed at a box factory and, apparently, during the Depression, did relief work in building the Abbotsford Public Swimming Baths.

After Dad had enlisted in the army, my mother, Deborah, and her sister, Lilly, took over a small corner grocery store on the Great North Road, Abbotsford. Zandra recalls that money was very short and that

Deb, Lilly, and baby Zandra lived over the shop. Lilly's husband, Bill, had also gone off to war. "Mom and Aunty Lilly, still in their early twenties, used to measure out things like sugar, flour, salt, etc. and always got the giggles when they had to bag the pepper. They made ice blocks out of milk and strawberry essence." Deb delivered the groceries on a bicycle with my young sister, Zandra, about three years old, hanging on the back seat. "The living quarters upstairs were sparse without much furniture, and there was no table, so we always ate 'picnic style'. I remember they used to put the radio on and dance every night."

Deborah and Polly Phillips at Bondi Beach not long after they arrived from England.

Zandra continues, "There was a tram stop out the front of the shop, and we used to visit both grandparents, the Fahey's and the Phillips', regularly. I remember returning home from the Phillips' at Bondi one night, and Polly had given Mom two eggs - a delicacy. Mom had put the eggs down her blouse to protect them, and all of a sudden, the tram lurched, and Mom, who was standing, fell against the side and broke the two eggs. She burst into tears, probably at the thought of me not getting the treat. I remember looking at the gooey mess."

The Phillips were living at 122 Hastings Parade, Bondi. Grandma Polly, Moss (22), Charlie (16), Lou (14), Clive (5). Jack, aged 20, had gone to war. Also living in the house was an English friend of Polly's called Hardy, plus his two daughters, Dotty and Thelma. The Abbotsford shop was becoming too difficult, so my mother, her sister Lilly and Zandra also moved into Bondi. Twelve people plus, when on leave, Uncle Bill Lindsay, Mom's brother Jack Phillips and Dad. Sixteen people almost made the three-bedroom house a village. Polly had one bedroom, Hardy shared one with his two daughters, and Auntie Lilly, Mom and Zandra shared the third bedroom. All the others slept on stretchers on the verandah. My mother would have been 28 then, and Zandra about four or five. Zandra thinks I was probably conceived in this house - what was one more in such a crowded house!

I was always Nana Polly's favourite and visited her daily when we lived in the Sydney suburb of Eastlakes (the second time). She and Sid lived in a granny flat behind Mossy and his wife Jean's place, across the road from their corner store.

I would arrive after school to the same scenario. Polly would be knitting one of her crochet creations - sofa covers, shawls, headwear, etc. - and sitting at the table with playing cards ready. Sid would usually be snoring heavily in another corner. He amazed me because he could sleep with his head under a heavy blanket, something I have never been able to do. Polly would beckon me in, put down the knitting, and start shuffling the cards. We played two-pack 16-card Polish rummy - quite a fistful for a young boy's hand - or poker. After a few games, she would walk over to Sid, still snoring like a train, extract his money roll; he always seemed to have a roll of notes, peel off a handful, which she put down her ample bosom, hand me a ten-shilling note, then proceeded to shake Sid violently encouraging him to wake up and join the game. I suspect he was already awake, knew the routine, and played along.

It seemed as if nearly all the Phillips family gambled. Polly and Sid loved their cards, and Nana even dared to take me to a professional, no doubt illegal, card joint in Kellett Street, Kings Cross, more than a few times. I went for the free chicken sandwiches and the excitement of going out with this larger-than-life woman everyone seemed to know and love. We stopped going after someone got murdered at the club.

There was singing, dancing, and cards whenever the Phillips family got together. Polly could also do card tricks. Sid followed the races, and the house was full of piano playing and the droning voice of radio race coverage. At one stage, I thought race broadcaster Ken Howard lived in the spare room. The races used to drive me nuts, and

I still run whenever I hear race broadcasts. Thankfully, I didn't inherit any gambling genes.

A gathering of the Phillips clan at Lou's wedding.

Sid was bald as a badger, which he passed on to all the males of our family, and, alas, I followed my mother's side since my father had a full head of wavy hair. Polly had the most extraordinarily long hair, which she washed in beer. Her hair fascinated me as I watched her comb the long tresses and weave complicated plaits she piled on her head. It looked something like a pile of sausages wrapped around her head. She held it together with elaborate, large, black decorative pins. Although short, Polly had more than an ample bosom - they were bazookas! She usually wore crocheted tops and sometimes a matching tam o'shanter hat. She was a short woman but never short of a conversation. Polly was a real charmer and storyteller.

I remember arriving at her place one day; they were living above a butcher shop on Anzac Parade, Kensington, and I was taken back to see two Catholic nuns sipping mugs of tea and laughing their heads off. The good sisters had been door-knocking for some local cause, and Polly, ever-keen for a chat, had invited them in. They had been there for over three hours!

After Sid gave up the barrow, he started selling stationery at Paddy's Market in the Haymarket. The old Sydney market was lively in those days, and I loved joining him whenever I could, despite the fact he got there at 4 am. He had his permanent spot and surrounded himself with pencils, biros, various-sized paper pads, envelopes, etc.

But this wasn't his real job. Sid knew everyone, and everyone knew Sid. I was never sure if he was operating as an illegal betting service giving or getting race tips, but I do know this was his main business. After the market closed, he would be off to the track, preferably Randwick, and then home to Snoresville.

Food was always an important part of the Phillips family life, but I don't recall Polly ever boiling as much as an egg. My sister recalled Polly as "...a dreadful cook. During the war years, there were a lot of mouths to feed and not a lot of money. They must have pooled any army allowances, and Lilly worked in a shop somewhere because she would sometimes bring home a stale cake, which was a real treat. Polly served up chops or sausages, mashed potatoes and gravy so often that I still remember the smell. She made the gravy in the morning and would remove the skin in the evening."

Sid was the cook in the family and a good one at that. His specialities were Jewish recipes, and I loved watching him prepare giant jars of pickled dill cucumbers, sliced tomatoes in vinegar and brown sugar, and making horseradish sauces (I was chief grater) and, on Fridays, great piles of beautifully cooked fish. After he had fried the fish, he used the same fishy oil to make the thinnest pancakes imaginable, sprinkled with sugar, then rolled and splashed with lemon juice. They were delicious. Another of Sid's specialities was the best-tasting 'Jewish penicillin' I had ever eaten. He called it 'lokshen soup' because of the wiggly little egg noodles. He boiled up the toughest old boiler fowls and occasionally a rooster, but they simmered for hours and were infused with the flavour of celery, peppercorns and parsley. One morning, I was watching him finish up the process when I asked what he was using to strain the 'muck' from the chicken soup. "Polly's old stockings." came the reply. My mind went spinning. I doubt if Sid ever bought any food - it was all swapped for racing tips at the markets.

The one thing Polly did prepare, as the old song goes, 'Polly put the kettle on, and we'll all have tea' (she always sang the song as she made the tea). We ate large Jewish matzo biscuits smothered in butter and honey or Vegemite. This was just about as Jewish as we got -

except for Polly's continual stories about which actor, actress or singer was Jewish. Everyone in films, on vinyl or staring at me from the television, seemed Jewish.

Polly always claimed she had a second sense. A gypsy heritage. She often read my tea leaves and talked about ghosts. One story that stayed with me concerned her son, my uncle Jack, an Air Force gunner. One night during WW2, Polly woke up shouting, "Jack's been shot down, Jack's been shot down." Two days later, the family received news that Jack Phillip's fighter bomber had been shot down precisely when Polly had her vision at 2.10 am. Thankfully, Jack survived the ordeal. The tale was told so many times it's challenging to separate fact from fiction.

Polly was always singing little ditties and old music hall songs. I have never tired of these family heirlooms, and I still carry them in my head and occasionally in my repertoire.

Susie, Susie, sitting in the Chinese shop,
The more she sits, the more she knits,
The more she knits, the more she sits,
Susie, Susie, sitting in the Chinese shop.

(Try saying these six times - I double dare you!)

She sells sea shells down by the seaside

Sister Susie's sewing shirts for soldiers
Such skill at sewing shirts
Our shy young sister Susie shows!

Some soldiers send epistles,
Say they'd sooner sleep in thistles
Than the saucy, soft, short shirts for soldiers sister Susie sews.

One ditty that made me laugh was her reference to American sailors stealing 'our girls' in Kings Cross.

Twinkle twinkle, little star,
Went for a ride in a Yankee car,
What she did I ain't admittin'
But what she's knittin'
Ain't for Britain!

Sid died in August 1970 from a stroke whilst coming home on the bus. Ever the star, Polly made a more dramatic exit three months later. We had several conversations about death, which she didn't seem uncomfortable about, and it usually ended with Polly saying she wanted to go "Just like Marilyn Monroe." I was never too sure exactly how Marilyn went, except she was found dead in a hotel room. When Polly's time came, and I swear this is true, I remember going to see the body. She had made herself up in the usual manner - hair coiled and pinned up, crocheted top, mascara, rouge, lipstick, etc. - with her arms across her chest. She looked very peaceful for a woman who had raised nine children against all the odds and had had what could only be described as a hard but fascinating life. I am convinced a simple note was placed on the piano, no doubt intended for me, inscribed 'just like Marilyn Monroe'.

Mossy was my favourite uncle, mainly because, being a local, I saw so much of him, although all my mother's siblings were extremely close. Mossy's son, Raymond, became a famous cricketer and sports manager. Mossy was also the most musical and interesting. He played stride piano and ukulele, sang like a music hall belter and seemed interested in everything from photography to aviation history. After his wife, Jean Brandon, died, he married again, and both he and his bride, Anne, moved into the Montefiore Aged Home at Hunters Hill. He lost his legs and was confined to a wheelchair but lived until he died in 2011, in his late nineties.

IN 2022, I did an ABC radio interview with Sarah McDonald. I was promoting my latest book, *Dead & Buried: The Curious History of Sydney's Earliest Burial Grounds*, and mentioned that Rookwood

Cemetery had a designated place for gypsy burials. The telephone rang hot, with listeners saying it was inappropriate to use the description 'gypsy'. I didn't think too much of it other than to make a mental note. Unrelated, my sister called me a week later and said, "You'll never guess what Amanda found?" Amanda, Zandra's eldest daughter, had been chasing up our family history, was unaware of my radio interview, and had found my mother's mother's birth certificate. There in print was 'Polly Solomons - 'traveller'. I now had the cultural trifecta - Catholic, Jewish and Gypsy!

2

A YOU'RE ADORABLE, B YOU'RE SO BEAUTIFUL

I was born at St. Margaret's Hospital, Paddington, on the 3rd of January 1946. My parents had moved from Hastings Parade, Bondi Beach, and lived in a small terrace on West Street, Paddington, which meets Oxford Street and, coincidently, the corner where I opened the first Folkways Music shop in 1973. We next moved to a house in the southern Sydney suburb of Eastlakes. This was Mom and Dad's first house and purchased with a loan for soldier resettlement. Dad had secured a job in his original trade as a box maker. Wooden boxes were used for all sorts of things in those pre-plastic days, and Dad was an accomplished handyman, having learnt basic carpentry and so many other 'shed' skills from his father. Necessity was always the best teacher.

We lived in a corner red brick house at 19 Florence Avenue until I was six. I remember the house because of the spacious backyard. We couldn't afford a car in those post-war days, so Dad penned part of the yard as a chicken run and, on festive occasions, would slaughter one for the table. I have horrific memories of headless chickens chasing me around the clothesline' line as blood spurted from their headless necks. Just as horrific was the sight of the slaughtered chook hanging on the clothesline to drain the blood and then the sight of feathers as they were plucked. I remember the dog going crazy. Zandra reminded me of the arrival of the first chickens. "Dad had wired off a section of the yard and bought two hens. He borrowed a rooster, and soon, there were several chickens. One day, two of the hens got into a fight - screams and feathers were flying so dad had to race in to stop the girls from killing each other. During the fight, one of the hens got badly cut so dad, ever ready with Jenson's Violet, an antiseptic family cure-all, poured the violently coloured violet dye all over the panicked hen. The hen remained violet in colour for the best part of a year and was affectionately known as 'Violet' thereafter."

We could never bring ourselves to eat her. Chicken was a treat back then, reserved for birthdays, anniversaries and holidays. Dad had to do the gruesome act of slaughter. If anyone has witnessed a chicken being beheaded, they will understand the expression 'running around like a headless chook.'

I REMEMBER the clothes props that held up the washing lines. Like any kid, I saw these long wooden poles as an important part of my dream world. They could take me up into the sky, like Jack up the beanstalk; they were my Superman launching rods, and, of course, I would occasionally break one of them in two as I swung like Tarzan of the Apes. These were the days when the clothes' prop man regularly visited the suburb selling new ones - his identifying street call of "cloooo-thhhh-es' p-r-o-p-s ", all drawn out and clipped at the end, would ricochet around the suburb.

IT WAS at Eastlakes where I gave my first public performance. According to my sister's reliable memory, a cement section in the Florence Avenue backyard was exactly the right space for an improvised stage.

Zandra and Warren when I really was adorable!

Zandra, who was then about eleven, and her school friends, Valerie, Beverly White, and Elaine Murray, produced a series of backyard concerts to raise money for the Red Cross and Legacy. Adorable wee Warren was the show's star, was presented half a dozen times over two years. I would have been between three and five during these years. The girls sang and danced popular songs, and my star act was to sing 'A You're Adorable', illustrated by generous theatrical actions. It sounds very Little Lord Fauntleroy and very camp! I still remember some of the hand actions and the song.

A you're adorable, B you're so beautiful,
C you're a cutie full of charms,
D you're a darling, E you're exciting and
F you're a feather in my arms.
G you look good to me, H you're so heavenly,

I you're the one I idolise.
J we're like Jack and Jill, K you're so kissable,
L you look lovely in my arms.
M, N, O, P - I could go on all day,
Q, R, S, T - alphabetically speaking - you're okay.
U look so good to me, V you're so very sweet,
W, X, Y, Z - It's fun to wander through the alphabet
    with you
To tell you what you mean to me.

Zandra tells me that they spent hours teaching me to sing and act out the song. Mom, always ready with the sewing machine, made a white shirt and a little black bow tie. Then, borrowing a theatrical trick from Nanna Polly, they blackened a cork and drew a tiny moustache on my face. I must have looked a sight!

Sis Z and little brother, Warren

I remember running wild in Eastlakes mainly because the suburb at the time was mainly swamp and bush. The Southern Cross Drive hadn't divided the suburb, and the nearby Mascot airport wasn't particularly busy or noisy. There were sand hills that we kids loved to slide down when we could manage to get our hands on large cardboard boxes. The Italian greengrocer on Florence Avenue used to give us a couple sometimes, but it always cost the same - a hearty pinch on the cheeks as he repeated, "Use-a-kids has gotta be-a-good kids".

Mom was always proud of her legs. Outside our house, Eastlakes.

Most of our neighbours were typical Aussie families and we kids ran barefoot, ever-defiant of bindi-eye prickles. We towed our billy carts around the sand hills and raced down the bendy streets. My mother's younger sister, Lilly, husband Bill Lindsay, and three sons, Graham, Ronald and David, lived a few blocks away near Maloney Street, Mascot. Zandra used to double me on her bike, and it took about ten minutes from house to house. The Lindsays didn't have a telephone because Bill was liable to place bets with the SP Bookie and lose the family income, so we were the family-to-family message courier system. No helmets or anything in those days, but the street traffic wasn't as frantic as today.

Dad had left box-making and joined a small scrap metal yard owned by his sister Mary's husband, Jack Kendall. Not long after, dad had a terrible accident when water spilled into the molten metal and splashed up into his eyes, nearly blinding him. It was this accident that caused severe eyesight problems in his later years. Jack, dad's best mate, died soon after, and the business was closed.

Dad eventually went to work for Albert G. Sims, an ex-railway worker, socialist and ALP member, who, during the Great Depression, had established a scrap metal business collecting old metals on his bicycle. Sims went on to buy the old shipyards at Mort's Dock, near Balmain, in 1959, and when dad joined the company in the early 1960s, they had relocated to a large depot on O'Riordan Street, Mascot. He became NSW Sales Manager. I always went with him to the annual Xmas party at Mascot, where Sims laid on sacks of oysters, prawns and baked chickens for all the staff. Simsmetal became a very successful international company.

Mom in cap and gown after graduating from the Sydney Conservatorium of Music.

Mom, who had a diploma in music - cap and gown - from the Sydney Conservatorium of Music, was teaching piano and working part-time for Harry Landis, a Jewish jeweller on Goulburn Street, Sydney. I remember my mother being grateful for the work and how I was shocked when she told me that some employment advertisements in the *Sydney Morning Herald* specified, 'No Jews or Catholics need apply.' I assume gypsies weren't welcome, either!

AROUND 1950, Dad announced that we were moving to Willoughby on the north shore of Sydney Harbour to open a shop on Penshurst Street. Fahey's Gift Shop and Lucky Lottery Service also had a hairdressing section at the rear and, like many barber shops, an illegal gambling operation - an SP bookie. We lived upstairs. I was young but, according to my sister Zandra, not too young to not get into trouble with 'bad types'. I am not too sure how long we stayed at Willoughby, but I do know that one day I got caught wagging school, probably the only time I ever did, and very soon after, we sold the shop and, in 1954, moved to Ramsgate on the south side of Sydney. Zandra says the main reason was that I had been caught with some other kids pouring sand into a car's petrol tank.

Dad outside Fahey's Gift Store (with me looking on). Willoughby.

Dad in the store (with bowtie)

Mom behind the counter.

My main memory of the shop is accompanying my parents on their regular buying trips to the Hoffnung & Co. emporium at 153-259 Clarence Street, Sydney. Built in 1936, it was an impressive multi-floored wonderland. Hoffnung & Co. imported and distributed everything from tobacco to giftware, sound recordings to beauty products. It had an exotic smell I have never forgotten.

SHORTLY AFTER MOVING TO RAMSGATE, my sister came home from school, Loretto Convent, and defiantly threw her uniform into the backyard incinerator. She had had enough of the church and the cranky nuns. She enrolled in a business course and, later, scored a job in advertising.

Superman ready to tackle the clothes prop

I LOVED GROWING up in Ramsgate on the edge of the Shire. We lived on Pasadena Street, a block from the beach on The Grand Parade and two blocks from Scarborough Park. It was Clive James' territory. Our neighbouring streets all had American Hollywood names: Monterey, Hollywood and Culver. Our house was part post-war bungalow and part Spanish Mission, including a fish pond fountain in the front garden. The rear garden was large, and we had a chicken coop, a big bird cage for budgerigars, an outdoor loo, and a yard big enough to grow vegetables. It also contained a large clothesline with two enormous wooden props. We also had a dog, a spirited fox terrier named Whiskey; yes, he was black and white and loved a fight. I grew up with the perfect boy's backyard.

My first backyard show is a blur, but not so my second performance in 1955 when I was eleven years old and a 'waving wheat' in the Kogarah Marist Brother's production of *Oklahoma*. Us wheat, there was a sheaf of us, waved enthusiastically on the stage of the Kogarah Victory, an art deco-styled cinema later renamed the Avon and, in 1971, Kogarah Mecca. It was a long way from Oklahoma and Mecca! My friend, Marita Blood, had a better story from her schooldays at Ballarat - she told me how pupils at her Catholic school formed 'beads' in a giant human set of rosary beads.

It was the 1950s, and most household requirements were bought from regular street vendors. The milkman came every morning, and the clop clop clop of the horse was a warning for me, as my father's voice usually followed it, "Warren, quick, get the shovel and sugar bag." One of my many jobs was to chase the horse and get the manure before Mrs O'Connell, our opposite neighbour, gathered it for her rose bushes. It was a friendly rivalry, and I assume we took turns; besides, there was always the baker's, rabbit-o's and 'John the Chinamen's' horse cart to follow. What astonished me about the milkman's horse was that it knew exactly which houses to stop in front of and for how long. In those days, the milk came in large tanks, and we had to stand at the rear and have the milk poured into a jug. The baker came every day and sold us either tank loaf (shaped like a water tank with corrugations in the crust) or Vienna high-top, which you could break right in the middle - that first slice of fresh bread was pure heaven. Sliced bread was only available at the local corner store and sliced in front of you 'while you waited'. The rabbit-o came every fortnight and had a tiny cart refrigerated by blocks of ice. The rabbits were two for three-and-sixpence. We had rabbit every fortnight, either crumbed, stewed or fried. After the myxo scare, we stopped eating rabbit, and the street vendor disappeared forever. John the Chinaman delivered fruit and vegetables - probably from the Chinese market gardens at Scarborough Park or Botany. Later I found that all Chinese market gardeners were called 'John the Chinaman'. He was a kindly fellow and sometimes accompanied by his son. We hadn't seen many Asians then, so it was always a curiosity. The ice man came twice weekly wearing a big, heavy leather apron and carrying large blocks with massive steel claws. He brought the blocks right into the kitchen. The primitive fridge was a combo of ice and kerosene; I still recall the smell. The Crystal Cordial man also came every two weeks. Passiona was my favourite. There was also a bright green one called 'G.I.' We called it 'green ink'. The last street vendor's cries seemed to coincide with the arrival of Mr Whippy and his muffled amplified recording of *'Greensleeves'*.

Fahey family home, Ramsgate.

The corner store was not on the corner but close to Monterey Street, next door to the butcher and hamburger shop. If I close my eyes, I can see all three shops and identify the different smells. Butcher shops in the late 1950s did all their prep work right before the customer. Blood and guts were everywhere, and big white paper sheets were used to wrap up the orders. Offal was popular (not with me), as were sausages and chops. Lard was sold and used for baking. Signs urged us to deposit 'sixpence a week' with the butcher as a lay-bye for the Xmas ham and chickens. The three butchers were jolly fellows and always spoke what sounded like Double Dutch. Year's later, I found that many butchers spoke what was loosely called 'butcher's talk' where they inverted words so "That woman has large breasts" was spoken as "That namow sah egrael stsaerb'. The hamburger shop doubled as a newsagent and sold stationery (brown paper was a big seller), school supplies, and newspapers and magazines: Daily Mirror, Daily Sun, Truth Newspaper, Australasian Post, People Magazine and Woman's Weekly and Woman's Day. Only the Woman's Weekly remains; paradoxically, it is now monthly. The corner store, owned by the Jensen family, was typical. There was no self-service; all the staff wore crisp white aprons, and Mr Jensen always wore a bow tie. The shelves offered Aunty Mary's Baking Powder, Mother's Choice and Sydney Flour, Bushell's and Lipton's tea (we had Lipton's because mom saved the redeemable coupons, yesterday's equivalent of fly buys), Sunlight and Lifebuoy soaps. The shop usually smelt of fresh bread, a delicious aroma, and the sweetness of Arnott's biscuits. There was a large tin of Arnott's Variety and another with broken biscuits - five pence a bag. They also sold cordial and Smith's Potato Chips, both novelties for us kids. There were also soft drinks in bottles, and we collected the empties in our billy carts and redeemed them at the corner store for lollies. The other corner store smell I remember was garlic sausage - what we called any preserved meat, although it was mostly mortadella and devon. A freshly sliced devon sausage or mortadella sandwich with pickles was a treat (and I still enjoy them).

MY LAST PRIMARY school years were spent at the St Thomas Moore convent school at Brighton-le-Sands. The Sisters of Charity were strict and scary. I feared my piano teacher, who repeatedly whacked my knuckles with a ruler. I refused to get my head or fingers around *Fler Elise*. In retrospect, I wish I had been a good piano student because, years later, I had to start at the beginning and teach myself to read music.

I ACHED to finish junior school and stop wearing shorts - I wanted long trousers and a more grown-up world.

3

CALATHUMPIAN

I went to Marist Brothers, Kogarah, whose uniform included long pants, a tie, and a felt hat. On the outside, I was a model student: neat, polite and ever-eager. On the inside, I was a devil: ringleader, comedian and revolutionary. I was the class vice-captain and class clown. I was a good student in subjects I liked, especially English and history, but useless in anything mathematical or scientific. This was to continue through my school years, where I excelled in history and English but couldn't even master basic general maths. I was brain-dead in the math department and banned from science after nearly burning the laboratory building to the ground. I suspect I am numerically dyslectic.

KOGARAH HAD A MILITARY CADET UNIT. Every Wednesday and Friday, we came to school in full uniform, including leather belts and gators that had to be painted with a foul-smelling khaki compound called 'Blanco'. Like my father, I rose through the ranks like a rocket and was eventually promoted to Regimental Sergeant Major.

Here I am behaving perfectly normally in my school uniform (1960) for Marist Brothers, Kogarah.

The role of RSM was a power trip, and I held the position for two of the three final years of my schooling. Every morning and after lunch, in or out of uniform, it was my role to bring the entire school to attention and, after the headmaster, Brother Laurence McKeon, made his announcements, order the school to march off to their respective classrooms. *'Colonel Bogey'* was played by the school band or over the distorted sound system. We sang a parody of the song,

"Bullshit! Was what the band would play,
Bullshit, they played it night and day".

If I was feeling cheeky, I could, and would, make a weird face or poke my tongue out at the entire school. Everyone relished the conspiracy, and no one ever dobbed me in. The Drum Major, a few years older than me, was a good friend, Brian Lynch, whom I maintained contact with throughout his life.

Cadets kept me busy. It also gave me another excuse not to play cricket - a schoolyard game I loathed. I was once hit by a cricket ball and swore off the game for life. More to the point, it provided an escape as non-commissioned cadet officers had access to the quartermaster's store, an expansive network of rooms under one of the buildings. It was an invitation to mischief and a 'private club'.

In my cadet uniform.

A couple of times a year, we went on bivouac to Holsworthy Army Camp, south of Sydney, and once up to the Singleton Army base in the New South Wales North West. It felt like we were going to war, and Captain Benildus, the Marist Brother in charge of the cadets, took the whole affair exceptionally seriously. Our main concern was the food - what would it be like? We were told the camp was to 'sort us out' - 'weed out the sooks' - and we were sent on route marches, cleaned rifles, listened to lectures, then to the rifle range (the 303 rifles bruised many a shoulder) and then more marching and parading. Rumours spread that the army cooks put bromide in our hot chocolate to reduce our testosterone. It didn't stop us from being randy little soldiers.

In my Marist Brothers Kogarah uniform.

I liked most of my teachers. They were generous with their time and patience and always looked for a likely candidate to join their dwindling religious ranks. I was not one of the candidates, as I realised early on in my youth, around puberty, that I didn't believe in religion or a higher being. I stopped going to confession and Mass in the year I studied for my Primary Certificate. I would have been fourteen.

I was never fiddled with at school apart from an over-touchy Brother Loyola, who, given an opportunity, had a habit of putting his twiddling thumb up our shorts. We had a young and handsome priest named Father Newman, who came to the school to give religious instruction and one-on-one chats about sexuality. I recognised he was different, and although he never corrupted me, he went to Long Bay Gaol for child molestation. My only other memory of sexual mischief was through my two invitations to dinner at the Rockdale house, where a group of Brothers known as the Gerard

Majella Order lived. John Hargreaves, the actor and a sort of school crush, and I went together, and both remembered it being very camp. The brothers and a priest dropped lots of innuendoes and flirted with us but never touched us sexually. Looking back, hearing all that gay talk and how they seemed to enjoy 'dressing up' their neck-to-ankle religious gowns makes me realise they were all as gay as goats. We were told the Order was founded in Italy, and the saint had a special interest in motherhood. The Australian chapter was disbanded after several cases of child sexual abuse and rebranded as the Redemptorists.

My parents were not religious on any account. Mom was Jewish, but I had never known her to attend synagogue, and Dad was a typical lapsed Catholic. When the time came for me to stop going to church, they said - "your choice." To this day, I do not understand religion's power and its hold over seemingly intelligent people. All I see is the havoc caused by religious belief, especially centuries of war. For me, religion is illogical, without evidence and seems to approve of a preponderance of suffering. My parents brought me up with a rationalist spirit and the motto: 'Do unto others as you would have them do unto you'. The old maxim still makes more sense than all the blithering blathering of religious zealots. Like my father, I became a self-declared 'Calathumpian'.

Dad advises young Warren about the ways of the world.

George Fahey was an inspiring man. He was part philosopher,

rationalist and humanitarian. He always told me there was *'No Indispensable Man'* and had a favourite verse he would recite - often! I have never forgotten it.

> Sometimes, when you're feeling important,
> Sometimes, when your ego's in bloom,
> Sometimes, when you take it for granted,
> You're the best qualified in the room:
> Sometimes, when you feel that you're going,
> It would leave an unfillable hole,
> Just follow these simple instructions,
> And see how they humble your soul.
> Take a bucket and fill it with water,
> Put your hand in it up to the wrist,
> Pull it out, and the hole that's remaining,
> Is a measure of how much you'll be missed.
> You can splash all you wish when you enter,
> You may stir up the water galore,
> But stop, and you'll find that in no time,
> It looks quite the same as before.
> The moral of this quaint example,
> Is to do just the best that you can,
> Be proud of yourself, but remember,
> There's no indispensable man.

The school disliked my not attending religious services, and it took some time for them to accept my parent's decision. There was talk of expelling me, but it didn't happen. Mind you, I still had to participate in the daily reciting of the rosary, attend the religious class for an hour daily, and sign AMDG (all my deeds for God) and JMJ (Jesus, Mary and Joseph) on every page of my workbooks. In later years, my religious and mathematics teacher was the headmaster, Brother Frederick McMahon, a frightfully boorish and unpopular clan member. He was thin, looked constipated and commenced nearly every sentence with the words "Now look now." We made a sport out of it; at least I did. The game was to count the number of times he said "Now look now" in a day. Every time the poor man uttered the words, there would be a scramble for a pen to tick off yet another entry. The first to 100 was to declare the results loudly. I can't recall anyone winning because we were terrified of cranky Brother Frederick, the school's principal authority, and his cane lashings were legendary and painful. I received many a canning as if 'Fred', that's what we all called him, seemed determined to belt the Christ into me.

Although I was an excellent student in the subjects I enjoyed (Geography, English, Modern and Ancient History and basic Economics), my brain was dead to calculations, multiplications, divisions and algebra. I now suspect it was something to do with Frederick being such a disliked teacher. One day, I was summoned to his office, a scary prospect, and berated about my low mathematics and religious exam marks. I had the honour of having the lowest marks in religion he had known - six out of one hundred. He threatened me, saying I would not pass the Leaving Certificate. I eventually passed with distinctions in History and English and more than a sense of self-satisfaction. I failed maths, which meant I didn't matriculate, which, at the time, prevented me from going to university. This, in itself, proved to be a blessing. God works in mysterious ways!

One morning, the "Now look now" contest was in full swing when a man appeared at the door and stood there. We were all conscious that he was not happy. Eventually, he said, "Brother Frederick, I want to speak to you." Frederick, mid-chalk on the blackboard, turned around and replied, "Now look now, I am in the middle of class....." He didn't get any further as the man yelled, "Now look now, 'Brother Now Look Now', I want you bloody well out here now! Or I'll come in and throw you out the bloody window." Brother Frederick rushed for the door and told us, "Now look now, do your work until I get back." There was a fat chance of that as our ears strained to listen to the man screaming at the headmaster. Apparently, his son, a star footballer, had been banned from playing in the competition because of his poor attention in class. It was a real donnybrook argument. After the break, we returned to class, and nothing more was ever said about the incident. It was a day of excitement.

WE PLAYED some terrible pranks on the more placid Brothers. We had one older teacher who was more of a carer than a teacher, Brother Charles, who took us to recite the rosary. Maybe he was a bit simple as he seemed to put up with much torment from us monsters, especially during the rosary. We all took turns to say a decade of the Hail Mary Full Of Grace; well, everyone took a turn except me. When it was my turn, most of my classmates would inevitably turn to me and poke their tongues out or fart or something that would set me off giggling. Eventually, Brother Charles would say, "Fahey, outside!" - and that was that.

Once, I found a pregnant stray schoolyard cat, and the St. Francis of Assisi in me came out to protect it. With some other boys, we set the cat up in the little nook under the Mother Mary altar in our classroom. For some reason, probably to store the chalk and duster, the altar had a door that seemed made for cats. A rug, saucer of milk and some leftover tuck-shop Devon seemed to make pussy very content, and two days later, she gave birth to five little pussies who sang in chorus during the rosary. The cat and her family disappeared that evening. On another occasion, we little devils brought in matchboxes full of those yellow and black stink beetles found on citrus trees. As the rosary got into full swing, we opened our matchboxes. The room crawled with the little beasts, including those crawling all over Brother Charles's cassock. He was so placid we became even more outrageous. It wasn't uncommon for someone to drive a tack through the sash that hung down from his flowing cassock. The moment he walked away, he was tacked down to a desk. We all looked very innocent.

The one occasion we couldn't escape his glare but still escaped rage was when a desk caught fire in the third decade of the rosary. The school switched from fountain pens and Steven's Blue Ink to biros, but our desks still had ceramic ink wells. We had to use these ink wells for something, so what better than a desktop barbecue? Someone discovered that methylated spirit gave a clear, almost invisible flame, so we made skewers out of paper clips and pushed them through Jaffas, a round lolly with chocolate in the centre. These were ideal for barbecuing! Two seats from me, Walter de Maria was busily barbecuing when the metho leaked into his desk, and the whole affair roared with fire. We all screamed with delight as Brother Charles frowned and tut-tutted, muttering, "de Maria! Put that fire out NOW!". We all thought Brother Frederick's cane would be thumping, but no more was said, and Brother Charles became our hero.

Despite my non-compliance with religion, I joined the St. Vincent de Paul Society. It wasn't a matter of finding God, more a case of finding John Hargraves, a self-confident, handsome and seductive student who had declared himself president of the Society. The real reason was we both hated cricket and schoolyard games, and the St. Vincent de Paul Society had privileged use of the bookshop under the main stairs. It was our private club, and about fifteen of us gathered most lunchtimes to gossip, yarn and talk about who we liked and disliked. John became a celebrated actor, and we retained a strong friendship off and on over the years until his untimely death from AIDS in 1996.

Food was always on the minds of energetic young boys like myself. At Kogarah, we had the tuck shop to end all tuck shops, or so it seemed. The mother's club ran it like a machine. We marched into the tiny space and pointed at what we wanted and could afford. I recall some shocker concoctions, including the 'wimpy roll' - no doubt named for the drooling, hamburger-munching character in the 'Popeye the Sailorman' cartoons and comics. It was a roll dribbling with a mess of hot baked beans and cut-up sausage. The smell was foul.

In retrospect, apart from the sweets on offer, the sandwiches were fairly healthy compared with many of today's school 'canteens' (whatever happened to the tuckshop?). My secondary years saw many 'new Australians' join the school, especially Maltese and Italian, and they played quite a role in changing my diet. Here they were in the playground with these whopping big sandwiches - huge slices of bread with mysterious fillings like cheese and salami that stank of garlic - and there I was with my regular sandwich of peanut butter and lettuce (a combo I still like) or Vegemite and Coon cheese. Joseph Zammit and I regularly swapped sandwiches and were happy with our newfound food. Then came the 'Oslo lunch' - a campaign aimed at a more balanced school lunch - introduced in 1940; it ran through until the rebellious sixties.

Throughout my school years, we were subjected to another health campaign, the School Free Milk Program, whereby every student was given a quarter pint of milk daily. The small bottles were given out every morning at what we called 'play lunch', and we dreaded the summer months when the bottles would be lukewarm with a revolting cream at the top. In those days, Australia had a glut of milk, and I imagine the dairy producers had a very successful lobby. The campaign was introduced throughout the British Empire, and locally in 1951, it stayed in operation until Gough Whitlam axed it in 1972. With an eye on Britain's financial well-being, British Prime Minister Margaret Thatcher also announced the program's demise. 'Attila the Hen' became Margaret Thatcher 'Milk Snatcher'. One of the bonuses of the School Milk Program was that many students, especially primary school kids, collected the aluminium tops. We made Christmas bells out of them by reshaping and threading them together in chains. We also pressed them around pennies until you could see Her Majesty's profile in aluminium. Our favourite use, especially for the older boys, was to roll them into solid balls, which we flicked at some unsuspecting heads during class. On special occasions, the silver tops would be replaced with coloured designs. The first I remember was for Empire Day and featured the Union Jack. These are now priceless collector items.

I revisited the school in 2009 for its anniversary. I had been asked if I would participate in an oral history program at the school. I took my neighbour, Brian Lynch, the old Drum Major. We were shocked that no religious brothers remained at Kogarah and that the open spaces were now covered with bitumen car parks and new buildings. Old desks were now computer terminals. I was even more shocked to learn that Brother Now-Look-Now was still alive and had participated in the oral history program. (I later learned he died in 2015 after 66 year of religious service.) The school seemed haunted. They made two videos of Brian and me talking about the school. The school's website now has me up as one of their most successful ex-students. To mark the school's centenary we both appeared in a filmed interview https://www.youtube.com/watch?app=desktop&v=a3IKXetXnss however because we told outrageous stories, they only ever put 'part one' on YouTube.

My best mates at school were Trevor Jensen and John Evers. Trevor disappeared; however, I occasionally keep in contact with John. He and his wife had a beautiful vineyard, Camyr Allen, in the upper Hunter for a while. I performed there a couple of times. John hated school and most of the teachers and is at a loss to understand why I give them credit. In truth, I enjoyed my years at Marist Brothers Kogarah and credited the Brothers, well, most of them, as dedicated and enthusiastic teachers. I still remember the war cries.

Kio Ora, Kio Ora, Kio Ora Katoo
Kio Ora, Kio Ora, Kio Ora Katoo
KOGARAH

And at school sporting carnivals, we yelled:

One , two, three, four,
Who do you think we're barracking for?
Five, six, seven, eight,
Who do you think we appreciate?
K-O-G-A-R-A-H!

And we had insults for our neighbouring schoolies, Ramsgate Public and Kogarah Tech High School:

Kogarah, Kogarah, yar yar,
Ortta be ortta be
Dipped in tar.

Ramsgate, Ramsgate, brave and bold
ortta be, ortta be dipped in gold.

Catholics, Catholics,
Ring the bell
While the Proddies go to hell

Trevor Jensen was from Muswellbrook, Hunter Valley, and his family had midget racing cars. He was handsome, an outstanding footballer and randy. On Saturday evenings, I would join the family in going to the Showgrounds to watch the midgets race the track, and, inevitably, I would sleep over at his house. We shared a single bed nearly every Saturday night for two years. No one seemed to think it was odd - except me.

The years of growing up in Ramsgate were full of adventure. Scarborough Park was a network of bush tracks and expansive lakes teaming with carp and monstrous eels. We raced our bikes through the forest playing cowboys and Indians and sought our favourite hiding places for our gatherings. Sometimes, older boys smoked Capstan or Ardath cigarettes and would let us have a puff. A recreational centre in the park, sponsored by the local council, had a full program over the summer holidays. I always associated the Scarborough Park bushland as edgy, slightly dangerous, a place where older boys hung out and smelt of youthful sexual misadventure.

THE MAIN 'ADVENTURE' was far from sexual. Behind the football grandstand was one of Sydney's largest Chinese market gardens. They grew melons and vegetables, and 'raiding the Chows', a dreadful cry of the era, was almost a sport. The aim was to crawl undetected along the always muddy pathways and steal something edible, anything, but especially carrots. Talk about stolen fruit tasting sweet - these tasted so fresh, but we had to wash them as we all knew the Chinese used 'night soil', better known as their own manure. We never knew if this was true or not. The Chinese no doubt saw us as pests and tried to scare us away by firing saltpetre rifles. Years later, I met a wonderful woman at the City of Sydney Historical Society. She was a daughter of one of the Chinese families, and I dutifully fessed up.

1959 when the 'Many Loves of Dobie Gillis' was screened on television. Wow, a Canadian Jacket and a Kookie Comb.

At the other end of the street from our home was the beach on Botany Bay. In those days, it was relatively clean and even had a healthy marine population of fish, rays, jellyfish and sharks. The sand was clean and white. Dad and I used to go to the Ramsgate Public Pool on the weekends for an early morning swim and then walk up the beach to find 'Bung-Eye' (or was it 'Bing-eye?), the local fisherman who, along with his son and daughter, sold their early morning catch of bream. 'Bung-Eye' was part Aborigine and had the curliest hair I had ever seen. No fish ever tasted as sweet as those bream - we would take them home, scale them and fry them up straight away. You'd be lucky to find anything edible in the bay today.

I loved the water and was spoilt for choice, with Ramsgate's ocean pool, Pemberton's Ramsgate Baths and the Brighton-le-Sands ocean pool all in walking distance.

The Brighton-le-Sands ocean pool, opposite Bay Street, was large and, at the time, offered many attractions. Opened in 1928 on the site of the original bathing enclosure, it became an instant success after a 3.38-metre grey nurse shark was caught just outside the enclosure the same week it opened, and three weeks later, a bronze whaler was caught nearby. What better advertising! The baths had an entrance fee but also a circular boardwalk, trapeze, diving boards, tower and fishing spots. Band recitals were staged on the weekends. The biggest attraction was the roller skating rink operated by Seymour Amusements. Another of its attractions was a 'pashometer' machine which, for a shilling, could measure your 'sexibility'. The baths were rebuilt in 1968 after a massive storm swept most of the enclosure away.

Pemberton's Pools, on the corner of Grand Parade and Ramsgate Avenue, has stuck in my memory all these years. Run by Mr Arthur 'Pop' Pemberton and widely known as Pem's Pools, there were three pools; we preferred to call it Pem's Piss Pools. Theoretically, salt water from Botany Bay (right across the street) was pumped into the various pools daily, but we doubted it. It turned sour after a few days and too many kids peeing in the warm water. Opened in 1926, it was one of those time-warp places you wish was still there with its slippery dips, dance hall, sun-baking area (with sand), distorted fun mirrors and mini zoo. I can still smell the exotic aroma of chlorine, fried potato scallops and monkey poo. The day's highlight came late afternoon when 'Pop' threw a handful of pennies into the pool for a 'penny scramble'. The zoo had an emu, various caged native birds, dingoes and too many monkeys. The monkeys on roller skates, usually smoking cigarettes, were the children's favourites. Pemberton's Pools closed in 1969 and was replaced by a Coles Supermarket. A friend, Dan McAloon, now runs a Pemberton's Pools Facebook group offering stories and photographs.

One of my passions at the time was roller skating. The Brighton-le-Sands Roller Skating Rink was above the entrance to the swimming pool, and you have never heard a racket like a hundred people skating around a wooden slated oval rink - especially to the sound of early rock and roll records by Brenda Lee, Bobby Vincent, Fats Domino and Little Richard. I could skate backwards, do the loop-the-loop and even swing dance on skates. I also remember the fashion. Girls wore wide clinch belts, blouses with neck scarves, and knee-length flounced dresses. Boys wore stove-pipe black pants, hideous luminous socks and button-down checkered shirts.

My mother and sister made most of their clothes, and our living room was often covered in paper cut-out patterns. They listened to music as they cut and sewed. I remember they once made an entire ensemble for a fancy dress party out of newspaper pages!

Zandra dressed in newspapers.

Incidentally, Zandra has great taste in music, and I was immersed in her recordings of Frank Sinatra, Sarah Vaughan, Dave Brubeck, Peggy Lee, Miles Davis, George Shearston and Ella Fitzgerald.

My gang usually went to the Brighton Cinema or Rockdale Odeon on overcast Saturday afternoons. We would walk or catch the electric trolley bus along General Holmes Drive and Bay Street to

Rockdale. I remember picture tickets costing one and sixpence, and you received a pink or green musk stick with your ticket. Our favourite films, which we never called movies, were the western or swashbuckling pirate adventures. The afternoon started with everyone standing for *'God Save the Queen'*, then the Cinesound or Movietone newsreel of recent events and the inevitable quirky 'would-you-believe' story. This was followed by the serial - *'Hopalong Cassidy'*, *'The Phantom'* or some dumb cops and robbers story that had us whooping in the aisles. If we were lucky, there would be a Three Stooges comedy. The second half started with two cartoons (if it didn't, the crowd would stamp their feet and boo until they were black in the face). My favourite cartoon characters were 'Heckle and Jeckle', the wise-cracking, cigar-munching, cynical crows. Interval was a sugar hit from Hell - you could choose packets of sherbet which you sucked through a liquorice straw, monster aniseed gum balls we called gob-smackers, long plaited strands of liquorice that you could assiduously peel for about thirty minutes, Choo Choo Bars, Hopalong Cassidy Bars, Wagon Wheel biscuits, packets of Minties, Jaffas and Fantails and, for those romantically inclined, small-hearted shaped sherbet flavoured sweets called Conversation Lollies, because each sweet had a message like "hello there..." or "I love You." At the end of the session, the theatre's floor resembled a garbage tip.

I WAS EXPECTED to do weekly chores at home, including cleaning the fish pond (knee-deep in slimy water), mowing the lawns, trimming the lawn edges, cleaning the bird cages and, of course, the daily routine of drying up after meals. Sunday morning was car washing, and the big Vanguard 'Ladybird' took forever. Washing the dog was another job. I received six shillings a week.

THE THREE MOST important events of the year were Christmas, the Royal Easter Show and Cracker Night. Our Christmas was probably typical of the average Aussie family as much as it centred on a festive lunch; in our case, that usually meant a large gathering, as my father used to joke, of the "tykes and yids". Once again, the Jewish aunts would arrive with truckloads of food and the Fahey's with bottles. We ate baked chicken at Christmas; it was considered 'special' in the forties and fifties, with the 'trimmings'.

Every Christmas mom would take me to the Anthony Hordern's Emporium, Sydney, to meet Father Christmas.

Mom always made a plum pudding (with obligatory six-penny pieces) as dessert, and we gorged on pudding and trifle until we nearly burst. We also had a huge ham, which we ate over the next month until it started to turn green. We had it curried, sliced into schnitzels, fried and fifty other recipes devised by my inventive mother.

On Christmas Eve, my father always made me leave out a piece of Christmas cake and a glass of brandy 'for Santa Claus'. I was always impressed Santa drank exactly the same brand of brandy as my father. I also had to hang up my Christmas stocking - a pillowslip. My eyes boggled with excitement when I saw the huge bag of presents in the morning. Christmas morning was a swim followed by preparations for lunch. I was always a ready assistant cook. Midmorning, we had a tradition of visiting the neighbours to share a piece of Christmas cake and cheer. My mother said, "For every piece of Christmas cake consumed in a friend's house on Christmas Day, you live a year longer." After lunch, we snoozed until the piano announced the singalong - which was approximately half an hour later, just enough time for the aunts to do the washing up. We usually sang into the night.

I was born into the Capricorn community on the third of January, far too close to that of baby Jesus for my liking, especially since everyone appeared financially exhausted from Christmas, and I tired of hearing my Christmas presents announced as "and that's also for your birthday." My father had a standing joke around this time that he was buying me a horse for Christmas. The joke wore thin after one year. He scattered a bag of horse manure on the back lawn and suggested: "The horse had got away." It sounds cruel, but I was very used to these family jokes.

The Royal Easter Show was held at the old showgrounds at Moore Park. We saved up our pocket money for months so we could 'go crazy' in the Showbag Pavilion and also have as many rides as possible. It was a day of high excitement. The Ghost Train, like the daredevil motorcyclist tent Wheel of Death, was a favourite, mainly because of the noise. In the morning, we usually arrived early. We patiently went to the Manufacturer's Pavilion for the Arts and Crafts, the Rothman's Theatre (where they tried to justify smoking cigarettes), woodchopping, livestock exhibitions (everything from dogs to cattle) and all the other 'important' exhibitions. We also caught some main show ring demonstrations, like the sheep dog trials and rodeo work. Lunch was usually Tasmanian Brownell potato chips, my first hot chips from a fast food outlet, and a hot dog. After lunch, we tentatively approached Sideshow Alley to the thump, thump, thump beat of Jimmy Sharman's Boxing Troupe. There was heightened excitement as we gaped at the parade of burly boxers, including the legendary Big Little Chief, a 'real Indian' in a feathered headdress, just like in the pictures.

Next were the freak shows: "Pygmies, look, I saw pygmies!", "Oh, there's a half man/half woman, and there's a woman's head without a body!". These were simple illusion attractions that appeared very complicated to us youngsters. My dreams can still muster up 'Princess Ubangi', 'Lanky Bill' - The World's Tallest Man, 'Mexican Rose' - The World's Fattest Woman, 'Betty Broadbent' - The Tattooed Lady with over 460 designs head to feet, The Pig-A-Dilly Circus, 'Tam Tam' the 'Leopard Man' from Ethiopia; and how could I forget Madam Zena's Circus of Performing Fleas? (She claimed her fleas came from the Kings Cross Picture Theatre and were extremely reluctant to learn new tricks). In 1997, the Show relocated to Homebush Olympic Park and took with it decades of memories. In 2021, I made a documentary video about the Royal Show and its sideshow alley. https://www.youtube.com/watch?v=QPLO6jgjGsk

After all the excitement and rides of Sideshow Alley, we hit the Showbag Pavilion, money still rattling in our pockets. We wanted to buy every bag, but news soon spread about which ones were the best. Nobody wanted bags with school stuff like rulers and pencil cases; we wanted the sweets: Cadburys, Jaffa, Minties and all those other familiar names. In those days, the bags were generous, and the producers included new products; there were also lots of free samples at the various stalls. We were sick with excitement and probably high on sugar. I rarely eat chocolate or such sweets these days.

I had a happy childhood, and my mom and dad had a happy life. Dad occasionally socialised with his workmates, especially on Friday evenings, but was never a boozer. When he came home, dinner was always in the oven, he brought a large bag of peanuts in the shell and a family-sized Small's dark chocolate. Deb and George never seemed to argue. It would have been difficult to argue with Dad, he was a saint (I take after him!), and if Mom niggled him too much, he typically responded with "Yes, Deb, yes, Deb". It's hard to argue with agreement. Years later, I still use this with my life partner of umpteen-dozen years, Mark Cavanagh, and if I need to bring out the heavy artillery in a disagreement, I look him in the eyes and say, "Yes, Deb, yes, Deb." and we both start to giggle.

Dad and Mom - a happy life.

4

FAMILY FOLKLORE

I look back on my early life and realise, what I recognise now as folklore, was all around me. I just didn't have a name for it. My family was walking talking folklore. From the moment we woke up until time for sleep. In the mornings we were greeted with "Rise and shine", no doubt an army reference to jumping out of bed and polishing your shoes. Incidentally, in polishing our shoes we were always told to brush one way in a certain direction (so as not to waste energy) and that we should be able to see our reflection on them. We were not allowed much slack in getting up. Maybe another leftover from Dad's army days, but it was almost as if Reveille rang out at 6.30 am. If I dared stay under the covers I was threatened with a glass of ice water on my head. Post breakfast, Dad would inevitably say, "Well, if that's breakfast, I've had it."

The evening meal was also met with a familiar comment from Dad, "I'm so hungry I could eat a horse and chase the jockey."

Mom also had a repertoire of old sayings. If we lost anything it was inevitably "Upstairs, behind the clock in Annie's room." We didn't have an upstairs or an Annie. If either parent was going out and I asked where they were going, "That's for us to know, and you to find out.". "What time is it?" was always "A hair past a freckle."

"What's for dinner?" had a stock response of either "Possum's guts and puppy dog's tails" or 'A duck under the table." I felt I lived in a curious world.

OUR FAMILY HOLIDAYS saw us pack the Vanguard and head north to the Shoal Bay Country Club at Nelson's Bay. In the 1950s it was situated in beautiful bushland and on a beach. I remember the smell of salty seaweed in the morning and the sound of cicadas at dusk. Mom loved these holidays and it brought out the wag in her - determined to have fun. There were lots of dress-up nights and lots of singalongs. Debby was always the light of the party, always full of energy and ideas, and was very persuasive in getting others involved - even on one memorable occasion - where she orchestrated fellow guests as a tribe of cannibals.

Oogie-Woogie Women dressed by mom (second from right) and their missionary prisoner.

Zandra and I also had to get dressed up. On one occasion mom made an outfit where I was 'night and day' - no wonder I grew up confused.

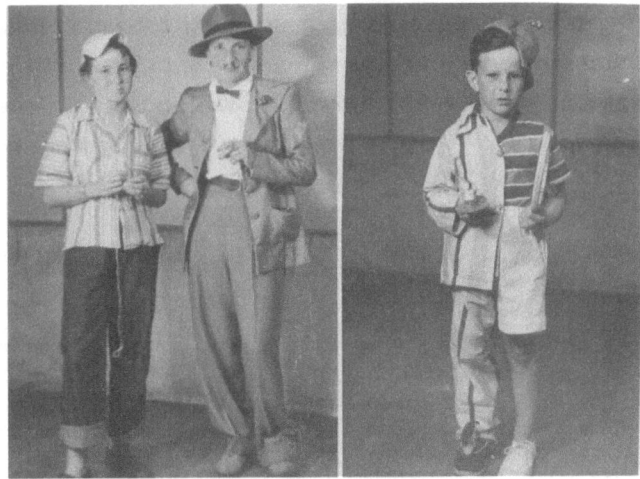

Zandra and mom in drag. Me as 'night and day'.

On trips to see Dad in the hospital, we had to take public transport as my mother never learned to drive. Inevitably, she would start a conversation with someone, anyone, on the tram, bus or train, and, inevitably, it would involve me - number one (and only) son. I am not sure if it was a Jewish mother sort of thing but it was embarrassing. I was always well-presented and polite but ever wary of looking like Little Lord Fauntleroy, a literary character Dad often ridiculed. Likewise, if we met a couple who appeared beyond their station, they were nicknamed 'Lord and Lady Muck' or, worse still, 'The Dockers', a reference to a vulgar rich couple, Lord and Lady Docker, who had a gold Daimler. 'The Gold Car' was a touring limousine covered with 7,000 tiny gold stars, and all the plating that would normally have been chrome was gold. The car came with them to Australia in 1951.

There were many family superstitions although neither mom nor dad would have admitted to being superstitious. Their parents were, and those superstitions were passed down to us. Shoes were never to be placed on the table, any table (bad luck), umbrellas were never to be opened in the house (bad luck), and broken mirrors gave you seven years of bad luck. Split salt was to be thrown over the left shoulder (because it will blind the devil who was always standing on the left); never touch eggshells because you'll get warts; place a slice of raw potato between your lips when slicing onions, and you won't cry. I remember, when walking the footpath up to the corner shops, not treading on cracks - because you'll break your mother's back.

One of my early visits to the 'bush'... at Taronga Zoo.

We had family folk medicines too. A teaspoon of cod liver oil for upset stomach (it tasted foul), Milk of Magnesia for indigestion (I always wondered how you could 'milk' magnesia), Jenson's Violet for any cuts; prunes for constipation and, the mighty tablespoon of black raw 'blackstrap' molasses every morning 'for blood.' If we had a cold we were given a teaspoon of sugar laced with enough eucalyptus oil to stun a koala. Dad also prescribed a nip of OP rum and warm milk but I never quite worked out what it was supposed to heal. Akta-Vite 'to improve vitality for the whole family' was always in the kitchen (we used to pour it on ice cream as a treat.) I recently discovered this Australian product, launched in 1943, is still available. Dad also believed in fresh air and at every opportunity, he would have me take a deep lungful, hold it, take another, hold it, and then another. It was no small wonder I could swim the length of the local swimming pool underwater.

To say George Fahey was stoic would be an understatement. He had no doubt seen poverty and hardship, had heard frightening tales of suffering from his father and had experienced the horrors of war. He was a considered man and modest and always ready to help a friend in need. "A friend in need is a friend indeed." Dad had a soft voice and a soft heart. He was very much the eldest son of his family, the responsible one in times of need. if I deserved a whipping, and occasionally I did, it was more likely administered by my mother. Sunlight soap or Keen's mustard in the mouth was very effective in getting me to own up or shut up.

Dad was pragmatic. If I stubbed my foot and hopped around in pain, yelling complaints, he would patiently wait and say, "I had a sore foot once and complained, until I met a man who had no foot at all." It usually shut me up.

Considering my family upbringing and stock answers to stock questions, it is probably no secret why I grew up with an inquisitive mind. I couldn't get a straight answer to anything, so I questioned everything. My probing "Why?" was met with "Y's a crooked letter, and you can't make it straight." To which I would respond, "What!" and, yes, the same response every time: "Watt invented the steam engine."

Another of his favourite sayings was a response to "I see." "I see, said the blind man, when he couldn't see at all." And if I dared to say, "That's not fair." The response was always "What's not fair?' To which the answer was always, "A black man's bottom!"

Instead of screaming, I always laughed. I knew these sayings were ridiculous but I also knew they 'belonged' to us.

My 'big' sister, Zandra, and I have always been close. Maybe it's because we are the product of such large families where aunts, uncles and cousins were so numerous. I remember being very honoured to have been asked to read the telegrams at her wedding to Alan Stanton in 1962. I didn't even think it strange they were getting married in a nightclub.

Dora Skelsey's Ace of Clubs Nightclub was opened in 1959 on the grounds previously occupied by her husband Bill's rather infamous nightclub called 'Oyster Bill's'. It was on the corner of Port Hacking Road and Prince's Highway. Situated just over the Tom Ugly Bridge - it was so far back in time Tom wasn't even ugly! I had turned sixteen and felt very grown-up at the wedding and even sported a dinner suit with a carnation. I still must have been a devil kid because the photograph reveals a very visible scar between my eyes - where I had been 'experimenting' with a double-bunger cracker, a marble and a bicycle pump. I should never have looked down the tube!

At Zandra's wedding. I read the telegrams.

I was never interested in participating in sports. Apart from surfing, I successfully managed to live my entire life without organised sport. Maybe being whacked with a stray cricket ball in the school playground sealed my fate? Maybe it is because sport typically places individuals or groups as winners and losers. Sure, I have watched the odd game of AFL and a bit of Olympic coverage, but most of the time I simply switch off from the daily Australian obsession. The government thinks nothing of spending our money on sports ovals and sporting facilities despite most sports being big business. I only wish the arts were given half as much media time and financial support. I wish!

I must have been channelling Les Darcy.

In my early twenties, I started to read books about folklore. I had already started my journey with folksong but wanted to learn more about traditions, customs and folklore. I also wanted to relate and understand the broad story of folklore to the Australian story. The more I read the further my mind travelled. A set of *'Funk & Wagnell's Dictionary of Folklore'*, a weighty tome I still refer to, was a good starting point and, over the years, I suspect I kept many rare book dealers busy with my growing demand for reference books. I pondered the idea of moving to America to undertake a university course in folklore (there were none in Australia), but, as usual, I went 'off-road' and eventually decided I would learn on the run. For over fifty years I have described myself as a graduate of the Dingo University of the Outback. It seems appropriate.

5

CRACKERS, BILLYCARTS & FAMILY SINGALONGS

Cracker Night, traditionally November 5, was the biggest night of the year by a long shot. It started as Empire Day and Guy Fawkes Night and then became Bonfire Night, but it was always Cracker Night to us Ramsgate kids. Sadly, it became a victim of the Politically Correct Police and was discontinued by law in 1987.

We saved up every penny we could, to buy fireworks from the local newsagent. There were lots to buy: Catherine wheels, jumping jacks, Vesuvius, sparklers, Roman Candles, Tom Thumbs, skyrockets and, of course, the mighty double-bungers. Nearly every street in Ramsgate had its own bonfire, and ours was at the top of Pasadena Street on the Grand Parade beachfront. All the kids in our street participated in building and guarding the bonfire which we built over a period of two weeks. Every bit of inflammable rubbish imaginable was scavenged from backyard sheds and sometimes even the shed itself. Old car tyres were prized because they created pitch-black, stinking smoke. Our billy carts went back and forth like soldier ants until we were satisfied our bonfire was taller and bigger than any other. We guarded the stack like dutiful sentries, ever-vigilant after rumours that the Monterey Street gang was set to make a raid.

On Bonfire Night, just about everyone in the street arrived for the firing, which took place as soon as it was dark. Every kid clutched brown paper bags containing fireworks, hoping none were fizzers. The adults enjoyed a barbecue and drinks, but we kids were usually too excited to think about food. Most bonfires had a Guy Fawkes at the very top - a wonky bag of a man stuffed with paper and rags, topped with a hat. The fire was lit in several places, and almost immediately, we started to light our crackers. There were sparkles and zooms and bangs left, right and centre. It was always a great night. In the morning, we couldn't wait to get back to the beachfront to search for 'duds' that we could resuscitate. We sometimes found frenchies (contraceptive rubbers) which added excitement to our morning hunt (not that many of us knew what they were for).

When we were older and bolder, we saw Cracker Night as a night of showing off and mayhem. We'd sneak away and play tricks on people we deemed neighbourhood weirdoes or cranks. The favourite was to knock on the front door, leave a lighted jumping jack, and run like the blazes. We also liked to put double-bungers in letter boxes and blow them to 'smithereens'. The worst prank of all was to put dog shit in a brown paper bag, light it, ring the doorbell and run. The poor respondent would open the door, see the fire, and, presumedly, stamp on the dog shit bag. We also experimented with fireworks, and to this day, I carry a scar from an accident that could have gone terribly wrong. I made a rocket launcher out of an old bicycle tyre pump, shoved a marble in one end and placed a double-bunger in the other. Bang! Straight between my eyes. I could have easily blinded myself. Maybe the PC Police were right in banning fireworks.

Billy carts were also banned. There was no room on the roads for both billy carts and cars. Dad, being a box maker in his youth, helped me make a dazzler of a billy cart, and despite the fact our suburb was mostly flat, I dragged it across the beachfront and back and forth to the local shops. I must have found a sizeable hill somewhere because my wrist still bears the scar of The Great Ramsgate Billy Cart Spill. I think the billy cart soon ended up in the incinerator or broken up for Cracker Night.

I didn't have a clue what I wanted to do when I would eventually leave school. I wasn't even sure I was equipped to do very much, or at least that's what I thought. I hadn't any particular skills and certainly nothing jumped out at me. One day a vocational guidance team arrived at the school, and each student was interviewed. I well-remember mine because I had to do a written test and then a physical test resembling a giant wooden jigsaw puzzle.

My vocational guidance interviewer finally spoke and asked whether I had "Considered working in a trade?" I must have started blankly at him because he kept going - "something like a motor mechanic or an electrician." I walked away completely shocked and disappointed and kept looking at my hands, thinking about how dirty they would look after an hour of meddling with motor grease. Friends will testify I am useless when it comes to fixing broken things. I am not good with a hammer, spanner or, as Dad called it, a 'whatchacallit'. I should also mention I have no sensible sense of direction, and if the GPS points one way, I'll head off in the opposite direction. I have become adept at following the mobile phone's Map app's bleating pulse. Oh, and I have rotten balance. Put me in the surf, and I will turn and zip, but never put me in a gymnasium callisthenics class or, for that matter, on a dance floor.

I was always good around the house and had a very happy home life. We were the ideal family unit of mother, father, sister, brother and dog. We also had the largest extended family in the world - more aunts, uncles and cousins you could poke a stick at. Since mom and dad were the eldest in each family - and because we always had a piano - we seemed to be the venue for most family gatherings. I lost count of the engagements, birthdays, weddings, anniversaries and holiday parties centred around our piano.

Parties at the Fahey household meant all the Jewish aunts arrived with food and the Irish uncles with booze. The Jewish side weren't big drinkers, but boy, could they tuck the food away! Huge trifles, pies, meatballs, fruit salads and chicken, lots of chicken (which was unusual in those days). My mother hardly drank, maybe one scotch and water before a party. Dad drank beer, whiskey, and, occasionally, that odd Irish concoction of rum and milk. I can't remember any wine or champagne in our house. The main focus at parties was always the piano. Most of my mother's family were musical clowns and took turns at the keyboards. Mom played everything from classical to popular and had a good musician's ear. Nana Polly played and sang like a 'Big Hot Mama' and could belt out a Sophie Tucker or Mae West song with the best of them. Uncle Mossy played the ukulele, guitar and piano and knew hundreds of songs, as did his wife, Jean. Uncle Clive played some dazzling styles but specialised in modern mainstream jazz. Uncle Sid Brandon, Jean's father, had dozens of music hall tunes from his parents, and I loved his unusual style. My sister Zandra played pop and jazz standards and still hits the keyboards whenever possible. Polly played stride piano, like Fats Waller, which was my favourite old style. Charlie, who we all considered a bit 'special', loved to sing Al Jolson songs which we all joined in on as he went down on one knee singing 'Mammy, Mammy, how I love ya, how I love ya...'

Our living room must have sounded like a music machine to the neighbours because we hardly ever stopped playing and singing at these parties.

We knew hundreds of old songs, including blues, jazz, popular, Irish and music hall favourites. As a kid, I was singing up there with the best of them, crowded around the piano, with 'Ida.....sweet as apple cider", 'Barney Google (with the goo goo googgly eyes), 'H-A double R-I G-A-N spells Harrigan', 'Sweet Betsy of Pike' and 'K-A-T-I-E, K A-K A, Katie...' There seemed to be a lot of stuttering songs!

Dad's side of the family sang typical Irish comedy songs like *'Paddy McGinty's Goat'* and *'If You're Irish, Come Into the Parlour'* and also songs I now recognise as traditional or folk songs. Dad also had a repertoire of semi-bawdy songs he would sing (quietly) after a few beers. It seemed my dad was always singing or whistling. He also had what I called a half-whistle - he would curl his tongue and issue a tune that resembled a kettle nearing the boil - he would do this when he was driving, in the shed, watering the garden or just walking down the street. I find I now unconsciously do it myself these days.

Dad's favourite place to sing was the shower, another habit I adopted, along with his songs. For several years after I started singing on stage, I used to describe myself as 'Australia's best-known shower singer'. He had quite a few songs in his repertoire. My favourites included *Who Killed Cock Robin?*, *Babes In the Woods*, *With His Old Grey Noddle A-shaking*, *Go Home to Your Mother You Red-Headed Bugger*, and another, *I Never Slept With Mary*, about the Holy Ghost claiming he wasn't the father of Jesus!

One song Dad sang, probably learned in the army, was a numerical folksong, one of those that count down or up. 'Whollop It Home' had an infectious chorus. The song contained no swear words, and I probably didn't understand its general intent, but I do know that every time Dad got to number eight, he couldn't quite allow himself to sing the line 'I gave her an inchy eight, ' she said, ' Put your finger up my date, ' without slurring the final part.

> I gave her an inchy one,
> Whollop it home, drive it home,
> I gave her an inchy one, whollop it home,
> I gave her an inchy one, she said I'd just begun,
> Put your belly close to mine and wriggle your bum.

I eventually recorded two albums of Australian bawdry (under the non de plume of 'Major Bumsore'). The two CDs (*Sing Us Anothery'/"Rooted in the Country*') offered a selection of songs and poems from my book *Sing Us Another, Dirty As Buggery*. The book traces the history of bawdy songs in Australia and, more importantly, has thousands of examples. Most of the songs are sexist, homophobic, ageist, racist and downright disgusting. I don't believe in censorship of traditional material and the bawdy songs mostly came from a different and earlier Australia. I feel obligated to document such songs, especially since the continuing shift to conservatism and political correctness has seen the disappearance of most bawdy songs. The environment for their singing has disappeared: the pubs are now mixed company and too noisy, and

The book and two CDs are a serious attempt to preserve a rapidly disappearing aural tradition.

television monitors blast music in every available space, even buses. In 2010 I staged a two-hour bawdy song free-for-all at the National Folk Festival, Canberra. I arranged for the National Library's Folklore & Oral History Unit to record the event. The recording is hilarious. https://www.warrenfahey.com.au/bawdy-song-verse-r-rated/

6

AS SIMPLE AS ABC

My cousins Graham, David, Ronald Lindsay, and I loved playing 'radio stations' whenever the weather was foul. We would get the big box of 78 rpm records and the wind-up gramophone player and set up the living room as our radio station. Ronnie and I were the main programmers, Graham, always the dour one, read the news, and young David looked after winding up the player. We had a lot of records, but our favourites were '*Tubby the Tuba*' and '*The Happy Prince*' and both were guaranteed to produce tears in the eye. Recordings by the Jewish philosopher humorist Dr Murray Banks were another favourite, as was the Victor Borge set. We gabbled away in our version of 'The Goons' with Graham reading our ridiculous news bulletins. We also made our own commercials. I'm not sure if all this playtime resulted in my lifetime association with ABC Radio, but it certainly didn't do any harm. I love the radio. The 'pictures' were and still are, better than television. We had a big console wireless at Pasadena Street, I think it was an AWA, and I loved those evenings when the family sat in the living room listening to radio serials and plays. Sunday nights were the only night we had dinner around the radio while listening to the Kraft Theatre play of the week. We probably had Kraft Coon Cheese on toast. Later, I got a crystal portable radio, a static-ridden thing, and then a stronger radio that allowed me to listen to short-wave broadcasts. I spent hours trying to tune into obscure broadcasts from around the world. I was also listening to local radio, which was far superior to the crap foisted on us nowadays. The only talking heads, and they weren't 'shock jocks', were the dignified opinions of people like Eric 'This I believe' Baume and news bulletins by James Dibbell.

Many of the Sydney radio stations had their own studio concerts and Amateur Hour programs. Terry Dear hosted the most popular. I was a regular listener to Roy 'Mo' Rene's *'McCackie's Mansion'*, *'Life With Dexter'* (starring Willie Fennell), *'Cop The Lot'* and, later, *'Pick A Box'* with Bob and Dolly Dyer, *'The Jack Davey Show'*, which seemed sidesplittingly funny, and 'The Bunkhouse Show', my favourite weekly hillbilly music session. Occasionally I would hear the serials like *'Doctor Mac'*, *'Biggles'* and *'Blue Hills'*.

As a young adult, I listened more to 2FC and 2BL, the two ABC stations that became Radio National and Local Radio 702.

When I was twenty-three, I made an appointment to see the Talks and Current Affairs Department of the ABC. I had already immersed myself in folk music and wanted to tell the world about it, leading me to radio's front door. Lord knows what the ABC production team thought of this somewhat cocky youngster who wanted to do book reviews about folklore and music. Still, they gave me a good hearing and an opportunity to contribute some meaty reviews. Stan Corry, Robyn Ravlich and Stephan Rapley, all proteges of the controversial left-wing departmental head, Alan Ashbolt, took me under their wing, and I became a semi-regular contributor. I was on the radio! The first reviews I did were of A. L. Lloyd's *Folk Song in England*, a serious look at the British folk revival and its working-class roots, and a series of ethnic music recordings issued by the American Folkways label. These reviews, usually about ten minutes a piece, often contained music or documentary sound bites.

A year later, in 1969, buoyed by the fact I was still on the air, I asked if I could contribute a series on the history of music from around the world. As a music program, it was unsuitable for

Ashbolt's department, so I was introduced to the head of ABC Music, the conductor John Hopkins. John was a classical music man but readily agreed to accept my program - as long as I presented it. That was a no-brainer, and I set about scripting twelve programs that featured the music of pygmies, Haitian voodoo, Italian choristers, Latin beats and just about anything I considered rare and fascinating. This was to be the first world music series broadcast on the ABC, and it was very successfully received and was eventually repeated by popular demand. I have never been game to listen to this series again as I must have sounded like a real prat!

I am so grateful to the ABC and the fine men and women who have worked there, sometimes unrecognised. I eventually made dozens of radio series, especially music programs, under the patronage of Harold Hort, who became head of music after Hopkins left. Classical music people usually appear mystified by folk music and its oral structure but not so many of the people I befriended in ABC Music. Apart from the support of Ashbolt, Hopkins and Hort, I had support from John Sullivan, Christopher Lawrence, Darrel Miley, Margaret Throsby, Alan Saunders, Richard Divall, Bill Flemming, Felix Heyman, Robert Paterson, David Mulhallen, Penny Lomax, Maureen Cooney, Andrew Ford, and so many others.

Harold Hort was a rebel and considered an odd bird by the music snobs but we got on like a house on fire, including regular liquid lunches at the Woolloomooloo Woolshed, where he would delight me by singing filthy songs. I doubt if his music department staff were too impressed.

Two of my most successful ABC radio series were the 12-part *The Australian Legend*' featuring Peter O'Shaughnessy and Declan Affley and the 16-part *While The Billy Boils*' where I used several singers and actors to recreate the stories of the bush and early cities. Both programs were broadcast several times, and *While The Billy Boils*' was released as an eight-cassette book. People still tell me they 'grew up listening' to these programs. One of my most challenging projects was an eight-program series titled *The Songs That Made Australia*', which featured my field recordings. It was made for the Social

History Unit with the encouragement of Tim and Ros Bowden. It was challenging because of the endless editing required in the days of tape. It took countless hours and, because of the foibles of radio programming, eventually broadcast on the Sunday evening 'graveyard shift' around 11 pm. Such a program is far easier nowadays with digital editing.

When, in 1976, the ABC announced it would launch an FM network, I was asked to contribute to a new regular Sunday program produced by Jack King. ABCFM had a broader charter when it was launched: classical, jazz, theatre music and folk however, this was changed after the appointment of Peter James, an ex-BBC executive who introduced Classic FM, a populist light classical format. All other music was banished.

The jazz fraternity screamed loudly, and their Sunday jazz program was saved from the chopping block. The folk audience, always fragmented, disappeared, as did folk music programming on ABC radio. By that stage, I was too busy with my record company to scream. Before the format changeover, I made hundreds of recordings with Sunday Folk, mostly with senior producers Jack King, Christopher Lawrence and David Mulhallen. It seemed I was in the studio with my group, The Larrikins, every few weeks. David and I were a solid team, and we devised special thematic programs on Australian animal songs, ghost stories, labour history and bush yarns. We received buckets of mail.

FOR A COUPLE OF YEARS, I scripted and co-produced a folk pantomime for Christmas, which was recorded in front of a very live audience, and broadcast live on ABCFM. I had flashbacks to my younger days around the wind-up gramophone. The 1990 production was 'A Wayside Christmas' and was set in a bush shanty run by Bertha Bother (Maggie Blinco). On the other side of the bar is a new chum, Bartholomew Green (Warren Fahey), a swagman known as 'Whinging' Willy (Chris Kempster), 'Old Henry' (Bob McInnes) and hard-bitten bush cynic, 'Hard Luck' Harry (Dave de Hugard).

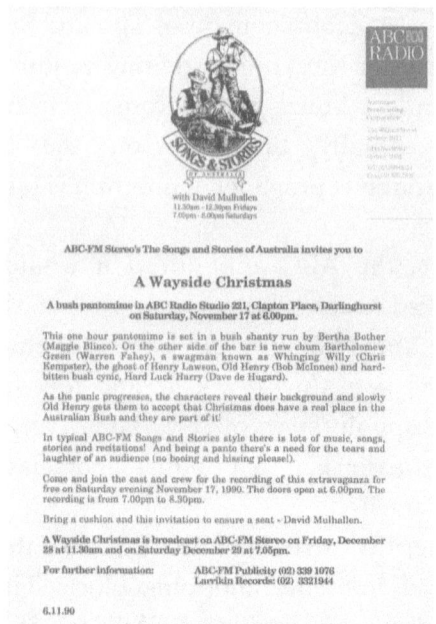

Flyer ABCFM's 'The Wayside Christmas' pantomime.

I continue to be an occasional voice on ABC radio, contributing to some of my favourite programs. I am also heard as a regular 'talking head' on all matters of folklore, music and bush history. I sometimes think I am the commentator on all things weird and wonderful. For example, I have chatted about everything from the Penrith Panther, bushrangers, Sydney eccentrics, dingoes, Cobb & Co., Polly-waffles and even the history of sliced bread.

The ABC has also been my record label and book publisher. I assume I have successfully paid my way, and it is an association I treasure. I can't imagine they made much revenue from my work, but it has been a cultural contribution that hopefully continues to fulfil their charter.

I have a face better suited to the radio. Still, I have done a bit of television work popping up in strange places like *'Simon Townsend's Wonderworld'*, *'The John Singleton Show'*, *'The Mike Walsh Show'*, *'Who Do You Think You Are?'*, *'The 7.30 Report'*, *'Collectors'* and even a celebrated appearance on *'Mr. Squiggle'* where I was dressed as a swagman and had to sing to a giant multi-coloured felt snail in a gum tree. In 1988, I was engaged as music consultant for a weekly program for ABC TV titled *'That's Australia'*. It was to be a television version of Ian McNamara's hugely popular 'Australia All Over' radio program and broadcast at 6 pm every Saturday before the news. 'Macca' was to host the program, but negotiations went sideways, and the actor, John Derum, was engaged.

'That's Australia' was made on the smell of an oily rag and filmed entirely at locations like Lane Cove National Park, harbour frontages and Centennial Park, and was essentially a 'magazine' format linked by John Derum. It was a huge success, and we received an extraordinary amount of mail, especially for the competitions. My role was to suggest and engage singers, yarn-tellers and poets. All the big and small names appeared, including Slim Dusty, John Williamson, Eric Bogle, Norma Murphy, Stan Coster, Bernard Bolan, The Bushwackers, Uncle Harry (Keith Garvey), Ted Simpson, and my group, The Larrikins. It was a unique hit and, for no explainable reason, unexpectedly yanked off the air after twenty-six weeks.

7

DUFFLE COATS, DEMOS & FOLK MUSIC

During the last two years of my schooling, I discovered folk music. It wasn't hard to find because, believe it or not, it was the most popular music of the time. Folk music, and I mean the English-speaking (and American-sounding) variety, was played on radio and television, and live music was performed at coffee shops, clubs and hootenannies worldwide, including Australia. The 'folk boom', as it was often referred to, was a curiosity with ancient songs and newly written songs in a traditional style, performed by artists with typically gleaming white teeth, neat hair and smart clothing. They were the type of young people you'd like to take home for dinner - never mind they were singing about oppression in the cotton fields, bawdy sailor songs and spooky ballads relating incest, trickery and murder. In my final school year, I used to catch the bus and train into the city to hear the music live and buy recordings of Pete Seeger, The Weavers, The Kingston Trio and Burl Ives.

Some fifty years plus later I am still passionately engaged with folk music and credit it as being one of the most important influences on my life's journey. I understand how many people, including my own inner circle, find this weird and possibly contradictory.

Performing at the Sydney Opera House Larrikin Folklife Festival, late seventies, with Cathie O'Sullivan and Jack Kevin's. I was singing Sally Sloane's 'The Wild Boy'.

I was never under the spell of popular music and still find most of it musically superficial. I even managed to avoid The Beatles, although I have been known to sing *'Blackbird'*. The Beatles, of course, in retrospect, were brilliant writers and arrangers. It's just that I had other, stronger musical distractions.

I HAVE WITNESSED SO many musical fashions come and go over the years and still keep an ear out, nodding sagely as music evolves and reinvents itself. For a short while in my teens, I even entered the world of the bodgie and early rock and roll, mostly that gritty, bluesy stuff from America's Sun Studios, but the beat soon disappeared. I did have a moment; well I hope it was only a moment when I wore stovepipe black jeans, snappy shirts, cockroach-killer pointed shoes and the crowning glory of luminous fluoro green or red socks. My hair and I had loads of it, was slicked back with Brylcream ('a little dab will do ya') or Spruso ('Spruce up on Spruso'), two hair goos that allowed for big cocky comb curls and a ducktail at the rear. If I've lost you with this description, I suggest you search 1950s male hair on Google image.

One of the first folk clubs I visited regularly.

Once I started to go to folk clubs, usually in coffee houses like the Greenwich Village at Kensington, near New South Wales University, or the Folk Attick on Darlinghurst Road, Kings Cross, I started to find flaws in the commercialisation of music. I wasn't comfortable with Australian singers impersonating English rural workers, American negroes and Irish tinkers, as if they were channelling the original song carrier. I was also confused and curious as to why so few Australian songs were sung. I am not sure if this fact was what started me searching out the Australian identity, but it certainly was instrumental. I tossed my bodgie look for blue jeans, a white tee shirt, a duffle coat and 'brothel sneaker' desert boots.

Folk music also led me to politics and, probably not surprisingly, to the left. I have never been a member of a political party and never will. I certainly favoured the Australian Labor Party in my younger days, but sadly, corruption and negativity in the party, especially in New South Wales, made supporting them farcical. I am a swinging voter and tend to support local politicians with an independent spirit. I have also supported the Greens in the upper houses as an independent voice. My father's maxim now determines my vote: "Whoever you vote for a politician gets in."

I was a semi-regular at Sydney Domain's Speaker's Corner for many years in the sixties and seventies. I was drawn by the craziness of it and also its history as a public forum for free speech. I experienced the last years of its heydays when up to five or six thousand people would gather. We had our favourite ratbags and rabble-rousers. Victor Zammit and John Webster were the big draws: ranting and raving on everything from the art of oratory to sexuality. These were no-holds-barred freak shows where audience members would scream abuse, attempt to take over and, quite often, perform weird dances to music no one else could hear. It wasn't unusual for these two speakers to attract crowds of 2000 or more. John Webster, a real crowd pleaser and eccentric, ruled his audience with outrageous comments and barbed humour, challenging his audience "on religion, free love and the individual inalienable right to be kinky". He declared himself one of Sydney's landmarks, along with the Harbour Bridge and Botanical Gardens, and demanded that his audience purchase his weekly newsletter. Unlike many speakers, these two men knew how to project their voices, command an audience and hold them. Zammit usually spoke on spiritualism, human rights and psychic phenomena. Other speakers sprouting 'Jesus Saves' usually ignited my rationalist interest. One Christian drum-beater was known as 'Bluey the bible basher', so named because of his high blood pressure that, whenever he got heckled, rushed to his face, turning it an explosive dark red, as he thumped his bible. Whenever this happened, and it was as regular as the GPO clock, the audience would shout, "Blood pressure, blood pressure, blood pressure," which only exasperated the situation. To Bluey's repeated cry of "What if you died tonight – where would you go?" the response was always the same, "The morgue!"

One of the most-loved of the Domain speakers was Sister Ada Green and her peculiar flock, who brought fire and brimstone to her corner near Art Gallery Road. They all had the dowdy, sour-faced look of people you wouldn't want to share eternity with. A small woman who always wore a flowered hat in the shape of a CWA sponge cake, Sister Ada would joyously shout out 'Praise Jes-us", to which the well-trained crowd would immediately follow with "And pass the ammunition"."I can save you!" cried Sister Ada, to which the inevitable response would come, "Can yer save me a pretty one?" Whenever she called out "Christ Jesus", the audience would respond with an equally loud "Kraft Cheeses". This was real old-time 'saving souls for Jesus' religion, and the interjections were nearly always boisterous and good-natured. Whenever one of her 'flock' spoke, the audience would groan in mock agony until Sister Ada started thumping her ever-ready tambourine.

One of my sixties favourites was a speaker we knew as 'The last of the Wobblies'. I never did record his name, but as a young student of labour history, I was fascinated by his theories on how the Wobblies could save the world. There was something sad in this old socialist soldier's fight as he yelled: "No God, no flag, no master." Whenever he cried out "I.W.W.," the crowds would call back an emphatic "I.W.W. – It Won't Work". We were like trained monkeys.

In 2020, I created a film on the Domain's history as part of my 'Sydney Stories' video series. https://www.youtube.com/watch?v=Hv2J5aO1fVc

AS THE OLD SAYING GOES, I readily 'carried the banner with Hannah' during my wilder years. I was angry about the idea of the world blowing itself to smithereens with a careless atom bomb, and I readily marched in Ban the Bomb demonstrations. I was also caught up in dozens of demonstrations against Australia's involvement in America's obscene war in Vietnam. In 2011, an old rebel mate, Bob Campbell, sent me an ASIO file photograph of me marching down Hunter Street, Newcastle, surrounded by protest banners.

ASIO file photograph. The young rebel, Warren (in sunglasses) marches against the Vietnam War.

I also sang at countless rallies. My favourite song then was Malvina Reynold's song *'The Bankers and the Diplomats Are Going In The Army'*. I still sing it occasionally. Like many idealist young people, I wanted to do my bit to change the world, and I saw folk music as one way I could contribute. I figured it would be difficult to shoot people if everyone sang, including the military front line. I thought about joining socialist groups like the Eureka Youth League but figured I was more of a quasi-socialist than a communist. Later, I accepted the fact I was more likely a 'Chardonnay socialist' or 'Bollinger Bolshevik.'

Folk clubs were reputedly dens of left-wing thought, but I never really found them to be that extreme. Certainly, some of the performers, like Gary Shearston, Jeannie Lewis and Declan Affley, were openly more than sympathetic. Folk music was never a lucrative business, and the idea of everyone sharing everything was idealistic and realistically attractive. Most of us were more interested in the community musical experience and, of course, determinately interested in the songs, especially the traditional songs. We were probably extremely boring and self-righteous about it. If you were going to sing or listen to a twenty-four-verse ballad, you needed such fortification! We also fortified our spirits with brandy and, god forbid, muscat and cheap claret. Most early venues were 'dry' but, fortunately, the day's fashion included duffel jackets with enormously large pockets. Some venues spiked their hot chocolate and coffee with alcohol in the service of more chorus singing!

I had my favourite Australian voices including Gary Shearston, who had a way with the old bush songs, Declan Affley, at the time a young Welsh-Irishman who was a consummate drinker, thinker and musician, and an eccentric Englishman named Mike Ball who played the English concertina and sang in a church-influenced almost magical style, especially when he sang his extraordinary interpretations of poems-turned-songs of Robert Graves. One song, based on a Graves' poem, '*Timothy Winters*', still haunts me with its bleak tenderness. I was always a sucker for a good story song, and the more I heard, the more I wanted to learn.

It was around this time my attention moved from American folk recordings to those of the British folk revival. I was never sure why they called the British commercialisation of folk music a 'revival', but it would also be incorrect to refer to this time as 'commercialisation'.

Compering an ABC Sydney Festival - Larrikin Folklife Festival concert at the Regent Theatre, Sydney. 1979. Where are those flared trousers?

Singers Mike and Carol Wilkinson and Mike Ball introduced me to the recordings of two British folk singers who were to dramatically change my musical direction. A. L. (Bert) Lloyd and Ewan MacColl were leading singers and interpreters of the English and Scottish tradition. Both were determinedly working class in their repertoire, communist when communism was based on something honest, and singers of immense drama and style that made most of their American counterparts sound superficial. Lloyd and MacColl had recorded Australian bush songs, accompanied by Peggy Seeger, for the 1950s Wattle label in Australia. They recorded countless recordings for the Worker's Music Association's Topic label in the UK. I was destined to become friends with both singers. However, at the time, all I wanted was to sing like Bert Lloyd and have every recording these artists ever made - and that was a staggering collection that included mining songs, songs of whalers, love songs and the most impressive collections of traditional ballads ever assembled and ever likely to be recorded.

I was staggered by the singing styles of Lloyd and MacColl and still am, although both are now dead and buried. Lloyd, the consummate Englishman, had a high voice capable of vocal gymnastics but took some listening to be appreciated. It was a peculiar style born of Lloyd's inert ability to replicate traditional song carriers as recorded by the great collectors of the late 19th century. He was not a copyist, for he made everything he sang a unique interpretation. The combination of this 'singing Englishman' and his extraordinary repertoire of balladry made for magical versions of old ballads like *'The Unquiet Grave', 'Long Lamkin'* and *'Six Dukes Went A Fishing'*, to name only three of hundreds he recorded. He was also a careful folkloric academic with a workingman's sensitivity that gave his song notes life. Lloyd had lived in Australia in the 1920s and had an extensive repertoire of bush songs. I corresponded briefly with him and eventually met him when he visited Australia in 1971. I presented him in two concerts in Sydney, in association with the NSW Folk Federation, and arranged for both to be recorded and broadcast by the ABC. One was a general concert, a mixed bag, the other a concert dedicated to 'The Erotic Muse'. To hear him sing '*The Two Magicians*', a ballad where two shape-changing magicians have a sexual 'battle', one turning herself into a ship, the other immediately turning into sails, and so on, was a triumph and drama worthy of any theatrical experience. Bert was getting short of breath by the time of his visit, but he still hypnotised his audience.

I took him to dinner at Harry and Rita Robertson's home in Balmain one night. Bert had heard Harry's album of original whaling songs ('*Whale Chasing Man*' Larrikin), and Harry had heard Bert's equally wonderful collection of traditional whaling songs ('*Leviathan*' Topic). It was a lively night of talk and song as we dined upon Harry's legendary bacalao, a Norwegian salted cod and potato stew. Harry's Rotterdam Shag tobacco gave the evening a distinctive aroma reminiscent of a whaling depot! Having these two men sing across the table was a unique experience.

I was fortunate enough to count Ewan MacColl and his then-partner, Peggy Seeger, as close friends. After years of listening to their recordings, especially their landmark BBC radio ballads produced alongside Charles Parker, their work with the Critic's Group, and a series of albums offering their renditions of the great ballads, 'The Long Harvest', I opened correspondence with them regarding a possible tour of Australia. I never wanted to be a tour agent; I already had my hands full with the record store and fledgling and always demanding record company. However, I reasoned that if anyone wanted to tour them, I did.

A. L. 'Bert' Lloyd, master singer of folk songs. Image via Mark Gregory.

Ewan had always wanted to visit Australia and was excited about the possibility. According to Peggy, who wrote most of the letter, he "never shut up about it."

I didn't have enough money to stage the sort of tour I envisaged so in 1976, I went to one of Australia's largest trade unions, the Amalgamated Metal Workers Union, and fronted their feisty national secretary, Laurie Carmichael and his 'fix it' offside, Marie Cunningham. Laurie was a dour man, a communist, a deep thinker, and a passionate lover of introspective classical music, mostly Russian symphonies. Marie had a background in New Theatre and was very aware of MacColl and Seeger. We did the deal over a cup of tea - the union would sponsor the tour as long as there were some factory concerts, and I handled all the tour management. It was a solid arrangement, and, of course, the union affiliation was welcomed by Ewan and Peggy as a unique opportunity.

The tour was an outstanding success for all concerned, with concerts in key factories in Sydney, Melbourne, and Adelaide, as well as major concerts in all states except Tasmania and West Australia. They also performed a special 'Songs of Struggle' at the Tom Mann Theatre in Sydney. I did the opening thirty minutes, and then Ewan and Peggy talked about and sang songs of struggle from history. It was fascinating, and thanks to the AMWU, it is now freely available on my website. https://www.warrenfahey.com.au/songs-of-struggle/

Ewan was interested in all things Australian and was like a big kid in a lolly shop. I knew that in England, he was considered aloof, sometimes cranky and usually dogmatic. Australian audiences found him none of these, and he went out of his way to reach out to anyone who wanted to chat. Both artists, and they were consummate artists, charmed most of the media. I say most because we maintained a fairly exhaustive media program, and some situations were ridiculous. On one occasion, Peggy was booked to perform on Adelaide's midday women's television program. It didn't take long for her hair to bristle at the pretentious nature of the host, who had no regard for her fellow workers, the ones she relied on the most. All charm and smiles, Peggy was inevitably asked to sing *'The First Time Ever I Saw Your Face'*, a song Ewan had written for her in 1957, which became a worldwide hit for Roberta Flack in 1972. Peggy, still smiling, faced her host and discussed the tour and the importance of songs, especially socially conscious songs. When the woman, teeth still grinning like a racehorse, asked Peggy to sing, and, looking straight into the camera, Peg announced that she had decided to sing '*I am a Union Woman*', a fiery Aunt Molly Jackson song, instead. The studio crew loved it, and the not-so-smiling host couldn't wait to get us out of her sight.

The next morning, still laughing, we were in the hotel dining room and talking about the insidious nature of Muzak as waves of bland, familiar music wafted over our muesli. Peggy softly asked the waiter if he "would turn the music down a little" while we ate our breakfast. Her polite request was met with a snarled, "There are other guests here, Madam." It was a red rag to a bull, or the female equivalent, so up Peggy gets and waltzes up to every table in the large room and asks whether they would mind if the music were lowered. Not one person objected, and most wanted it turned off. Point made.

The most popular songs of the tour were Peggy's *'I Wanna Be An Engineer'*, a song which has become a mini anthem of the women's movement, and a Ewan and Peggy co-write, *'Legal Illegal'*, about Joh Bjeke-Petersen, the conservative Queensland politician with notions of grandeur. Their concerts were definitely audience pleasers with a broad spectrum covering ballads, humorous songs and some of their most successful original songs like *'Shoals of Herring'*, *'I'm A Freeborn Man'*, *'Manchester Rambler'* and *'Dirty Old Town'*.

Ewan MacColl and Peggy Seeger, Sydney, 1976.

Travelling with Ewan and Peggy, and we made a lot of car trips, was always a mixture of history lessons and singalong. I was privileged to be immersed in their knowledge, music and friendship. I was also fascinated by how they approached their songs as performers, and I was given 'lessons' whenever I wanted more insight. I was surprised to see both artists prepare for the stage with limbering-up and breathing exercises. I was fascinated to see how Ewan used the Stanislosky acting approach to songs - delivering the story songs from different vocal efforts. For example, if singing a love song, he would tend to sing in a higher register - flitting through the verses like a hummingbird; the darker ballads usually called for a more theatrical approach and a vocal effect that could be stabbing, ponderous, threatening, etc.

We stayed at a beach hut near Green Point on the NSW north coast for a few days between concerts, and these were some of the most wonderful times. We sang and talked into the night and walked the beaches during the day. The tour had been a success in more ways than we expected.

A couple of years later, I visited Ewan and Peggy in England and joined them on a concert tour of Scotland. After staying a few days at their home in Kent and experiencing one of the most hilariously weird nights of my life - we dined on pickled onions, stilton and claret as we listened to a compilation of around one hundred bizarre renditions of 'The First Time Ever I Saw Your Face', and there were some complete horrors including versions by The Kingston Trio, Chad Mitchell Trio, Peter, Paul & Mary, Elvis, Brothers Four, and Johnny Cash - we set out for Dumfries where they owned, as Ewan described it, "a cow shed with a house attached to it." We then drove down through picturesque Scotland, my first visit, usually eating Indian curries at night (where was the Scottish food?) and doing a bit of sightseeing before the concerts.

In 1982 Ewan and Peggy returned for a second tour.

Ewan died in 1989, leaving an enormous legacy of books, recordings and original thought. Peggy's legacy will be equally impressive as that of a singer, recording artist, author (her biography is a sensational read), accompanist, and thinking activist. Peggy was devastated when Ewan passed. I have kept in contact with Peg and see her when she visits Australia. Peggy eventually found a new partner in Irene Scott, a move that surprised and possibly shocked many but also brought her new admirers for her music and her determination to be her own person. Irene has a house in New Zealand so Peggy, who lives in England where her children are, visits regularly. In her eighties, she understandably no longer wants the hassle of air travel. She remains among the youngest, busiest and brightest seniors I have ever met. Like many of us 'old guard', she maintains an active online performance schedule.

Because of my activity as a performer, observer, commentator, producer and, of course, my years operating Folkways and Larrikin

Records, I have maintained contact with the people and organisations contributing to the development of folk music in Australia. I reluctantly use the word 'scene'. Still, by its nature, it is a fragmented movement including State and Territory folk federations, music clubs, numerous festival organisations, folk music-related businesses and a host of artists. I am seen as one of the folk 'elders'. I attended the first festival in what has become the National Folk Festival, the large festival event staged in Canberra every Easter. The first Port Phillip Folk Festival was staged in Melbourne in 1967. I continued to attend each year as it moved around the country, including being involved on the organising committee in Sydney in 1970. After the festival's success, we established the Folk Federation of New South Wales to coordinate and promote folk arts. I hold membership card number 3 and have since been awarded a life membership. In 1973, I was the program director of its second Sydney festival, The Port Jackson Folk Festival. I had just established Folkways, and it doubled as the festival's office. Over the years, I have performed at national folk festivals numerous times and in 2022, to celebrate its permanent home of the past twenty-five years, I presented a thematic concert, 'Tracks We Have Travelled'. I am one of the few actively remaining from the first festival. In 2019, the Folk Federation of NSW asked me to be the festival producer for the Sydney Folk Festival - the first in thirty-five years. It was an outstanding success.

I am getting to the age where I am starting to feel like a folk 'curio' - especially since so few performers seem to value or explore the old songs and stories that I see as the backbone of our folk treasury, the bush songs and stories.

If I've learnt anything over the years, it is that the various branches of folk music, and its many twigs and leaves, need the nourishment of media exposure. Social media has provided a much-needed platform for emerging artists; however, I strongly believe the ABC has neglected its charter of encouraging all cultural expressions, particularly folk music. With the changeover of ABC FM to a classical format, the reconfiguration of Radio National to primarily talk, and the emphasis of the ABC capital city and centrally-programmed regional stations to playlists similar to commercial stations - Elton John and his cohorts - music under the umbrella of 'folk music' does not get much airplay. Dedicated (and extremely popular) programs like *The Planet* and *Daily Planet* were axed and never replaced. I am critical of musical elitism, which stifles musical availability. I believe the time has come for our ABC to establish a digital radio station for folk music (in all its wonderful expressions) - there's certainly enough music, demand and talent. ABC Jazz does a terrific job with jazz-related music. Oh, is someone going to tell me jazz and classical music are more culturally 'important' than folk music? Memo to Aunty - just do it!

8

YOU ARE WHAT YOU EAT

Although I am a city-slicker, I have always loved the bush, and in my late teens, I became an energetic bushwalker and joined the Youth Hostels Association. The YHA operates hostels across Australia, mostly in bushland conducive to walking. These dwellings offer basic accommodation and for a few dollars, you can stay for up to three days. In the sixties, you brought your own 'hostel sheets', food and they supplied the rest. Everyone had to accept 'hostel duties' which could be anything from sweeping, preparing firewood, cleaning kero lamps and even toilet duties. Some of the characters I met in those years are still fresh in my mind and some I still value as friends. There was an odd bird called Harold who always volunteered for toilet duties as it was usually a quick job emptying the pans down a slush pit and sluicing with lime. One day at Garie Beach, Harold wandered off to do his usual job and ceremoniously hoisted the half-full pan up on his head and then we heard screams, ungodly screams, coming from the bush. Harold had hoisted the pan onto his head and the bottom of the pan had rusted and collapsed - he had his head covered with shit. We all wanted to vomit but knew Harold felt worse. He ran down the hill, still screaming, until he jumped in the surf, fully clothed.

Evenings around the kitchen table or campfire reinforced my love for folk music. The YHA was a broad church - non-religious, non-political and non-ageist. All you needed was a membership hostel card stamped every visit. I eventually became Chairman of the Sydney Cumberland Region and, later, a board member of the national organisation. For some reason, I never used international hostels, primarily because I couldn't afford to travel overseas until I was in my late twenties. My YHA card, with stamps of Katoomba, Garie Beach, Thredbo, Little Marley, Tharwa, Carrington, Towler's Bay and so many others was deposited in the first instalment of my National Library manuscript collection in 2004.

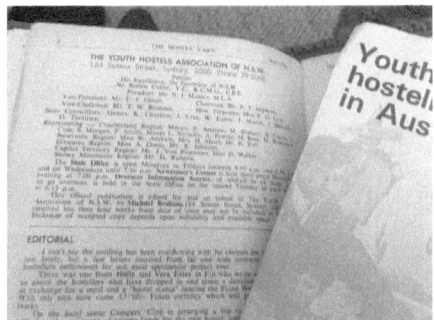

There's my name on the list of NSW YHA directors.

I was always a keen body surfer. As a young kid, my sister and her friends regularly took me to Maroubra Beach on Sundays. I guess it was the closest drive from Ramsgate. Maroubra in those days hadn't been built up and the beach was surrounded by sandhills. To earn my keep, it was my 'job' to tramp from the beach up to the shopping centre with lunch orders. There was a Greek deli that sold baked rabbits. Chicken was still a luxury, and roasted chicken takeaway was virtually unheard of. The baked rabbit was often dry, but it was delicious for someone surfing for three or four hours. In late high school, I started to hitch from Ramsgate to North Cronulla beach on weekends, usually with a schoolmate, Anthony Givney. We must have been crazy, hitchhiking back and forth, but we always got a ride. Tony and I stayed mates, and after leaving school, we bought motor scooters, a much more efficient means of travel. Tony also went into the record industry as finance manager for Festival Records. I continued to body surf throughout my life although I look back at my wasted days spent baking on Tamarama or Bondi Beach, sometimes covered in coconut oil like a potato chip about to be deep fried. I hardly go in the sun these days.

My first job after leaving school was with the Commonwealth Bank at Kogarah Bay. I had obtained the Leaving Certificate but failed mathematics, and here I was counting money. In those pre-decimal days, we had lots of heavy coinage. Most kids I knew had a tiny tin savings bank model of the Commonwealth Bank's Martin Place head office building. I had to pour the coins into a big shaker device that separated the pennies, halfpennies, two shillings etc. Smallest at the top and largest, the penny, at the bottom. I then had to count off the required quantity and roll them for the tellers. I also had to put all the day's trades, withdrawals and deposit slips into ledgers. It was boring work, and I lasted six months. I was distressed that this could be my life, anyone's life.

My sister Zandra worked at an advertising agency called Canny, Paramor & Canny, and I decided that the advertising world needed my extraordinary talent. I went to interview after interview, but, according to most, at nearly eighteen, I was too old, as they usually took trainee boys on after their Intermediate Certificate. With my sister's encouragement, I enrolled in the Sydney Technical College Advertising Certificate course, a three-evening-a-week intensive course. I probably had no idea what I was doing, but I persevered. Eventually, in 1963, I found a job as a despatch boy at Jackson Wain, an agency at Miller Street, North Sydney. There were five of us trainees under the tight control of a Scotsman named John Mackie. We'd huddle together in the Despatch room, waiting to be summonsed to collect and deliver inside mail and memos and outside runs to the city. In those days, everything was done by hand, including the all-important preparation and delivery of production parts to printers. I knew every lane and street in Sydney CBD and how to get there and back quickly. After six months, Mr Mackie advised me that I would move to the agency's Typographical section. I was excited and a bit scared as there was so much to learn, and much of the typesetting came down to mathematics. I was okay with working in the department and learnt many artwork and print skills that I still use. I was already making some freelance contributions to ABC Radio. I kept sniffing around the Radio and Television department of the agency, which was managed by a towering man named Neville Merchant. One day, I caught the lift with him, and I blurted out, "I want to work for you and produce radio commercials." He looked at me, my knees were shaking, and his booming voice replied, "Well, no other bastard does! Come and see me on Monday."

I started as a radio producer that week and assisted a Frenchman, Jacques de Vine, 'Jack of the wine', who intrigued me with his Citroen and hardcore breakfasts of strong coffee and chocolate croissants (I'd never seen a croissant). He was good to work with as he wasn't interested in work - so I did everything he didn't want to do. After a while, I became the main radio producer because everyone wanted the glamour of producing television. I was still a youngster, still green around the gills, but I worked on Rothmans, Peter Stuyvesant, Qantas, Sunbeam, Johnson & Johnson and dozens of other major accounts. I also did my fair share of television, including a stint producing the 'Galloping Gourmet', Graham Kerr, and the remarkable Maggie Tabberer for 'Woman's Weekly'. Maggie was a one-take wonder and would record the weekly 30-second commercial in one take, wave, and be off. I still occasionally see Maggie T. in 2011, Graham Kerr and I communicated via email. Jackson Wain had a string of Creative Directors, and two became lifelong friends: Donald Horne and Leo Schofield. Jackson Wain changed hands several times and eventually became part of the international Leo Burnett Advertising conglomerate.

In 1967, I was ready for a new challenge. I took a two-year contract to become the Activities Officer of the first student's union associated with a technical college, the Tighes Hill campus, recently vacated by Newcastle University. My brief was to plan and implement a program of activities for mind and body for the student community. My bushwalking and folk music experience came into use, but I also arranged festivals, talkfests, beauty parades, debates, sporting events etc. I also managed the student shop, which sold stationery, books and snack food. I had some memorable times in Newcastle, especially in setting up the Newcastle Folk Club, a weekly gathering that spawned some major weekend festivals like 'The Wild Colonial' weekends. I also made some lifetime friends in the area.

I had become a vegetarian before I headed for Newcastle, and I recall my first flat at Mayfield was behind a butcher's shop. Not the best location for a non-meat eater. My flirtation with vegetarianism lasted around eight years until I was seduced by my mom's baked lamb dinner.

I ALWAYS HAD AN INQUIRING MIND, and vegetarianism appealed to my inner sense. I think a combination of health and humanity pushed me over to the green side. I also had a medical situation that troubled me. As a teenager, I suffered strange lumps on my hands for a few years. They didn't cause pain, but as a teen, you think everyone is looking at you, and I was very conscious of the them. Doctors had given me pills, paints and potions, but the warty-looking lumps refused to budge. At the time, I had been a regular at the Bligh Street Cinema, a small art theatre screening avant-garde films by Fellini, Visconti and Bunuel and others, and I took to frequenting the Theosophical Society Adyar Bookshop. The bookshop was down a staircase next to the cinema, and its aromatic smell of incense made it very exotic. I picked up a leaflet from the Natural Health Society of New South Wales, an organisation that promoted vegetarianism. They had weekly dinner meetings where the buffet offered Hunza pie, baked vegetables and salads. For drinks, they served almond milk, although I later learned they didn't encourage drinking anything with food, not even water. In those days, an interest in a diet for health was associated with being a 'food crank'. I became a regular at these dinners as they coincided with my weekly Wednesday meeting of the YHA. One of the NHS members noticed my hands and suggested I make an appointment with their naturopath, Kenneth Jaffery. I had given up on a cure, but after the initial interview and iridology (I had no idea what he was looking at) he said I was healthy. If I wanted to eliminate the lumps, I needed to give up dairy food, especially the pint of milk I consumed daily. Miraculously the lumps disappeared in three or four weeks and never returned. I became a sceptical convert. Today, I prefer almond milk over cow milk, but I am a sucker for good cheese. To my mind, I was never a crank and saw my food detective work as just another path of my curious mind. I attended some crackpot and not-so-crackpot talks on health, including Dr Paul Bragg's Sydney Town Hall talks, where he espoused the benefit of apple cider vinegar. I always felt he was onto something.

If I wanted real oddities, I listened to the Theosophical Society's Sunday night broadcasts on radio 2GB. The society held the broadcast license for the station for many years. The Liberal Catholic Church also broadcast on Sundays and between them and the Liberal Catholic Society, my head spun with stories of astral flying, ectoplasm, clairvoyance, fairies and seances—theosophical leaders like Annie Besant, C. W. Leadbeater, Madam Blavatsky and Jiddu Krishnamurti. The Rev. Charles Leadbeater, a member of the Order of the Star in the East, a spiritual group associated with the Theosophical Society, later became the Australian Presiding Bishop of the Liberal Catholic Church, a spiritual version of the Roman Catholic Church, which denounced anthropomorphisms and expressions of the fear and wrath of God. This group built the Star Amphitheatre at Balmoral Beach in 1924. Urban myths surround this site claiming it was built for the second coming. Tickets were sold so Sydneysiders could see Christ walk on water. This was untrue. It was built as an outdoor lecture theatre. As you can imagine, my nineteen-year-old brain was spinning!

Strangely enough, the NHS and YHA were to meet when the YHA took over the disused NHS Hopewood Children's Home in Bowral. I remember my first inspection tour of Hopewood and the grand house with rooms with apparatus used in health hygiene procedures. It looked strange. The 'stable' was a separate building where 86 babies, 43 boys and 43 girls, were raised from 1942 to 1951 by the Youth Welfare Association of Australia YWAA) under the guidance of its founder, Mr L. O. 'Daddy' Bailey, a somewhat eccentric and successful character who wanted to prove that healthy living could cure the world. The children were raised on a natural diet, primarily fresh fruit and vegetables. Fortunately, Bailey owned the Katie's chain of women's wear and could finance the project. The YWAA was connected to Bailey's Natural Health Society. After Bailey's death, the society was run by his assistant Mrs Madge Cockburn. Years later, in 2019, Max Cullen and I took our two-man play, *'Dead Men Talking'*, to Hopewood, now owned by renowned artist, Tim Storrier and his talented wife, Janet, who manages the extensive gardens.

The Hopewood story has always fascinated me, especially after discovering my friend, Rebel Penfold Russell, dated Paul Cockburn, son of Madge. The kids may have been healthy in body, but history shows many of them found adult life difficult and unfortunate stories abound.

My interest in healthy food led me to become a regular at the Child Health Study Centre on George Street, Sydney. This was a real-timewarp history lesson. Operated by two elderly gentlemen who wore long white coats and sported equally long white beards reminiscent of ancient members of Z. Z. Top, these men darted to and fro in the dark wood-lined store supplying customers with herbal remedies. The shop itself had hundreds of small pull-out drawers labelled Irish Moss, Liquorice Root, Sage leaves, Fennel etc. and had a deliciously old-world smell. In the window was a life-sized boy with ruby cheeks and his hand out - and in his hands were a sweet they called 'Little Normies'. It was a non-sugar ball made out of nuts and dried fruit and rolled in carob and coconut. I became friendly with the two brothers, and they used to invite me into the back room, where I'd watch them put the ingredients through a meat-mincing machine. I was always intrigued by the massive painting of an old man with a long grey beard, just like theirs, that hung on the back wall. I later realised it was George Bernard Shaw. The shop eventually closed, and the brothers retired to Vineyard, near Richmond, on the lower Blue Mountains. I often wonder whatever happened to 'Little Normie'.

In the mid-eighties, I telephoned my sister Zandra and asked if she wanted to start a business with me - a health food shop. Grandma Was Right was right for the times, and Paddington's bustling commercial strip was the right location. An old-style shop had become vacant, and since I already had Folkways Music in the same block, it seemed a good idea. Z had raised three daughters and was ready for a challenge, and I had what I thought was a catchy name for the business. We plotted out the store layout and what things we wanted to offer and opened a month later. It was an instant success, and the tiny store quickly built a regular clientele that appreciated we were trying to do something different. Zandra managed the whole affair, and I occasionally played shopkeeper. I also sourced loads of products normally unavailable, including the American Tom's range of soaps and toothpaste (I still hanker for their cinnamon toothpaste), specialty foods and healthy sweets. We became a major outlet for IKU fresh whole foods and the Spiral Foods macrobiotic range. I doubt if either of us knew how much was involved in such a store, but it seemed there were always boxes to be unpacked and shelves to be stacked. Neither of us made much money out of the venture, but we certainly ate healthily and well. Zandra closed the shop in 1994 after unpacking one box of sultanas too many.

I am still interested in food, and I am one of those people who read the ingredient list on the food I purchase (or, more often than not, don't purchase) at the supermarket. If it has colouring, flavouring, emulsifiers or obscene amounts of sugar, which seems to be most products, it goes back on the shelf. I only use virgin olive oil and rice bran oil. Where possible, I buy organic fruit and vegetables and only buy what I need. Fortunately, I have a Harris Farm and Woolworths close to my apartment. Having the Wayside Chapel and St. Canice's, two charities that feed the homeless and hopeless, as neighbours have made me very aware of food wastage. I support them both.

I still eat meat, but, once again, I am selective in what I buy. Always free-range chicken and lamb. I don't eat pork, even bacon, because I have read too much about the lousy lives most farm-bred animals have, especially pigs. Asian and Middle Eastern cuisines are my favourites, and avoiding pork on the fork is a struggle.

I HAVE WRITTEN two books on Australian food history. One, *When Mabel Laid The Table*, published by the State Library of NSW Press in 1992, gained a fair bit of notoriety as it was a relatively untouched subject. Incidentally, its title comes from the Dad & Dave sexist line: "Get off the table, Mabel, the money's for the beer." The second, *Tucker Track (The curious history of Australian food and drink)*, published in 2005 by ABC Books, was more of a nostalgic read and, as Margaret Fulton kindly offered for the cover, 'What a joy to be reminded of so much lore and wisdom from our childhood'. Food writer, Leo Schofield, launched the book at the Country Women's Association's Sydney headquarters. My friends supplied recipes from the book for the launch, including pumpkin scones, porcupine (half a pineapple studded with cabanossi and cheese sticks), lamingtons, angels-on-horseback and some other scary stuff from indigestion central.

It reminded me of an old rhyme when you burp:

> 'Pardon me for being so rude,
> It was not me, it was my food,
> It just came up to say hello, a
> And now it's gone back down below.'

9

LIFE ON THE FRINGE

After completing my contract in Newcastle, I returned to Sydney. I was slightly shellshocked because, in my final year after I had turned 21, I accepted I was homosexual. I had been going out with a gorgeous Dutch girl and thought it was love, but I also knew something else was at work. I suspect it slammed home to me after I had taken Karlyn to meet my parents. I'm not sure how it happened, but a friend, Robin Connaughton, had loaned me his classic British racing-green Morgan to drive to Sydney, and after a weekend staying with my folks, my father farewelled us with a genial, "I guess the next time we'll see you will be in church." I drove back to Newcastle and hardly spoke to Karlyn, my mind spinning like a top. When we reached her house, I blurted out that it was over. She was sympathetic but must have thought me a very odd goose. A few months later, after my 21st birthday party and too much wine, a neighbour put me to bed and tried to get in with me. I vomited all over him in horror. I was still confused but knew I had to move forward.

Back in Sydney, I got a job as the coordinating head of the radio and television department of a large advertising agency, Hansen Rubensohn McCann and Erickson. My job was to assess scripts, allocate them to the various in-house producers, coordinate the budgets, and prepare final presentations for the account executives and clients. I was well paid, had a large office and enjoyed the challenge. I became friends with the elderly Sim Rubensohn, who mentored me and gave me insights into the often crazy advertising world. Sim was unpopular with many of the staff and had a reputation for barking orders in a high-pitched dictatorial fashion. He liked me for some reason, possibly the tenuous Jewish connection or my already leftish tilt. His pet account was the Australian Labor Party, and he asked me to produce their radio commercials personally. I had a terrific working relationship with the team of television producers, many of whom became lifelong friends. Bryan Westwood, who was also a distinguished portrait artist (he produced a stunning painting of Prime Minister Paul Keating), David Elledge, an American bon vivant who later bought Patrick's Restaurant in Paddington. George Pugh, a thinker and writer who became a senior director with ABC television, and, finally, 'The Baron' Count Hans von Alderstein, husband of *Vogue* magazine's matriarch, Marion von Alderstein.

The serious young advertising man.

Life at the agency was hectic and competitive. Having my own office allowed me to also prepare scripts for my ABC programmes during downtime or early mornings. I have always been an early bird; arriving at the office at 7.30 am wasn't unusual.

When I returned to Sydney, I moved into a Paddington terrace house and shared it with a radio announcer, David White, and a very randy English boy named Leo, who seemed to have hot and cold running girls. They were good lads, and we had great times until

David left to accept a country radio job, and I had had enough of Leo's bedroom stories.

I loved Paddington's organic architecture, quirky dunny lanes and robust pub culture. My father always said: "Paddington born, Paddington bred. Strong in the arm and thick in the head." I suspect he meant it the other way around!

There was a gay bar on Oxford Street, just around the corner from our terrace on Regent Street and right next to the Paddington Post Office. It was called Enzo's after its charismatic host. The bar was owned by his partner, Ray, who owned butcher shops. Enzo's was a wine bar. The licensing laws only permitted wine-based drinks, and ninety per cent of the clientele drank Dry Cinzano and Dry Ginger, 'Dry and Dry'. It was always packed, and I must have walked past it hundreds of times, too terrified to walk in the door.

I'd been at the advertising agency for about six months when, one night, I plucked up enough courage to enter Enzo's door. The music was blaring, and the joint was jumping. It was only one of a handful of gay venues in Sydney then. Shaking like a leaf, I walked in and weaved my way down the bar, trying not to be noticed and certainly not looking at anyone. Halfway down, a hand reached out, and George Pugh and David Elledge, both openly gay men, gave me a big smile and said, "Welcome - we were expecting you!". Four weeks later, I moved into a spare room at David's terrace house in Little Brown Street, Paddington. Bruce Donnan, who was to become one of my best mates, shared the other room. We were family. David, a terrific host, was like a mother hen, always inviting friends around and always looking after everyone's needs. He loved all sorts of jazz and classical music, and the house was always alive. On Sundays, he would cook giant pots of Italian sausages and fried onions for lunch. We usually listened to a reel-to-reel tape he cherished of a dynamic choral Bach Mass in B minor. He played it at full volume. Afterwards, usually a bit pickled, we would wander up the road to check Enzo's out.

These were the days of gay clones. Most wore moustaches reminiscent of Tom Selleck's Magnum character. It was a strange western denim, checkered shirt, macho tribal working-class look. The Village People took it to new sartorial heights. At one stage, even drag queens appeared with moustaches!

I came out effortlessly, and being gay was never an issue in my life, apart from the dramatic realisation in Newcastle. I have never let it rule my life. I am too much of an individual to become attached to a tribe. I was not a club person, although I've done my fair share of carpet crawling. Sissy talk and gay culture are not my styles. I never discussed my sexuality with my parents, but my mother often said I did not need to marry. They knew I was married to music and, as mothers often do, knew more about me than I realised. My dad, ever the saint, was always happy that I was happy. I did tell my sister. I took her to dinner at David's restaurant, Patricks, and when I told her I was gay, she started to cry. I felt awkward until she got up and kissed me, saying, "I'm so happy. I knew, but I thought you didn't know." If only coming out was that easy for everyone.

Young gay life was and, to some degree, still is powered by recreational drugs, including far too much booze. Late-night dance clubs are hunting grounds and, in so many ways, strangely, be they around the corner or in a foreign city, they are 'familiar'. Sometimes, when travelling in a strange city, it is reassuring to walk into a gay bar, be anonymous, and be welcomed into a community. My main problem was always the music, as most gay bars play inane, endless dance music which drives me batty.

The history of gay Sydney has been fairly well documented, especially from the more visible 1970s. The sixties were more secretive, closeted, and prone to fantastic rumour mills. It wasn't unusual to hear that such-and-such was gay, including Prime Ministers and one Governor-General. Every male actor was guilty before opening his mouth; even some women were hushed. As they say, "where there's smoke, there's fire", and I have been privy to many the revelation. I have never seen it as my role to be a gossip, and certainly not the type to discuss anyone's sexuality.

For a moment, I flittered to Sydney's Oxford Street clubs, reassuring myself as gay, celebrating with the tribe, and always looking in as an outsider at what looked like a parallel universe. Capriccio's, known as 'Cap's', was the main club, and it had over-the-top drag shows every night of the week. Opened by LGBT entrepreneur Dawn O'Donnell, in 1969, just after Ivy's Birdcage, Taylor's Square, and before Patches, Flo's Palace and the club where 'feathers met leather', The Midnight Shift (sometimes colloquially called 'the Midnight Frock'.) As they say, 'there were feathers and glitter from arsehole to breakfast!' A friend, a large 'gal' inspired by 'Divine', dragged herself into the job of 'door bitch' of Cap's, primarily to keep the straights out of the club. Lorraine Campbell-Parade perched herself at the top of the stairs leading from Oxford Street and would greet customers, insisting any straight boys had to kiss her to gain entry to the club; it worked a charm. The shows were held in a separate showroom, and each table had the obligatory 'food with alcohol' dish of stale jazz biscuits and chopped-up cabanossi, which, regulars knew, was never to be eaten. It was probably recycled daily. David Mitchell and David Penfold produced many of the shows; undoubtedly, the star performer was Rose Jackson, who, Tony Sheldon said, was his inspiration for the role of Bernadette in 'Priscilla, Queen of the Desert'. Karen Chant and Trixie Lamont were the other two regular showstoppers. Other high-kicking gals included Corrine Day, Honey West, Red Lesley, Jay Jay and a cast of male dancers (led by Polly Petrie) in shows like 'Star Whores', 'Circus' and 'Tropical Nights'. These were low-budget spectaculars. I also recall a drag named 'Barbara' who was the cleaner at Cap's and, quite possibly, the worst lip-sync-er I have ever seen. If the song went one way, her lips went the other - and it was impossible not to look at her lips! She had a regular Sunday night spot at Chez Ivy, a rough-and-tumble gay club at Bondi Junction, a few doors down from one of Sydney's early gay steam baths.

Many other gay venues opened up across Sydney, including several in Kings Cross. The 'Bottom's Up' Bar at the Rex Hotel, The Barrel Inn and the Chevron Hotel all attracted a gay clientele. Around the corner from Oxford Street was the Taxi Club, a strange, very late-night destination for drag queens, drug-fucked dancers and the deranged. It was a strange and alluring destination.

I recall stepping out to a new club that opened on the legendary Martin's Bar site opposite the Supreme Court. Martin had hung up his big overcoat (he wore it nearly all year round), shooed off the topless waitresses and sold the lease. A three-level gay club, Trilogy, opened with a bang. Gays love a 'new venue', and the place was set to compete with Dawn O'Donnell's Capriccio's - not a wise move in fire-prone Oxford Street. A friend turned to me and whispered, "When Dawn sees this crowd, the place will be renamed 'Torch Song Trilogy', and so it was. It was never a good idea to cross Dawn O'Donnell. Over the years, I got to know Dawn quite well. She was a tough old gal. Short, reputedly had had a mastectomy to give herself a chest, drove a Lamborghini sports car and owned bars, brothels, sex shops and a gym. She milked the gay community and had a reputation for giving back through gay charities. It was somewhat strange. Whatever her story, it was well known that it was advisable not to get between Dawn O'Donnell and a dollar.

I lived at David Elledge's Brown Street, Paddington, terrace for a few years, and then, when David relocated to the Sunshine Coast, I decided to rent a terrace of my own and share it with a friend, Keith Dyson Smith. Keith was a funny gay man who looked purposely prematurely older - it was his look. He used silver-grey dye on his hair and beard. This was unusual for a gay culture usually obsessed with youth. We had many parties, especially card nights, and probably too much alcohol. Keith had a regular boyfriend, a married man named Tony Edwards. Tony had a men's clothing store in Double Bay and was, as they say, fairly camp.

Tony and Keith had some weird thing going, whereby Tony would call Keith on a Friday morning, and Keith would act as if he had never heard of Tony. After some prompting, Keith would ask something like, "And do you have references as a housemaid?" or "And why were you dismissed from the Moulin Rouge?" Tony, always ready to go along with the fantasy, would have to spring into action and improvise - something he became very skilled at. The fantasy continued when Tony arrived later that evening. It was all a bit much for me, and I used to shoot through. Tony told his wife he was playing poker and would probably drink too much and sleep over. At least one of those excuses was right. Tony and I became great mates - he was extremely funny. At the last call, he had a men's boutique in Shanghai. However, truth be told, I now assume he has departed this life.

I'D HAD a few casual affairs by this stage and realised I was more of the monogamous type. My next move was to Loftus Road, Darling Point, where I moved into a large Spanish Mission apartment with now long-term friends George Pugh and John Allingham. Another friend, Richard d'Apice, lived down the road. These were some of my wildest years; I had started Folkways and had started exploring life. We were always entertaining and had a wide group of friends. After a few years, an opportunity to move further down New Beach Road, Darling Point, opposite the park and on the water, the three of us moved lock, stock and barrel. I'm unsure if we tossed a coin, but I ended up with the largest bedroom. We continued to have fun, and George and John remained friends. Richard has moved to Manar, Elizabeth Bay, where I now live. We have come full circle.

IT DIDN'T TAKE me very long to hook up with my first partner, Kevin Powyer. He was stocky, reasonably masculine, cheeky and had a smile as big as the moon. We moved in together and stayed together for a couple of years. He was one of the early casualties of the AIDS epidemic. I was also an on-and-off lover of Bobby Goldsmith, a charming, smart and athletic lad who became the first documented death from AIDS in Australia. With rotten historical timing, Bobby became a frequent visitor to the flesh pits of San Francisco. Australia's first AIDS charity, the Bobby Goldsmith Foundation, was named for him. My next relationship was a few years with a cheeky brat named Stephen McGee. He, too, died of

HIV complications. I was always careful (and lucky) in my sexual encounters.

BRIAN MOORE WAS my first long-term partner. We lasted around nine years: seven solid ones and two wonky ones. Brian had great taste and was interested in the arts. He worked at the David Jones Art Gallery alongside the revered Robert Haines. He was also a nester, so we rented another apartment in the Darling Point block of four and set up a home, including a couple of dogs. Brian was always sentimental over dogs; even when we split, he had crazy dog stories. I remember him calling me some years later, imploring I take a stray Alsatian he had found wandering in Centennial Park. I already had a dog (he had three) and refused the offer. A week later, I ran into him and asked if he'd found the pooch a home. He looked embarrassed and explained that he'd put a 'lost dog' advertisement in the local newspaper, *The Wentworth Courier*, and the Centennial Park ranger called him - and asked him to bring back his family dog! Brian eventually established his own gallery, the Brian Moore Gallery, in Paddington, but sadly, his long-standing non-Hodgkins lymphoma eventually caught up with him, and he passed away in 2003. I spoke at his funeral.

After breaking up with Brian in 1981, I was introduced to Mark Cavanagh, who was nearly seventeen years my junior. He had just turned eighteen, and I was thirty-five. Forty-four years later, we are still together. Mark and I hit it off immediately; it was love at first sight for both of us. Remarkably the flame still burns. He had been studying at The Sydney College of the Arts and moved across to the marketing section of Qantas, but he was still floundering about what he wanted to do to earn a crust.

Brian Moore, mom and Pepé le Fahey

My record company was expanding, and he came to work at Larrikin as a publicist, a job he held for fifteen months before deciding to work in public relations. A friend, Marita Blood, offered him a position at her well-established agency, and he learnt on the hop, step and jump. He remained with Marita Blood and Associates for five years until he opened his own public relations company in partnership with Fiona Coogan. After a year, he went solo as Cavcon Consulting, a boutique agency he ran with his sister, Suyin, developing strategies for major fashion, beauty, alcohol and style brands. He was very well-regarded in the industry. He did public relations strategy, marketing and events for some of Australia's leading brands, such as Absolut, Jamieson Whiskey, Calvin Klein, Omega, RayBan, Marie Claire Magazine, QT Hotels, Napoleon Cosmetics, and Hemmes Merivale Group, to name a few. In 2018, tired of dealing with shrinking marketing budgets and advancing technological change, he wound his business up. He took a breathing space until, in 2019, he launched himself back where he started: interior design, taking freelance projects. He now enjoys working solo, having no staff and a different creative challenge. Word-of-mouth has seen him working continually. It helped that our own apartment was awarded Belle 'Apartment of the Year'. He is a clever cookie.

I could write a book about Mark and my adventures (this isn't it). We are compatible in most ways: energetic, curious, tidy, affectionate and probably predictable. We enjoy reading, adventure holidays, art, foreign cinema, theatre, food and animals. We are not necessarily totally compatible in music, and I can't say any of my partners have entirely understood my music. After forty-plus years of listening to me singing and playing the concertina over the past twenty years, including a couple of painful years when I was determinedly teaching myself the elusive instrument, I can't blame him. He is, of course, hugely understanding of my passion for folklore and traditional song, and he often comes to my talks and concerts, but it is not *his* passion. Maybe because he worked in public relations, where the 'shock of the new' is essential, his taste is more contemporary. That said, we often listen to ABC Classics or ABC digital Jazz while reading. He could not have been prouder when the Australian government awarded me the Don Banks Award for Lifetime Achievement in Music in 2010. It all probably clicked at that stage.

Mark and I got married in 2024 - after a 44 year engagement - it was more a case of 'tidying things up'. We are sympathetic to those who want those golden rings - neither of us has ever worn jewellery. Referring to each other as 'husband and husband' doesn't sound right. We're partners in life's journey.

Togetherness, me and Mark, 2017

Although Zandra is my blood sister, I also have a faux sister. Rebel Penfold Russell and her family are also Mark and my family. We've been a unit for nearly forty years. Firstly, when Rebel was married to Stuart Quin. Then, in 1996, she introduced me to her now partner, Ian Low. Ian plays the guitar and sings, and we've had some memorable music-making sessions accompanied by some fine wines. His son, my godson, Jasper, calls Ian the 'backpacker who stayed'.

Warren and Rebel at Palm Beach

I briefly met Rebel's mother, Rada Penfold Hyland - a writer, businesswoman and a woman larger than life. Rada's life was conducted at high speed. The last time we met, she was on horseback accompanied by her best gal friend, Lizzie, and man-about-town, Charles Widdy. I was lunching at John Marsden's home near Ingleburn when the threesome rode up to the poolside table. The horses, possibly confused by the newly laid green astroturf, shat everywhere. It was a somewhat confused lunch and a speedy retreat for the riders. Sadly, Rada's story was complicated; she died comparatively young, aged 58. Lizzie, Rada's closest companion, ended up living in Paddington, around the corner from Folkways, and we would occasionally meet for a chat.

Rebel is a Renaissance woman. Strikingly beautiful, opinionated, forceful, generous and talented. She studied at NIDA, but her real lessons in life have been experiences. Left a modest amount from her mother's estate, she set about improving her fortunes through real estate and ethical investment. Her great loves are travel and theatre, and she has a history of impressive philanthropy for festivals, large and small theatre companies, and worthy projects. In 2018, she set up the Vine Foundation with her family, a philanthropic foundation with ideals in climate change and environmental awareness through the arts. As a filmmaker, Rebel has an impressive producer's list, including the film and the stage show of *Priscilla, Queen of the Desert*. Our naughty friend and eternal trickster Stephen Elliott wrote and directed the film. When Rebel first gave me the script to read, Mark and I shook our heads, saying, "It's too gay - won't work!" How wrong we were.

Before the film began production, Rebel and Stephen hosted a small dinner party at Bondi, and I sat next to 'an English actor' and asked, "And what do you do again?" To my horror, it was Terrence Stamp. I never had much of an eye for recognising famous faces. It wasn't the first and probably not the last faux par. I recall Mark and I being in Marrakesh in the eighties. I was writing travel articles, and we were guests at the famous La Mamounia Palace Hotel when Mark started walking surreptitiously back and forth, looking at someone. I said, "What are you doing! who are you looking at?" Seated on a sofa surrounded by dogs was the designer Yves Saint Laurent. It could have been Attila the Hun, and I probably wouldn't have recognised him either. Mind you, I did spot Mick Jagger and Jerry Hall around the pool.

In 2013, Rebel announced that she was making a one-hour documentary about my work. I squirmed a little, but 'Larrikin Lad' received repeated cable screenings on Arts TV, an ABC DVD release, screenings at the National Folk Festival, and a three-month season on Qantas Inflight. The ever-curious Pat Fiske directed the doco, and the film is still in circulation. The most impressive part of the film for me was an ancient clip from an ABC '*A Big Country*' episode which showed me wearing a shearer's singlet, standing in the back of a ute and playing a lagerphone. I had forgotten that seventies film footage. Thankfully, they didn't dig up the segment I did for 'Mr Squiggle', where I was made up like an old swaggie and conversing with a giant felt snail.

As an 'extended family,' we are very close and spend many weekends away together. Some of our most enjoyable times have involved long lunches with lots of singing. I am not one for astrological readings, but January does bring us together as Rebel, Mark, Ian, Jasper, and I are all Capricorns. We goats have also spent several holidays together, including a memorable trip to Vietnam. During COVID, we all bunkered down, and 2020 went flying past in often glorious isolation.

Some things I have seen in my gay life would probably make readers blanch, even some gay readers. I have seen it all: crazy Studio 54 parties in New York, Fire Island fantasies, The Mine Shaft sex club in the meat-packing district of New York where people allowed others to piss on them (and worse), people taking pharmacies of drugs until they fell over, lesbian catfights - you name it, and I have probably been on the sidelines.

I was far more interested in tasting bohemia; maybe the gay underworld goes hand-in-hand with that strangeness. I love freaky people and am incredibly fortunate to have met some of the world's greatest self-declared freaks. My celluloid heroes, Frederico Fellini and later Andy Warhol, Paul Morrissey and John Waters, set the standard for my introduction to freakdom. I used to see foreign films at the Phillip Street, Sydney. Cinema. It was a small art cinema and not a picture theatre, and to prove the point, they sold espresso coffee in the foyer. I saw *8 ½*, *Rocky and his Brothers*, *The Leopard* and *Momma Roma*. I was devastated by the characters on the screen: ugly people, beautiful people and beautifully ugly. I saw Andy Warhol and Paul Morrissey's *'Trash'*, *'Flesh'* and *'Heat'* at the equally tiny Paris Cinema on George Street or Glebe's Art Cinema and John Waters's *'Polyester'* (in glorious odorama) and *'Pink Flamingos'* at the Valhalla. The sight of Divine eating a piece of shit revolted yet fascinated us. 'Edie, the egg lady' was another shocker - a sixty-something overweight woman dressed in a diaper and eating bowls of boiled eggs was not normal.

'Larrikin Lad' a documentary film by Rebel Studios.

Years later, in 1984, I became friends with Warhol and Morrissey's star, 'Divine'. Glenn Millstead, the man behind the woman, was performing a season at Kinsela's nightclub at Taylor Square, and there he was flicking through the LPs at Folkways. I introduced myself, took him out for lunch, and no doubt chewed his ear off with questions. We became friends. Another Kinsela's 'freak', and I mean the description in the best possible way, was the American drag artist Joey Aria. Joey, a New York institution, claimed to channel Billie Holiday - and he just about could! He toured with another exotic creature, a drag with a completely shaved head, Robert Sherman, whose main claim to fame was having been photographed by Robert Mapplethorpe for his 'Bald Heads' series. My longtime friends, Graham Howarth and Richard Fotheringham, were part-owners of Kinsela's by then, and we all had several big nights out. It was with Richard and Graham that I saw my first underground Warhol/Morrissey porn film. It was a privately distributed 16mm film we saw at somebody's house and featured a short, very handsome boy with a long blond ponytail. His name was Joe Dallesandro and the film showed him being fucked doggy style. We were all fairly shocked and even more shocked to see him as 'Little Joe' in a later Warhol/Morrissey film where he starred with Sylvia Miles. He later starred in Morrissey's trilogy *Trash, Flesh* and *Heat*. Everyone fantasised about 'Little Joe'. Yikes! I just Googled him and noted he is still alive, married with two kids, and is two years my junior!

A Rat Party poster - tickets available Folkways!

Sydney had its freak brigade: Jack Vidgen, and his partners Billy Yip and Reno Dal, were the talented trio that produced the outrageous Rat Parties of the seventies and eighties. The irrepressible Simon Reptile, Brenton Heath-Kerr, a massively talented costume maker and performance artist who created a life-size version of Tom of Finland for an 80s Mardi Gras party, the amazing Doris Fish, and three moustachioed glamorous drag queens who performed in the nineties as 'The Planet Sluts'. There was also Harold 'Kangaroo' Thornton, a loveable man in his late seventies, who dressed eccentrically (he painted his clothes) and pushed a wheelbarrow proclaiming 'Greatest Artist Who Ever lived' through many parties. Fortunately, on-the-spot photographers Mazz Images and Robert 'Rabbit' Rosen captured much of the madness for posterity. There were also the old-school drag queens like Carlotta, Simone, Carmen and Beatrice, but they were all far too straight for my liking.

Tony L'uomo, Jack 'The Rat' Vidgen and WF at the 'Casino Royale' party, Top of the Town. Photograph Paul Ferman.

Sydney's bohemia could be elusive. I was a little young to be a serious onlooker at the Sydney Push, although I subsequently became friends with some of its members, including filmmaker Margaret Fink and folk singer Declan Affley. My bohemia was in Paddington and Balmain. The late sixties and early seventies were rebellious, hashish-hazed with pockets of social radicalism that prompted spirited discussion, poetry and music. Chris Hector, a young, affable, kaftan-wearing, poetry-sprouting intellectual, held irregular Sunday gatherings at his rambling home on Duke Street, Balmain, where he would make huge vats of vegetable curry, and all were welcome. The poets Nigel Roberts and Robert Adamson joined with singers and musicians, and the afternoons were always stimulating. Actually... I think some were *on* stimulants!

In the early seventies, before the Mardi Gras made Sydney gays and lesbians 'party mad', there were private invitation parties hosted by Sylvia & the Synthetics. The 'Synthetics' were led by the imposingly tall Danny Aboud and featured a cast of outrageous characters, including Doris Fish. The first parties, usually held in Darlinghurst warehouse spaces, were more like improbable happenings. I remember being gobsmacked when I witnessed a leather boy come onto the stage and bend over so the audience could see a small chain protruding from his anus. Another man, also dressed in leather, pulled the chain out until a small mountain of chain was on the floor. They then vanished into the wings as quietly as they had appeared. On another occasion, the 'Synthetics' took over Paddington Town Hall and turned it into a bizarre circus. Giant artwork resembling television sets would frame live shows where the irrepressible and very tall Danny Aboud would crawl on his knees dressed as a six-foot-eight North Shore housewife having a cleansing attack. Rinso powder, sprays and foams were everywhere, including over the audience. There was no point - and that was the point.

By 1978, Sydney's gay scene was boiling. It was also becoming increasingly political as the banging of opening closet doors reverberated across the city. The sixties television series 'Number 96' had already shocked Australia by introducing LGBT characters - including Australian television's first male-to-male kiss. The times definitely were a-changing. In 1978, Tom Robinson released his *'Glad to be Gay'* single. In June, a gay and lesbian demonstration rally was staged to commemorate the 1969 New York Stonewall riots. Although it had obtained permission from the police, it was revoked at the last minute. That same evening was the birth of Mardi Gras as a semi-illegal parade, led by a flat-bed truck with a sound system playing *'Glad to be Gay'*, drove down Oxford Street.

A few hundred marchers shouted, "Out of the bars and into the street" as the motley crew headed to Hyde Park. To say the police were menacing would be an understatement, and what was intended as a celebration became increasingly ugly. I was with Richard Fotheringham and Graham Howarth. When we reached Hyde Park, it became clear the police were intent on serious hassling. Some people were arrested as most of us dashed up William Street and headed to Kings Cross and the Fitzroy Gardens. It was all very exciting as we were revved up to the max, angry, and scared. The police started dragging people into paddy wagons, and the three of us decided to split before we ended up in the Darlinghurst lock-up. We had no idea how many people had been arrested or why. The following morning, June 25th, *The Sydney Morning Herald* reported 53 demonstrators had been arrested. We also got unofficial reports that many protestors had been physically and verbally abused.

Unbelievably, the following day, the SMH published a list of names, occupations and addresses of the people arrested. Like many of my gay generation, I continue to hold an uneasiness about some of our city police.

Alternative parties were staged at Stranded, a city nightclub, 77 William Street, and even the disused railway workrooms at Redfern. The music changed with the fashion, and the most notable deejays included Stephen Allkins, Ben Drayton, David Hiscock, Gemma, Groovi Biscuits, Robert Racic, Seymore Butts and Kate Munroe. Folkways Music was a ticket outlet for many private parties, and I was always 'on the door list'. Later parties to continue the strangeness included 'Frank the Bagelman's' Sub-Culture parties and often the weird and wired 'Jamie and Vanessa' parties. 'Vanessa Wagner' was the creation of the very talented Tobin Saunders. 'She' started as a dedicated housewife and part-time hostess. Vanessa was crowned Sydney Mardi Gras Miss Fair Day 1993. Another 'star' of the nineties was 'Pauline Pantsdown'. Created by political activist Simon Hunt, 'Pauline' parodied Pauline Hansen. Larrikin distributed Pauline's singles *'Backdoor Man'* and *"I Don't Like It'*. If the endless dancing didn't finish you off, there was always the Midnight Shift (then owned by my old Marist Brother's classmate, Terry Patterson), Patches, Flo's Palace, The Manacle or the Phoenix at the Exchange Hotel. I am exhausted just thinking about it.

The Sydney Mardi Gras and Sleaze Ball became international phenomenons attracting huge crowds dancing their tits off from 10 pm to 10 am. Well, in retrospect, many staggered more than danced. Massive halls with deafening sound systems, confetti dropping from the heavens, and a parade of local and international guest artists prevailed. Mark and I attended most of the early ones until they blurred. The most memorable was probably 1988 when our friend, the theatre director, Richard Wherrett, produced a spectacular show where half-a-dozen drag queens, all dressed identically as Diana Ross, appeared on stage miming *'Chain Reaction'*, then, from the other end of the giant Sydney Showground's Manufacturer's Pavilion, another six identical Diana Ross drag queens appeared. Heads were spinning as thousands joined in singing and dancing. It was quite some show.

One aspect of my life that people find difficult to reconcile with my bush persona is my social life. Maybe it is the gadfly in me, but I was lucky to have been on 'lists', although many were opportunistic public relations events. I shudder when I think of the number of parties I have attended and the people I have met.

First, the parties. I would be very embarrassed if I added all the dollars associated with entertaining me. I have consumed buckets of French champagne and fine wine and whiskies to wash down bellyfuls of caviar and canapés. Without a doubt, the most extravagant parties were the Cointreau Balls staged during the late eighties and nineties when each year the party organisers, mainly Nikki Andrews and Deeta Colvin from Colvin Communications, celebrated the famous French liquor by breaking the bank to produce the most outlandish parties imaginable. The guest list ran as a who's who of society, from the establishment ladies like Lady Sonia McMahon and Lady Susan Renouf to the brightest new things. And, amen, a few old farts like myself.

Mark 'Jack' Jackson, footballer and actor. photograph Robert Rosen.

The fact that each year the venue, always a well-kept pre-party secret, changed so dramatically was part of the mystique. One year it was the old Naval stores at Alexandria. The Matraville Army Barracks, Pier 8 and then, one of the wildest, had us all transported, toothpaste and pills in hand, on a magical mystery bus tour that ended in Wollongong at a Basketball Stadium where we partied and were accommodated before, after a quick nap, we bussed it back to Sydney for a sit-down grand breakfast in an old disused church in Darlinghurst. I boogied down with then SBS newsreader Indira Nardoo, Deborah Hutton and Jill Waddy until some obscene hour and was carelessly late for the last bus back to Sydney. I arrived late for breakfast but also had a headful of stories. The Cointreau Balls were always a costumed theme - a real challenge to the social set, and some of the costumes and make-up were spectacular. One year, a group of us went as members of the cast of a popular television comedy, 'Hogan's Heroes'. I was Colonel Klink, a befuddled swastika-wearing Nazi, and Mark and Jonathon Ward went as his high-heeled frauleins. It was the height of bad taste, especially me being of Jewish heritage, but scandal and outrageousness knew no boundaries at these parties. Writing for *Mode* magazine, Maggie Alderson quite rightfully gave us the bad taste award.

Warren de Maria - a towering inferno. Cointreau Ball. Photograph Robert Rosen.

The launch of new magazines, the relaunch of tired old journals, landmark editions, new Foxtel lifestyle channels, television station program launches and, as they say, the opening of an envelope all demanded a lavish party celebration. Product launches always guaranteed invitations in the mail to welcome new perfumes, hair products, electrical products, gadgets and gizmos. The bigger the brand usually translated into a bigger party budget, and the international fashion labels of Gucci, Pucci, Burberry, Armani, Chanel, Tiffany & Co and Hermes offered regular flings. Hermes, under the stylish Karin Upton Baker, ruled the roost in the 2000s with her 'Hermes on the Beach', an annual affair at Neilson Park, which miraculously became Hermes Swinging Fifties in 2013 with a wonderful themed party at Luna Park, where vintage 50s Cadillacs and Chevrolets decorated the park as guests, over 200, sipped French Champagne before being ushered into Coney Island where James Morrison's Big Band pumped out the music as singers and swingers danced the night into action. At one stage, the Japanese girl group 5 6 7 8's that had appeared in Quentin Tarantino's film 'Kill Bill Vol.1' knocked the crowd sideways with their raunchy rock.

Some of the most fabulous parties were produced as private affairs with no commercial connections. These were tightly controlled guest lists that drove the wannabes crazy. Three themed private parties organised by Mark Cavanagh, Jonathon Ward and Geoffrey Parker were the most famous - 'Vanity Fair', 'Casino Royale' and 'Pineapple Crush'. These were parties staged for no other reason than to party.

Pineapple Crush - one of Sydney's most memorable private parties.
Two 'gals' and Miss Pineapple contestants, Kerrie Lester and
Sandra Ferman. Photographs Paul Ferman.

These private parties demanded everyone dress to the theme. Many went beyond the call of duty and remained true to their character throughout the party. This was particularly so with 'Casino Royale', which took its theme from the well-known James Bond film. The venue, an old high-rise hotel called Top of the Town on Victoria Street, Darlinghurst, next to the fire station, had a top-floor Korean restaurant with some of the most dazzling views of Sydney Harbour. The owners, not quite expecting a full-dress party, agreed to hand the party over to the team. An army moved in on the party day, turning their restaurant into a chic Bond-styled casino. The tables were hauled away, and the nasty walls were covered. Everything was 'glamourised' and made plush. Gambling tables and croupiers moved in; a stage was built for the entertainment, which included performances by The Rat Pack, impersonators of Frank Sinatra, Sammy Davis Jr, Peter Lawford and Dean Martin. Handsome waiters with pink Cosmopolitans and martinis - shaken, not stirred - greeted the arriving guests, and the evening never stopped buzzing until the 3 am shut down. The first of these parties was 'Vanity Fair' and staged at a bistro where the Apollo Restaurant now rules in Macleay Street, Potts Point. It was previously the site of the Texas Tavern. The party was themed around the social reportage of New York's *Vanity Fair* magazine. The guests included 'Ann Bass', 'Graydon Carter', 'Truman Capote', several women straight from *Breakfast at Tiffany's*; famous actors and a triumphant 'Grace Jones' as interpreted by jewellery designer Ray Griffiths, who arrived black and all teeth from 'her' limo waving at the amazed onlookers crowded on the footpath who believed it was the real thing. 'Pineapple Crush' was another spectacular party. Staged on the Imperial Peking floating Chinese restaurant anchored at Rose Bay, the theme was 'kitsch resort', and the attendees did the theme proud. Sandra Ferman and Kerrie Lester were memorable as contestants in the Miss Pineapple Crush contest. The Golden Circle Pineapple Factory girls were also in for the big prize.

I was an enthusiastic participant in the world of cabaret and strangeness. Kinsela's restaurant and nightclub were one obvious focal point. Kinsela's was a funeral home built in 1933, bought by venture capitalist Leon Fink in 1982 and converted into a venue. His timing was impeccable in as much as he transformed the establishment, including its mortuary, into the liveliest joint in town. The showroom and office space became a sensational bistro by Tony Bilson - combining great food, wine, winning service and style, and craziness. The cocktail bar, reputedly where the bodies were displayed, was chic and beautifully designed and lit by George Freedman; upstairs was a theatre cabaret. The combination of excellent food, fun elements and a working cabaret was magic. Graeme Blundell, the actor and television reviewer, was instrumental in producing the cabaret and musical offerings - and they surely flowed from brave attempts at a serious theatre to totally wacky. After Leon sold the place, a consortium purchased the business and bravely attempted to maintain the flavour, but times had changed. As they reached out to young club audiences, the restaurant floundered, and the cabaret became more of a space dominated by very loud doof, doof, doof dance music. Some of the standout shows for me were The Trios Del Ray, a trio of advanced-age sisters from Miami who sang and played some of the strangest songs I have ever heard; Divine, the star of so many Paul Morrissey/Andy Warhol films, was magic as she steered the audience through a program designed around her personal journey; Joey Arias, more of a drag queen than a female impersonator, channelled Billie Holliday; George Melley played wonderfully camp jazz as he related his life story; Mark Murphy, camped up his jazz too, and a stream of drag queens just camped it up completely. There were The Globos (Wendy de Waal and Mark Trevorrow, who, in 1984, emerged as the campy and sometimes brilliantly creepy 'television host and personality' Bob Downe), Renee Geyer, Wendy Saddington, The Flying Pickets, Glen Shorrock and even a season when the Sydney Dance Company graced the stage at Kinselas.

Sadly, I attended far too many funerals and memorials in those years. Too many friends, young and old, fell to the horrors of AIDS, many checking out early to avoid the agonising later progression of the disease. Some thirty years ago, I decided to stop attending funerals. Being a non-believer in things godly, I accepted that the deceased, however close, wouldn't mind nor notice my absence. I celebrate their lives and our friendship in my way. I have instructed that when I finally shuffle off, there will be no funeral service and no final resting place. My ashes are to be scattered over the ocean or bushland. Undoubtedly, some will find this strange, especially since I spent over a decade as a cultural historian for Sydney's Rookwood Cemetery, producing a dozen documentaries on the necropolis and some of its notable 'residents'. The fact is, Rookwood's 160-plus year history is Sydney's history, covering everyone from the wealthy to the homeless and hopeless. Over the years, I made videos on pioneer retail merchants David Jones and Anthony Hordern; newspaper baron John Fairfax; musicians and entertainers Roy 'Mo' Rene, Peter Dawson and Peter Dodds McCormack; Chinese businessman and philanthropist Mei Quong Tart; pioneer feminist, Louisa Lawson (Henry's mom); and on the Mortuary railway that ran from Redfern to the centre of the necropolis. They are available on the Rookwood website. https://www.rookwoodcemetery.com.au/about-us/videos

10

CELEBRATING THE BUSH

I n my late teens, I started attending the weekly meetings of the Bush Music Club, an organisation that champions Australian folk music. The BMC was established by pioneer folk music collector John Meredith and his Bushwhacker Band comrades. When I started attending the Club, its gatherings were held at the Australian Realist Writer's Hall on Sussex Street. It celebrated its 70th anniversary in 2024.

Singing at the Bush Music Club in the sixties accompanied need by Ken Greenhalgh, John Dengate and Jamie Carlin.

THEY WERE strange evenings reminiscent of an oddball religious meeting. We all had our 'hymnal', a bound copy of various *Singabout* magazines. This irregular BMC publication included collected songs and poems and we sat around the walls of the hall whilst the central musicians started each song. Everyone was encouraged to join in, and every so often, an old-time dance like *'The Galopede'* or *'Circassian Circle'* would be called. John Meredith, Alan Scott, Jamie Carlin, Eric Bolton and Frank Maher were regular faces and, occasionally, older musicians like tin whistle and accordion player Herb Gimlet would appear.

Members of the Bush Music Club (I am in the middle) under Henry Lawson's statue, Sydney Domain. Photograph Bob Bolton.

I first met Sally Sloane, the remarkable traditional song carrier recorded by Meredith in the nineteen fifties, at the BMC and eventually made my own recordings of some of her songs and stories. Meredith and I eventually fell out. Coming from a communist background, he didn't like the fact I was a 'businessman' and then, I suspect, he saw my increasing interest in folklore and my association with the ABC as a threat. He bitterly objected to me recording Sally Sloane, but since Sally had invited me, I didn't give two hoots. It was a good move because John had not recorded any speech from Sally, and I believed this was important to document. In response, John rumoured that I had used his recordings on an ABC program without permission. This was not true, but the damage was done. I was doubly damned a few years later when my record label, Larrikin, released an LP of Sally Sloane featuring his recordings compiled and edited by sound archivist Graham McDonald. The label had absolutely nothing to do with the access of the material and had issued 'A Garland For Sally' because of its cultural importance, and besides, I was over Meredith's melodramas. There was another hidden agenda- the fact that I was openly gay and he was closeted made for a very uncomfortable relationship. I believe he was terrified I would 'out' him, although this is something I would not have done. "Too late now, she cried."

My greatest influencers were my 'Melbourne mates'. Maybe because I was from 'up north' and possibly because they too had fallen out with John Meredith at some time or other. I was a regular visitor staying with either Wendy and Werner Lowenstein or Pat and Norm O'Connor. Together with Jim Buchanan and Shirley Andrews, we were a gang. The conversation was always brisk, with a left-wing wink and usually with a lot of music and laughter. We talked a lot about folklore and bush songs. Norm and Pat played me some of the gems they had collected, which, thankfully, are now deposited in the National Library of Australia. Wendy's oral history and folklore recordings are also in the National Library.

Norm O'Connor provided most of the tracks Edgar Waters used on the vinyl record *Traditional Singers and Musicians of Victoria*, issued by Wattle Records in 1963. The compilation was reissued as a CD in 2004 as a collaboration between the Victorian Folk Music Club (est. 1959) and the National Library of Australia. I remember when Norm first played me some of his recordings of Simon McDonald - I was flabbergasted and set about learning most of them, including 'Old

Man Kangaroo', 'Lost Sailor', 'Golden Vanity' and 'Ginny on the Moor'. I still sing them over fifty years later. When I established Larrikin Records one of the first albums I issued was the LP *'Bush Traditions'*, where I offered similar field recordings from my own collection. I still believe singers of traditional songs should, wherever possible, listen to the raw field recordings of songs. Initially, they may sound simplistic, but they often treasure waiting to be heard.

Norm and Pat dropped out of the 'folk scene' (gawd, I hate that description), but Wendy, Shirley and Jim remained close friends until, one by one, they died. They also introduced me to Bob and Mavis Michell, who had moved from Melbourne to Brisbane. Bob was a patent attorney and all round nice bloke. He shared his collecting experiences and entrusted me with his field tapes. Bob encouraged me to record Cyril Duncan. Bob and Mavis are also long gone. The other collector in my history was Ron Edwards. Ron lived in North Queensland and was a genuine character. He energetically collected, self-published and annotated everything from traditional leatherwork to yarns. He and I shared many laughs and were regular correspondents. In 2023, at the National Folk Festival, I 'cut the ribbon' on Keith McKendry's book on Ron Edwards and, at the same festival, introduced Martie and Richard Lowenstein's documentary on their extraordinary mother, Wendy Lowenstein. Sometimes I feel like the last man standing.

Wendy Lowenstein and Shirley Andrews - I took this when we went bushwalking in the Blue Mountains in the 1980s.

The old bush songs are resilient devils in as much as they served their original purpose, mainly in the last two decades of the nineteenth century, as stories created by and sung by people just like those in the songs they were hearing. The songs of shearers, drovers, bullockies, timber cutters, shearer's cooks, boundary riders and farmers were 'owned' by the pastoral workers of Australia from rouseabout to squatter. The earlier songs from the convict, pioneering settler, maritime and gold rush periods served a similar need, typically expressing frustrations, aspirations and, occasionally, documentation. Later song catalogues steadily developed for coal mining, railway building, and other industries. There were also songs about unionism, socialism, republicanism and just about every other 'ism'. City life also produced songs documenting factory and office life, leisure time and political shenanigans. All these songs and ditties had a common thread: storytelling. Some are angry songs; others romanticise bush life. The latter was particularly true of the early part of the twentieth century when poets like Henry Lawson and A. B. 'Banjo' Paterson reminded city-dwelling Australians of their debt to the bush.

The bush songs served their original role, but that doesn't mean they are to be forgotten. Sure, they are mostly sung these days to celebrate the bush, mostly by urban singers, but their value as a conduit to our identity is as strong as ever. They help remind us of the pioneers who forged modern-day Australia. They give us a taste of what life was like, what frustrated people and what they hoped for. They also remind us how the songs documented events like mine disasters, wars or political and social changes.

Old songs are a powerful treasure chest I call upon when discussing history. Singing a song provides colour, allowing an audience to imagine and possibly step back in time. I fear the average Australian (whatever and whoever that is) has been conditioned not to think about our colonial history. Sure, some will always rejoice in the old stories, but generally, Australians see themselves as modern, too smart to look back at history. Sadly, our schools and universities do not address the subjects well and, as they say, if you want to bring people on board, catch them early. We have all missed that boat!

Often the tunes of the songs are very secondary to the words, and just as often, the same tune will be used in different songs. Through the magic of traditional music, these songs all sound different. Subtle

The bushman

changes produce big effects to enhance the storylines. For example, 'The Wearing of the Green' appears as the tune base for a Kelly Gang bushranging ballad and again as a shearing song. The same tune claims around twenty different songs. By slight variation, they all claim their individuality.

Some of the most powerful songs in the Australian song swag are those associated with unionism and socialism. When I first went out with a tape recorder, I aimed to find some examples of industrial folksong, songs about mining, factory work, strikes, etc. I felt earlier fieldworkers had overlooked them in their enthusiasm to collect the songs of rural workers. In a stay in the coal town of Lithgow, west NSW, I met several retired miners who had all been staunch unionists. Jack 'Twinny' Mays and Jim 'Champ' Champion were typical. They had worked the mines all their lives, suffered from black lung, survived the Depression and held solid memories of the early pit mines. One story related to the history of the Hoskin's Mine strike. It concerns the bitter 1911 confrontation when Charles Hoskins, the mine operator, responded to the union's request for an additional tuppence a ton by reducing their rate by tuppence a ton. This led to a battle for many months and ended when the strikers attacked the scab labourers charged with keeping the mine operational. The Lithgow Brass Band assembled at the pit head every morning and played *'The Death March'* (from *Saul*) as the scab labourers arrived. In the final confrontation, when the scabs started dancing to the music, the unionists couldn't stand a day longer and attacked. The scabs were locked in the boiler rooms, Hoskin's new T-Model Ford burned to the ground, and the attending police were thrown in the nearby water slush pond. Jack and Jim gave me a song from the time called *'When You Give That Tuppence Back,*

Charlie Dear'. Appropriately, considering the scabs' fate, the song's tune was the hymn *'When the Sheep Are In The Fold, Jenny Dear'*.

Another of my informants, Joe Watson of Caringbah, NSW, had been a member of the ALP since its establishment in 1901. Joe had been a travelling picture showman and visited shearer's strike camps. He had many songs and poems, including several directly related to unionism, including a unionist version of *'Clancy of the Overflow'*. His version of A. B. Paterson's *'A Bushman's Song'* emphatically endorses unionism, and it is the version I sang in my play with Max Cullen. Every time I sing the song I feel transported back to the troubled times of the bush and, in a way, channel Joe Watson.

I have compiled several books and radio series using my collected songs. I see myself as a populariser, a packager, and a folklore recycling unit, making the songs and poems available in accessible and attractive formats. My first book, published by William Collins in 1977, *Pint Pot & Billy*, offered some of my collected songs. It sold over 50,000 copies (mainly from a deal with Scholastic). My last songbook, a large format job and my best songbook to date, *Australian Folk Songs & Ballads*, sold out the first and only print run of 2000 in ten months. My publisher, ABC Books/Harper Collins, explained this was okay as they wanted to steer consumers to the three e-books of the same work. Book publishing is frustrating. For me, it is not about the book income, it's about ensuring the songs are available, especially for young Australians.

One of the earliest line-ups of The Larrikins. Tony Suttor, Jack Fallis, Ned Alexander, Paddy McLoughlin, Liora Cliff and Warren Fahey.

I still find it extraordinary I have had a career as a performer of bush songs. For over thirty years, starting in the late sixties, I performed with The Larrikins, a group I established in late 1968 to present bush songs, poems and stories. Although it was often called a 'bush band' it was far more musically sophisticated than the term implies and also original in its repertoire. I was fortunate to work alongside some of the 'folk revival's' (another term I dislike) most talented musicians and the family tree of the group's membership is a virtual who's who of Australian folk music, including, at some time or other, Dave de Hugard, Declan Affley, Jacko Kevans, Cathie O'Sullivan, Bob McInnes, Pete Hobson, Tony Suttor, Liora Claff, Marcus Holden, Garry Steel, Clare O'Meara, Mark Oats, Michael Atherton, Cleis Pearce, Brad Tate, Phil Moore, Andrew de Teliga, John Morris, Lionel O'Keefe, Ian White, Andy Saunders, Tom Rummery, Steve Ellis, Roger Firkin, Kate Delaney, Gordon McIntyre, Richard Brooks, Bob Meadows, Paddy McLoughlin, Jack Fallis, Ned Alexander, Martin Halley and George Washingmachine. My apologies if I have left anyone out. No doubt others joined for specific projects, including ABC radio specials. The group toured extensively in Australia and internationally through Musica Viva in the seventies and eighties. The Australian regional tours took us everywhere, but particularly to remote areas, including many Aboriginal communities in West Australia and the Northern Territory.

Two later Larrikins, Ian White and Declan Affley.

Our concerts were generally structured thematically to show the diversity of the Australian tradition and would include some unaccompanied ballads, folk songs, tunes, bush poems and yarns. I also wanted to break the bush band mould and always had a female member in the group. I was also aware of including contemporary songs that fitted the storyline, told stories of contemporary Australia, including political songs, and could show that the tradition continued. Whilst I was the main presenter, each member usually introduced their item. It was a very successful formula. The Larrikins did three or four regional and international tours a year.

Touring the bush also allowed me to do some folklore collecting. On one memorable occasion, the group was booked to fly from Adelaide to Broken Hill and then across to Perth, where we did an extensive West Australian tour and then across to the Northern Territory. In Broken Hill, I arranged to do some recordings at the retirement home while the rest of the band did a promotional spot on the local television program. Things went a bit sideways when the over-eager and pretentious female presenter's first on-air question to the group was aimed at Tom Rummery and his concertina, "Tom, tell us about that fascinating thing between your legs." Tom and the group were speechless.

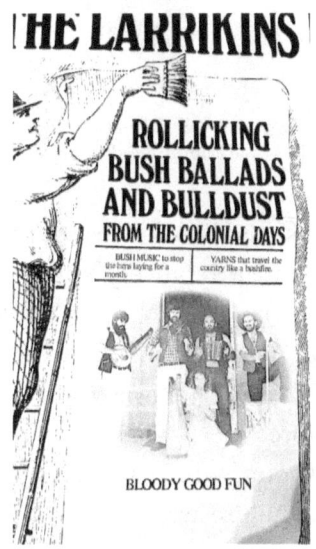

A 1977 Larrikins tour of remote areas for Musica Viva and regional arts councils took us from Sydney to Adelaide, Broken Hill, Adelaide, Perth, Newman, Roebourne, Karratha, Derby, Port Hedland, Wickham, Goldsworthy, Shay Gap, Broome, Kununurra, Darwin, Snake Bay, Bathurst Islands, Maningrida, Gove, Katharine, Tennant Creek, Alice Springs and back to Sydney.

Another memorable performance on that tour saw us at the remote mining town of Newman, where the group performed an evening show using the local supermarket loading dock as a stage. We were on the edge of a desert, and when the arc lights were switched on, every insect in West Australia descended on us. Our beards and hair were alive, and every time we tapped our feet, there was a distinct squishing sound. Worse still, we could hardly open our mouths to sing without insects propelling themselves into our gobs.

Another bunch of larrikins - WF, Liora Cliff, Tom Rummery, Steve Ellis, Kate Delaney, Gordon McIntyre.

Roebourne, a town in the North West of the state, is the home of the Ngarluma people and a relatively small white population. We didn't get off to a good start. Arts WA had booked us into the town's main hotel, and we had made the mistake of going into the back bar to talk to the locals. The back bar was the black's bar, and the local art's group wasn't impressed. I was probably considered double trouble as in the afternoon, whilst the group did a sound check, I visited the local Aboriginal 'reserve' (still can't believe this is what it was called) and did some recordings of a local singer, Winnie, who accompanied her songs by hitting an old metal pie tin. A very strange thing happened. I was seated on a blanket on the front lawn of her home, surrounded by kids eager to see the 'white bloke recording Winnie', and I heard myself singing on their radio. I said, "That's me singing." They looked toward the house and then back to me in amazement. I was as confused as they were. The ABC was broadcasting one of my songs.

That evening at the golf club, we were taken back to see the audience was entirely white and rather frosty. It was obvious news of our transgression to the Aboriginal bar, and my visit to the community had reached the town's conservative ears. When the interval came, we all went outside to escape them and, to our delight, lined along the fence were about a hundred black faces. They had come to listen to us. We went and talked to them, went back and did our second half to a stony-faced audience, and then packed up and returned to the hotel as fast as possible. The next day I received a message from the head of WA Arts saying he had received an official complaint from Roebourne Arts - and congratulated us on our stance.

The trip to Darwin happened in the middle of a national airline strike, and we ended up in small delivery planes to maintain our schedule. On the way from Darwin to Maningrida, an Aboriginal community at the very top of Australia, the pilot, who claimed he had been working triple shifts, had me sit in the co-pilot's seat and asked me to nudge him if he looked like he was dozing off. I was terrified. He was a joker and the same bush pilot who advised, "if anyone was feeling sick and needing to vomit, could you do it inside your shirt rather than across the plane - that way, we can contain the mess." We all felt ill at the thought.

I ENJOYED TRAVELLING the bush and still do, although daily long drives, bush hotels and motels, and usually dodgy food were hard to take in the early days. I recall a trip through the Victorian outback where a hotel arranged an early evening meal (there was never anything open by the time we finished our shows). The affable woman manager told us the train had brought fresh vegetables, and we were craving salad. As we tucked into the salads, we all looked at each other in shock and agreed it tasted like fly spray. When we questioned the woman, she nodded and said, "Well, how else did you expect me to keep the flies away?". It reminded me of the bush yarn where the hotel cook asked the drover what he wanted to eat. "A couple of eggs will be fine." The cook replied, "Okay, I'll boil up a dozen, and if they're no good, I'll boil up another dozen."

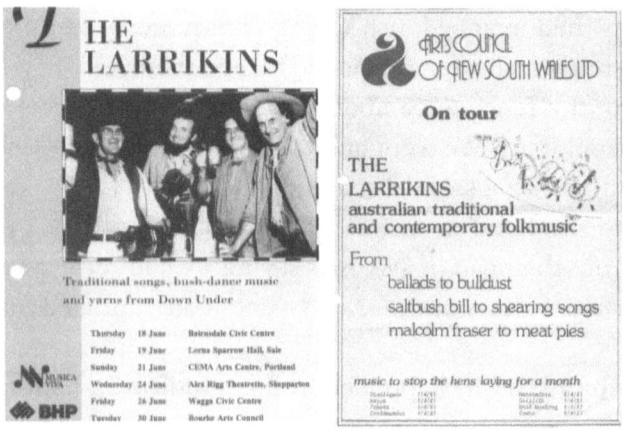

Early Larrikins touring flyers (WF, Bob McInnes, Dave de Hugard & Chris Kempster)

We were regularly invited to join locals for a meal, but nothing compared to our visit to Nyngan, West NSW, in the mid-seventies. We arrived early on a Friday and called into the local pub to see if they had a counter lunch. As we were standing at the bar, chatting to the locals, a bushie came in carrying a sugar bag which he casually left at his feet as he commenced drinking his beer. We continued chatting, and before we knew it, we had all jumped on top of the bar - as about six whopping big snakes crawled out of the sugar bag. The bushie smiled and asked, "You'se blokes staying long in town?" We had been set up, and the bushie was a local character, a wild pig and rabbit trapper of some notoriety. He casually put the snakes back in the bag, tied the bag, and said he'd come to invite us to lunch tomorrow at his place. Lunch was also a surprise - held in a campsite, he had boiled up buckets of yabbies. They were delicious. As you probably know, yabby heads are as hard as steel, and every time there was a pile of yabby heads, the bushie would chuck them into the cages of his yapping, tough-looking dogs parked near the fire. The dogs, pit bulls, chewed through the yabbies like marshmallows. I pitied any pig caught by those buggers.

In 2014 the celebrated actor, Max Cullen, contacted me and asked whether I would be interested in being in a play he was writing. I knew Max from his illustrious reputation with the *Kings Cross Whisper* and his radio, television and theatre history. He was famous for his "oils ain't oils" television commercial. We had also shared a stage a couple of times as Senior's Week Ambassadors (not that either of us believed we were 'seniors'). He told me he had been doing a one-man portrayal of Henry Lawson and had an idea to bring Lawson together with Banjo Paterson. He had trialled the idea with a bush poet, but it didn't work out. I was interested, but the idea of acting terrified me. The thought of making a fool out of myself didn't sit right. I decided to visit Max and his talented artist wife, Margarita Geordiadis, at their Gunning home near Yass. After a weekend of endless chatter, wine and laughs, I said I'd give it a go. I'd be Banjo Paterson to his Henry Lawson as long as we could both write the script and I could also handle the producer role. I knew there wasn't enough money in it to hire an agent or even through traditional theatre seasons. Besides, I liked the idea of taking the play to the bush and working with local communities.

Apart from the subject matter, the play's success was that it was a two-man show, one hour and fifteen minutes, required minimum production, could be staged just about anywhere and appealed to an older audience not necessarily catered for by touring theatre.

Dead Men Talking - Max Cullen as Henry Lawson and Warren Fahey as 'Banjo' Paterson.

Dead Men Talking was a terrific idea: the two celebrated poets meet in the Leviticus Bar & Grill, Heaven's Gate, reminisce, have a few drinks, sing and recite some of their works and generally question their literary legacies. In some ways, Lawson and Paterson were chalk and cheese, and as the play developed, a year later, we were rewriting the script to create more drama between the two characters. Lawson is a hopeless, drunken genius, and Paterson is a city-slicker lawyer and commercially successful writer. The play was a success from the start and got better and better as we continually tweaked the script and our performance skills. I was terrified in the first performance, sweating profusely, fearing I would forget lines, freeze up, or trip over a stool (I think I did all of those!). Max reminded me I had also broken an actor's golden rule: never whistle backstage. Somehow or other, probably 'other,' I emerged out the other side as a credible actor, and newspapers started referring to us as 'veteran actors'. It was a trifle weird at first, but after five years (rudely interrupted by COVID), it was nothing but a joy.

Working with Max taught me much about stagecraft, especially being prepared for anything. Whatever happened, we always enjoyed the play and especially the opportunity to ensure people did not forget the great legacy given to Australia by Lawson and Paterson.

2020 was the year for our 'last hurrah', and we had plans to take the play to Queensland and return to northern NSW, where we had started our first tour.

In 2018 we collaborated on a second play, Dead Men Laughing, where Max would play the great humorist Lenny Lower, and I would be Roy "Mo' Rene. We gave the play a test run in the south coast towns of NSW and at the Cobargo Folk Festival but soon realised hardly anyone remembered Lower, and the script wasn't working.

At least we had the look right. Max and I as Roy 'Mo' Rene and Lenny Lower. Photograph: Margarita Geordiadis.

We put it aside and returned to *'Dead Men Talking'* for another two successful years. Several towns invited us to return and, as they often remarked, "It's different." They were right; over the years, we changed the play considerably.

In 2020, just before COVID stumped us, we did a successful tour of Victoria and then a season at the Adelaide Fringe Festival. We have never been short of an audience. As the producer of the regional tours, I broke all the accepted rulebooks. Generally, I avoided established theatres, preferring to work with the local arts, heritage groups, or service clubs. The play was performed in various venues, from sheds to gaols, barns to swanky living rooms. More often than not, we performed in halls like Masonic halls, community halls, church halls and school of arts halls. We travelled light; all we needed was a bar table, two stools, a spotlight and an audience. The play appealed to older Australians, and Max and I had a running joke as we peered out from backstage at the arriving audiences - "Yes, that's our audience", reckoning it's the same group who followed us by bus for every performance.

Times changed, and so did the bush. Nowadays, especially in coastal towns, you can find excellent cafes and restaurants, although most slam shut after 6.30 pm. Coffee has improved too, and espresso machines have travelled far and wide. One thing that hasn't changed is the openness and friendliness of bush people, who are generally welcoming and up for a chat. The smaller the community usually means, the friendlier. Maybe surprisingly, we also found the smaller the community, the larger the audience. Dalton, population 106, is a good example and in 2020, we did a *Dead Men Talking* performance in their newly renovated hall with an audience of 102.

One of the play's highlights was a rendition of 'Waltzing Matilda' - a pigeon-indigenous version I had collected from Herb Green, in 1973. Over the years, I have often been asked about our national anthem. 'Advance Australia Fair' is unsingable, jingoistic and old-fashioned patriotic nonsense. On the other hand, our 'unofficial national anthem', Paterson's 'Waltzing Matilda', holds a special place in the heart of Australians. It is intertwined with our story as a modern nation. I am not specifically referring to the words because the 'song' bridges the bush and the city. I am talking about

Warren Fahey as A. B. Paterson.

its emotional hold on Australians, old and new. Australians abroad inevitably sing the song at every opportunity to celebrate their 'Australianess'. In the lead-up to the 1977 referendum on a suitable anthem, I suggested that the time had come to do away with sung anthems. Surely, in this day and age, when hardly anyone sings socially, we are unaccustomed to singing, especially as a group. I further suggested that the stirring tune of *'Waltzing Matilda'*, acknowledging its confused origins, was probably enough to encourage sporting and other massed gatherings to their feet. The non-compulsory vote, with a very badly worded question, declared *'Advance Australia Fair'* as the winner. Fewer supported the idea of a song about a sheep-stealer appropriate. It took until 1984 for the song to be officially recognised. Today, hardly anyone knows the words, and if called upon to sing, the general population will mumble a few familiar lines and become incoherent. In a letter to the SMH in 2014, one of the ballot scrutinisers said, 'many of the 1977 ballot papers came back with 'I Feel Like a Toohey's' scribbled across the form'.

Warren with his concert-screamer. Photograph: James Gleeson.

11

TRAVEL TRIPS & STUMBLES

I have been extremely fortunate to travel the world. My first trip was in 1974 when I was 28, relatively late considering I had always planned to go youth hosteling in Europe. Suffice it to say I got sidetracked. When I eventually did travel, it was to Athens. I had always held a love affair with Greece, probably stemming from my immersion in ancient history in school. I didn't have much money and, in those days, you didn't need much money in Greece. I stayed at a flea pit hotel on the steps of the Plaka and the smell and excitement of that city have never left me. Athens was fairly run down in those days. The colonels and their right-wing junta had just been evicted, and most of the city looked and felt neglected. The Plaka, by contrast, was alive.

On the first night, exploding with youthful excitement, I walked up the Plaka to see nearly everyone in costume. It was Apokreas and the start of their mardi gras season. I assumed this was Greece every Saturday night and my head was spinning. The climb was a cacophony of people yelling, music blaring, smells and laughter. Halfway up the climb, I heard what was unmistakably rembetika music. Rembetika is essentially underground music steeped in tradition, hashish and rebellion. Through my Sydney connection with musicologist James Murdoch, I befriended Gail Cork, an authority on rembetika music, and with its distinctive sound I knew I had discovered something special. I followed the music up a staircase and, at the top of the stairs, was a poster of Che Guevara, the Argentinian revolutionary. I gingerly walked into a room full of people seated at tables listening to a very large woman singing her soul out.

I was riveted and felt every eye on me. Fortunately, a man ushered me in with "Yassou, come in." and, with not a word of Greek except Yassou, I spent the next three hours in the Greek equivalent of nirvana. I spent three weeks in Athens, didn't have the money to go further, and with the Acropolis, Plaka and the Benaki and other antiquities museums my life was full. Embarrassing as it now sounds, my second overseas trip, a couple of years later, was to Greece again, but this time, I visited Delos, Sparta and Delphi. Back in Athens, I climbed to the very top of the Plaka where, according to my *'Spartacus Guide'*, a pre-Internet printed gay guide, was a gay bar. It was the size of a small hotel room with about a dozen patrons, mostly foreigners. It was a disappointment but I needed a beer more than a queer. An American soldier stationed in Greece chatted me up but fussy me decided it wasn't to be.

Greeks seemed to be fascinated by my R. M. William's boots. In those days my preferred dress was R M William's trousers with stud pockets, a bushman's shirt, an Akubra hat and R M William's Cuban-heeled boots. It sounds a bit contrived now but I was more often travelling the bush than being in the city. I had started to collect folklore and was also performing. I guess I did look different, especially in Greece. Years later, I went to Cuba as a guest of the Cuban Department of Culture. I was importing Cuban music way before it became popular, and my hosts were also fascinated by my boots. When I explained they were 'Cuban heels,' they laughed nodding their heads, "Oh, like Russian salad". Apparently, their Russian guests had never heard of Russian salad.

By the mid-seventies, Folkways Music shared an office with my record importing and newly-hatched Larrikin record label. We were fledglings but growing rapidly. To expand the business I had to fly to America and meet with independent labels who had expressed interest in a distribution deal. I visited New York, Chicago and San Francisco and came back to Sydney with Australian rights to Bay Records, Flying Fish, Folkways USA and Rounder Records. I already had rights to the French Ocora catalogue and the British Topic label. One of the advantages of travelling and connecting with independent record labels was the possibility of attending local shows with their artists performing. I remember going to San Francisco to see Arhoolie and Bay Records, it would have been around 1980, and I was able to see one of my idols, Big Mama Thornton. She was playing at a small bar in Oakland. Big Mama Thornton had a deep modern R&B sound, and she powered songs like 'Little Red Rooster', 'Hound Dog', 'Let's Get Stoned' and her own composition 'Ball & Chain'. The bar was packed, sweaty and throbbing, and it wasn't until halfway through the first set that I realised I was about the only male. I was in a lesbian bar.

As my label grew, so did Larrikin Entertainment, the distribution side of the business. The label was a labour of love (or insanity) and needed imports to balance the books. I was also starting to export a few Larrikin titles. The Australian government was active in supporting the export of Australian music and part-funded an industry stand and some of the costs to get independent labels to the industry's Midem international showcase held annually in Cannes, France.

Midem became an annual trip and, apart from showcasing Larrikin's export catalogue, it also provided access to likely distribution partners from across the world. Midem was crazy. The 'big boys' of the industry stayed at the plush and very expensive hotels on the Croisette opposite the beach and threw money around - the Australian dollar was low and a round of drinks at the Carlton International could cost around $800. It was far too expensive for my meagre wallet. I found an affordable serviced apartment a few streets back and returned each year like a homing pigeon. Cannes is a peculiar place, but over the years, I started to see through the facade and find a local community. Yes, there was one price for locals and another for the rich. So it goes.

I went to Midem every January for over twenty years. I made some lifelong friends and also had the opportunity to do an annual side trip after the festival. Over the years I knocked off my hit list of Britain, Czechoslovakia, Spain, Italy, Netherlands, Austria and Germany.

In 1986, I had an invitation from the Cuban Ministry of Culture to visit Havana and meet with the national record label Egrem. This was a decade before Ry Cooder's 1996 Cuban-inspired album which introduced many veteran performers, including some members of the Buena Vista Social Club and Rueben Gonzalez. I imported records and also Cuban percussion instruments, which I sold in Folkways. Larrikin also went on to distribute Nick Gold's World Circuit Records and had considerable success with 'Buena Vista Social Club' and the label's many African recordings. Flights from America to Havana were not possible in 1986, and I had to fly from Los Angeles to Mexico City and onwards to Havana.

A Larrikin Entertainment catalogue.

I spent ten days in Havana listening to live music, walking the city and retracing the steps of Ernest Hemingway. The Ministry even took me to lunch at Hemingway's favourite bar, El Floridita. One highlight of the trip was a night at the famous Tropicana Nightclub which was sheer 1940s camp madness with about seventy-five girls in top hats and tails walking overhead across wooden bridges and playing violins and guitars - very Busby Berkeley. At one stage, a member of the ministry leaned over and said, "In the old days, those women were men." I could imagine seventy-five drag queens.

In Havana, I stayed at the Hotel Libra, previously the Hilton. It was 'interesting' as the hotel had seen better days and there were even bullet holes in some sections of the walls. It was also a statement of communist full employment with hotel staff at every turning point who dispensed tickets to me as I entered the lift, where I gave the ticket to the lift operator, who gave me a new ticket, which I gave to the woman waiting to take me to my room. The restaurant was the same rigmarole of ticketing. There wasn't anything sinister in it, just a system to employ people.

Cuba seemed a happy place. It also felt safe as I wandered back lanes, unashamedly peering into people's living rooms to be met with the same photograph of Fidel Castro and, typically, a smiling local face. One of the surprise finds was the National Napoleonic Museum in Havana. The exhibits are housed in the 1920s Villa Fiorentina, the original residence of the main benefactor, Orestes Ferrara. When I visited in 1986, the objects on show included arms, militaria, furniture, bronzes, porcelain, paintings, sculptures, coins, personal items belonging to Napoleon and his entourage, books, engravings and autograph letters. More than 7000 pieces go to make up this extraordinary museum. The saddest part was the beautiful Napoleonic furniture which had not coped with the humid and hot Cuban climate. The wood was warping and veneers lifting. It was a sad sight, and I was tempted to whip out the beeswax and polishing cloth.

Leaving Havana was an adventure all in itself. I learned about a 'secret' United Airlines flight that left every Sunday evening at 1 am for Miami, which is almost in spitting distance. I had decided to visit a friend in Key West. The ministry advised me to get to the airport early as the flight schedule was somewhat dodgy. I arrived at 10 pm and the airport was already crowded with a mixed group, including several nuns and priests. An announcement advised the flight had been delayed, no one seemed to know about a rescheduled departure, and there was a sense of apprehension in the air. No one dared doze off; the only alternative was ordering another mojito, the wonderfully sharp Cuban cocktail. They cost about fifty cents each, and everyone was drinking and drinking and drinking. The flight was eventually called for 4 am. We boarded and, exhausted, immediately collapsed into sleep. Half an hour later, we landed in Miami in a very dazed state.

I am fortunate and still surprised that my occasional travel writing and performing have taken me around the world several times. Later, I became a guest speaker on high-end cruise ships - it's a lurk and perk I still enjoy.

Cruising down Milford Sound on Seabourn Odyssey.

In the 1980s David Gool, a mate who worked for the French Shipping Line, arranged for me to go as a guest on a 16-day cruise on the QE2. I had been writing the occasional article for Conde Nast in Australia, and it was my first taste of cruising. It wasn't to be my last. I loved everything about ship life and, most notably, being able to unpack the bag and stay put as the ship travelled from port to port. The fact I had been booked into the Princess Grill, the middle tier, was a bonus enhancing the experience and, as they say (referring to aeroplanes), 'once you've turned left you find it near impossible to turn right'. I look back with disbelief at that first cruise and the eccentric people I met. One charming woman dressed every evening as an animal. Apparently, as she sailed the world, she bought life-sized stuffed animals and, in the evenings, dressed like them and they accompanied her to the cocktail lounge! On her Australian visit, she purchased a life-sized koala, kangaroo and platypus. The crew discreetly told me the woman, obviously 'as rich as' had two cabins - one just for her 'zoo' animals and matching clothing. Another, a widowed heiress, always wore Chanel and Dior and dripped with jewellery. One evening I noticed she had gigantic art deco lapis lazuli rings on every finger, both hands. I said they were exquisite and she immediately withdrew her hands saying, "Oh, thanks, but I don't want to sell them!" Lord knows what she was thinking.

In 2001, Larrikin's GM, Geoff Weule, recommended me to a friend of a friend who worked as cruise Director on the prestigious Regent-Radisson line. They wanted someone to talk about Australia. Geoff suggested I could do it underwater! Barry Hopkins, the Cruise Director, was a delight to work with and after five Regent Radisson cruises, he jumped ship to another line and asked me to jump with him. I became part of the Seabourn guest speaker circuit and have held that honour since 2005. I do two or three cruises a year and have developed a unique catalogue of talks. I love speaking on the small ships, and by all accounts, my fellow guests enjoy my whimsical historical bites. I sing in some talks, especially the Australian and New Zealand circuits. Cunard still invites me, and occasionally, I join the ocean cruisers Queen Victoria, Queen Mary 2 and Queen Elizabeth — four old queens in total. I also remain a guest speaker with Regent Seven Seas, the high-end ships of the Norwegian Cruise Line. Cruising has become my international travel ticket.

High-end cruising is not cheap by any standard, and Seabourn and Regent deliver a first-class experience in every respect. The lectures are well-attended, and the audiences respond to some brain fodder between the pampering. My lectures, typically 50 minutes, are illustrated with Keynote and where applicable, I like to throw in some songs, poems and stories. In 2017 Seabourn invited me to talk on their Hong Kong-Taiwan-Philippines-Japan cruise and asked what I'd be talking about. I suggested I present a session on the History of Footwear as a tribute to Imelda Marcos and her fabled shoe collection. They loved the idea, and I loved the research and the eventual sharing of knowledge and folklore. One of my most popular

Just out of Nice, France, exploring a beautiful harbour township.

talks is on Aboriginal and Islander Australia, a subject most lecturers shy away from because of its complexities. I tell the indigenous story, warts and all, and finish with the inevitability of constitutional acceptance. I always have Aussies in the audience, and many congratulate me on telling this shared history as it is. Other local lectures cover Cook Island and Maori history, bush traditions, international food folklore, military stories and humour, folklore collecting, children's folklore, maritime history and, of course, several talks on the history of recorded sound and the music industry. When I cruise, I tailor my talks to the region. For example, in Asia, I have a talk titled 'Asian Game of Thrones', where I discuss the various heads of countries, be they monarchs, dictators, prime ministers or whatever, as I place them in a territorial 'Game', where the 'prize' is the South China Seas. In the Adriatic, I might talk about the history of headwear, antiquities, or foodways, tracing them back to their earliest forms. I also present snapshot talks on our itinerary taking in history, landmarks, and political and social history. My talks are purposely a mix of entertainment and education. I even have one on the history of boozing!

During a typical 20-day journey, I deliver eight talks (I have a list of over 50 available talks and am always refreshing or adding new ones) - the rest of the time, you'll find me at the gym, poolside, writing, albatross and dolphin watching or smelling the fresh ocean breeze. My cruising has taken me to just about every port in Australia and New Zealand, Los Angeles through the Pacific to the Cook Islands, All around South Asia including Japan, Shanghai, Hong Kong and up across to Indonesia, Malaysia, Thailand, Vietnam, India, Sri Lanka and Dubai. I have also cruised up the Red Sea, through the Greek Islands, through the Adriatic, everywhere in the

Mediterranean and across to France and Spain and Morocco. I was scheduled to visit India and South Africa before COVID pulled the plug on cruising. In November 2022, I returned to the high seas with three back-to-back cruises in New Zealand, then around Asia and then back to New Zealand. In 2024 I added India, Sri Lanka and Africa.

Jill Waddy, Melissa Hoyer, Mark Cavanagh and myself - in beautiful Montenegro.

Many people go cruising to escape work. I go cruising to take my work with me. Writing on board is a guilty pleasure. I find a quiet place and settle in. Head down and tapping away, I am usually left to and *with* my own devices.

Mark Cavanagh and I have made many cruise journeys together, including European segments. One of our favourites is the Venice to Barcelona run which takes in the Adriatic, Ionian Islands and Mediterranean. We did this in what we refer to as our 'gap' year 2018. The original plan was to spend a year in Europe living in one place and arranging mini-tours, but then we reasoned it was better to do a half year and keep on the move. Neither of us needs the frills of fancy hotels, restaurants or whatever to get from point A to B or even Z. After the Regent Seven Seas cruise dropped us in Barcelona, we hoofed our suitcases, mostly by train and bus, over to Portugal, back to Spain, across to Morocco, back to Spain, across to Italy and then to Athens, where we boarded a Seabourn cruise which took us down the Suez Canal and, eventually, dropping us in Dubai. We figured we wouldn't be in this part of the world very often, so we flew across to Amman and spent a week in Jordan including the 'must tick off' visit to Petra. From Amman, we flew to Tel Aviv for a ten-day visit. Throughout our travels, we hardly stayed at a hotel, preferring Air BnB wherever possible. We did a lot of homework and, all things considered, the train, bus and Air BnB accommodation worked extremely well. We got to know our suitcases extremely well too.

I generally like the people who cruise on Seabourn and Regent Seven Seas. They tend to be smart. interesting and appreciative of the cruising advantage. Over the years, we have made friends with fellow speakers and guests, including the legendary music producer Clive Davis, who casually chewed my ear off over his new book, adding, "And I finally came out as gay." (a secret near everyone in the music industry already knew); race car heroes Jackie French and Stirling Moss (Stirling delighted everyone by borrowing a passenger's disability scooter and doing wheelies around the pool deck), actress Anne Miller ('*The artist*'), newsreader Dan Rather, Apple co-founder Steve Wozniak, lyricist extraordinaire Tim Rice - to casually drop a few familiar names. There is always a parade of historians, biologists, authors, retired pollies (Julia Gillard speaks on Seabourn), and UNESCO heritage experts. Unlike my fellow 'conversationalists' I am very difficult to label.

Lord knows travel has become a nightmare, especially airports, and, post-COVID, it will probably never be the same. However, we still need to explore our world, and as long as small cruise lines are environmentally and socially responsible, I feel okay.

If pressed to nominate a favourite destination, I would probably lean towards Istanbul, although I have only visited twice. I had been to Bodrum, near the Greek Islands, many year's ago as a guest of Club Med (don't ask) and had always planned to visit Istanbul and the ancient sites of Ephesus, both great cities of Asia Minor, but never made it. In 2016, Mark and I did a couple of European cruise engagements for Seabourn and were headed for Turkey, the same year as the failed coup d'etat against Recep Tayyip Erdogan's Islamic government which had been steadily eroding Turkish secularism.

The cruise line rightly decided to cancel the Turkish segment of the itinerary. We decided to continue under our own steam to Istanbul, where we had booked an Air BnB for two weeks. We figured we would be okay if we avoided large crowds and the area where the demonstrations were held, Taksim Square.

Our apartment, on a very steep street, was in the middle of old Istanbul near the 67-meter Byzantine Galata Tower. The inexpensive apartment had three bedrooms and views across the European and Asian sides of Istanbul looking down to the Bosphorus. The area was vibrant, colourful and beautiful. The apartment was large, very chilly and prone to electrical failures. As it happened, Taksim Square was a stone's throw away, and we visited it regularly as the main street led straight into it. Nothing prepared us for the vitality of Istanbul with its street musicians, exotica, fabulous restaurants, Turkish Delight shops and friendly people. It was hardly hardcore Islam, and women were unveiled and relaxed. Highlights of the city for us included walking through the crazy Grand Bazaar, visiting the Topaki palace and other historical sites, the Islamic museums and, of course, the great mosques. We also had the benefit of a beautiful Swedish ex-model as a guide. Tova was a friend of a friend from her time as a model in Sydney and had married a wealthy Turk. She was in the midst of a divorce and wanted to play. Her car and driver dutifully arrived every second day or evening to take us to some special spot - the hidden side of Istanbul. We had fun.

I had visited a few hammams in Morocco, but the Turkish bath at the Kilic Ali Pasa Mosque in Istanbul was the most spectacular ever. Spotlessly clean, architecturally beautiful and madly relaxing, the spa treatments with foam, hot slabs and alternating buckets of near-boiling and ice-cold water, combined with deep tissue massage, made our bodies feel very alive. Another surprise was the Istanbul Modern - one of the best contemporary art galleries we have ever visited.

My head still spins with thoughts of Istanbul, where ancient truly meets modern. There was one scary aspect of our visit. Mark had been talking to two young Turks, and they joined us for dinner in a local shisha cafe. After dinner, they insisted we come to a bar for a beer. I am always suspicious of such invitations, and when we arrived at an underground bar with half-stunned dancing girls, I wanted to run. They insisted, and we agreed to one drink. Before we knew it, the table crawled with Russian girls offering their services. Food arrived, although we said no, and a round of drinks. I insisted we leave after one girl jumped on my lap. Boy, was she barking up the wrong tree! As we made for the door, five bruiser thugs appeared, and the manager gave us a bill for something like a thousand dollars. It was ugly. The two boys were petty pimps who did this all the time to receive a kickback. The Japanese and Koreans dancing enthusiastically with the girls were in for a costly night. I never carry much cash with me at night and only carry one credit card. There was much ado at the stairs, and one thug even brandished a gun. At one stage, I took control, saying to Mark, "Just walk up the stairs." Easier said than done with five goons barring the way and the Russian owner demanding payment. I denied having a credit card as I knew they'd march me up to an ATM, so I fished out my cash, about $200, threw it at them, and we managed to escape. With thumping hearts and silly grins on our faces, we jumped into a taxi. I had hidden my credit card and another $100 down my pants. I didn't think the thugs were going to look down there. Mark and I still laugh about our night with the Russian hookers of Istanbul.

Mark and I found a 'dress up' photo opportunity in the Grand Bazaar, Istanbul. How could we resist?

Our farewell to Istanbul was far more rewarding. The street where our Air BnB was situated had a mosque, synagogue, and what we assumed was another mosque. It was a Mevievi Sufi meeting lodge built in 1491. Walking past to get our daily fifty-cent glass of freshly pressed pomegranate juice (bliss), we noticed a leaflet advertising a public performance of the Whirling Dervishes. We booked immediately and that evening, at six o'clock, sat with the faithful and about twenty other foreigners for a two-hour performance of hypnotic Sufi ritualistic music and dance. Best of all, the master musicians, perched on the mezzanine level, played exquisitely on traditional instruments: ney flutes, kanun boxed zither, oud and darbuka drums. At one stage, the dancers whirled in their mystical trance for twenty minutes, eyes fixed, heads slightly askance, and round and round they spun. Sharing in culture, especially ancient culture, magically spins my head.

My heart aches for the people of Turkiye after the horrific earthquakes of 2023 levelled over 55,000 buildings in Istanbul alone. Museums and galleries have reopened, and most of the significant heritage sites thankfully survived. In 2023 we returned to Turkey to tick off our list. It is still wonderful.

Music has been my other great international travelling partner. My singing and my ability to gather other singers have allowed me to travel widely and sometimes wildly. For many years, from the early seventies, my performance group, The Larrikins, were represented by Musica Viva and participated in several cultural mission tours for the Department of Foreign Affairs. This meant the group would perform in various countries representing Australian culture. A typical performance would involve me explaining Australia's uniqueness, how, despite our British heritage, we had developed our own folk music, and the importance of our own story and then we would perform story songs and play tunes. We performed at schools, universities, community gatherings, on local radio and also to the ex-pat community. The Larrikins, in one form or another, toured twice to New Zealand, three times to Indonesia, Malaysia, Philippines and in one tour, in 1980, to the Solomons, Vanuatu, New Caledonia, Tonga, Samoa, Nauru and Kiribati. In 1986 the group performed in Edinburgh, Scotland, for the Commonwealth Arts Festival and, in 1989, I took an ensemble of artists to the Vancouver Folk Festival in Canada. In 2006, the Australia Council asked me to produce the Australian Spotlight of the Festival Celtique, Lorient, Brittany, France.

The Festival Celtique celebrates Celtic music from all over the globe, and 2006 was Australia's turn. Over 700,000 people attended the ten-day festival of music, song and dance. The streets of the small coastal town were packed with impromptu and staged performances, the pubs hosted dance and song, and in the town centre a village of tents representing each participating country. There was also a grand parade, which took up to four hours. I programmed the Australian pavilion for ten days and nights. It also had an Australian kangaroo and emu BBQ, which, I have to say, was unbelievably popular. Australian Rugby Union also arranged giant screens to show the Bledisloe Cup. Fosters and Australian wines flowed from several bars. The highlight of the annual festival is the Gala Concert of the toast nation. Staged in a 3500 modern theatre, I devised a thematic concert telling of the Australian Celtic experience. Tickets sold quickly, and a rarity for the festival, a second show was arranged, which also sold out.

I produced the Showcase on a shoestring budget with support from the Australia Council for the Arts, the Department of Foreign Affairs & Trade, the Australian-France Association and the Paris Embassy. We had 150 musicians and dancers, including John Williamson, Mara & Llew Kiek, Fiddler's Feast, Martyn Wyndham-Read, Brother, harpist Christina Sonneman, Queensland ceilidh band Murphy's Pigs, The City of Adelaide Pipe Band, the Ipswich Thistle Pipe Band and the Queensland Irish Pipe and Drum Band. Dave de Hugard and I supplied the bush song segments. Indigenous culture was represented by didgeridoo masters Mark Atkins and Wongi Forrest, and two young North Queensland dancers, Joshua Thaiday and Sean Carter. I had my work cut out for me organising 150 performers to be in the right place at the right time. Herding folk performers was often like herding cats, but I was experienced and always optimistic. We did it.

There were some memorably funny international touring experiences. In 1976, after a week of performances in Jakarta, Cathie O'Sullivan and I decided to travel down from Yogyakarta to Bali by public bus. We must have made an impression at the Surabaya bus terminal because they gave us the 'special seats' directly behind the driver and alongside the raised motor. All was well as we chugged along, often stopping without a timetable and waiting for more passengers to take the empty seats. Passengers carried everything from massive baskets of fruits to live chickens. It was all good until we hit the mountains. It was apparent our fellow passengers were not regular public transport users, and several started to vomit. It was fine when the bus went uphill, but every time it headed downhill, so did the sea of vomit, which, frighteningly, edged onto the stinking hot motor at our feet and commenced to sizzle and fry. It was nauseating. An experience neither of us would want to repeat.

We met in Bali with Dave de Hugard, who excitedly told us he had nearly been robbed. He had been sleeping, and an arm came through the window, reaching over to take his wallet when he woke. The startled thief screeched at Dave and tried to shake him, yelling, "Watch out! I wanted to warn you - don't leave your money around. There are terrible thieves in Bali."

The trip to the 1989 Vancouver Folk Festival saw me take a contingent of Australian artists to the prestigious festival, including Eric Bogle (with Brent Miller and Andy McGloin), Kev Carmody, Judy Small and The Larrikins (Dave de Hugard, Cathie O'Sullivan and myself). It was a very well-attended and organised festival set on the foothills of Jericho Mountain. The festival really looked after its artists with meals, massages and prime seats. During our Australian showcase, there must have been around 5000 people seated on the ground in a field, and the heavens opened. It poured solid, yet the hardy Canadians remained seated. It was a weird experience, and if in Australia, we would have been looking at an empty field.

On the way home from the festival I was scheduled to go to New York to meet with Nick Perls of the Yazoo blues label and to see Folkways USA founder, the legendary Moses Asche. Being a long weekend, the queues at the Vancouver airport were endless. People were extremely frustrated and getting vocal about their discontent. Pete Seeger and his wife, Toshi, were in my queue, and Pete turned to me and said, "Watch this, I'll sort them," as he casually took his banjo and climbed up on one of the dividing stands in the middle of the lanes. He plunked a few notes and started playing *'Living in the Country'*, a lovely guitar tune he had recorded, and a silence gradually fell over the airport. Obviously, many people didn't realise who was playing - "It's Pete Seeger" was passed on like a Chinese whisper. At the right time, easy as pie, the troubadour started singing a children's song about 'waiting', and smiles erupted across the airport. It was an extraordinary moment in time. The story doesn't stop there, for Pete and Toshi, the bluesmen Cephus & Wiggins and folksinger Patrick Sky were all on my United Airlines flight headed to New York. Forty minutes into the flight, the Captain announced we were making an unscheduled stop at Chicago's O'Hare airport because of 'technical difficulties'. Offloaded, the airline arranged overnight accommodation and a meal voucher in the airport transit lounge. A quick confab and our group decided to make the best of a bad situation and meet in the airport's Mexican cantina for dinner. That evening turned out to be one of the best concerts of my life. We all took turns singing, storytelling and playing, and it was, to use a bygone word, a hoot.

I COORDINATED A 'FOLK BOAT' cruise for P&O in the late seventies, taking some musicians and fans around the Pacific circuit. It was a trip from Hell for most of the passengers and performers because we hit a week-long typhoon that had the boat rocking and rolling in all directions as we came down the Timor Sea and Great Barrier Reef. The performers included Ted Egan, The Flying Emus, and my group, The Larrikins. People looked green, and vomit flew in every direction. Ted Egan and I, tough old buggers that we are, never got sick and usually ate dinner in the three-quarter empty restaurant as people groaned around us.

Through my musical travels, I have known so many fine musicians. Some of my favourites, as people and performers, include the songwriter Louden Wainwright III, old-time singer Mike Seeger who, incidentally, according to his sister Peggy, 'could fold himself up like a cricket', Tom Paley, an original member of the New Lost City Ramblers, Ewan MacColl and Peggy Seeger, Tallis Scholars, Michael Nyman, Martyn Wyndham Read, Jody Stecher, Shirley Collins, Blossom Dearie and .... so many more.

I COULDN'T EVEN START a list of favourite Australian performers - far too many to count.

I DID GET a regular showcase to feature Australian artists when, in 1992, I had my own Qantas in-flight audio channel. The program combined country, folk (and many genres in-between) music and was recorded and played for three months. I did this for several years, and it was a good deal as it meant I nearly always bagged an upgrade. I was flying high.

12

DRAW BACK THE CURTAINS

I have twirled around the social dance floor more than once and this has no doubt confused those who barely know me other than from my folklore and performance personas. By 'society' I mean the so-called Sydney 'A List' as reported by the Sunday newspapers and magazines past and present like *Mode* and *Vogue* (or *Mad* and *Vague* as we called them). I have no idea who came up with the concept of a Sydney social register nor how the heck I ended up being on it but I was there in the 80s and 90s and enjoyed the ride. For over forty years, I was invited to some of the great parties of Sydney, including the famous, fabulous and somewhat notorious, including the previously mentioned Cointreau Balls (I went to ten). These extravagant events, sponsored by Cointreau, were the invitation of the year and always full of surprises. Around 400 invited guests came dressed for the theme but never knew where they were to party. One year, with instructions to bring "a toothbrush and a change of clothes", we were bused down to Wollongong, where we partied in a basketball stadium until we dropped; then, after a quick refresh at the stadium hotel, we were bused back to an old disused church in Darlinghurst for a breakfast feast. In other years we found ourselves in the old army base at Pagewood, the Navy stores at

Alexandria, and the Sydney Showground at Moore Park. The Cointreau Balls were produced by David Grant who always delivered style, surprise and extravagance. We were given themes - country, western, cosmic etc. and one year everyone had to build and decorate their own table. Our bloodthirsty group constructed a butcher's shop complete with chopping boards, carcasses and bloodied butcher aprons.

MANY OF THE major Sydney parties had prizes for the most outrageously dressed, and one year, to celebrate the opening of chef Neil Perry's Star Grill at Darling Harbour, Mark Cavanagh and I won a trip around the world flying business class with Qantas. Mark dressed as a yum cha Chinese trolley dolly, and I went as 'Charlie the head waiter'. We weaved our steaming trolley, borrowed from the Kam Fuk Restaurant, around the party for an hour as I yelled, "Table for how many?" before we were declared the winners.

Channelling Roy Orbison. Amazing what a wig can do!

I lost count of the number of times photographs appeared in magazines and newspapers, and we considered them more of an embarrassment than a social asset. Robert Rosen, a talented social photographer, has catalogued them and occasionally presents one from the archive. There's one of Richard Branson and myself, smiling to the camera like pranksters - it is now on the wall at the Sheraton on the Park, Sydney. I have absolutely no idea where or when this was snapped.

Richard Branson and WF

When I first started to receive invitations, and there were hundreds, they came addressed to 'Warren Fahey and Guest' then, after Mark Cavanagh and I were obviously an item they began arriving as 'Warren Fahey and Mark Cavanagh', then, as I retreated and Mark became a successful public relations operator, they were addressed 'Mark Cavanagh and Warren Fahey'. And finally, as I decidedly slipped into oblivion, they arrived as 'Mark Cavanagh and Guest'. Today, social diary invites are a rarity and we're non-plussed. Don't get me wrong, I love a party, love air kisses, love organised mayhem and love seeing old friends and meeting new ones; however, the mantle of the 'big' event parties, rightly, has been passed to a new generation, and, personally, I don't want to be stuck in a room full of 'influencers'! Nowadays, a good night for me is a small dinner party with stimulating conversation or a couple of glasses of red wine as we watch the sunset.

Party mode with Mark Cavanagh, Kerrie Lester and WF. Photograph Robert Rosen.

I made some good friends on the social roundabout including Sonia McMahon who was ever the lady and a great drinking mate; Red Bond, ex-wife of Alan and always a scallywag; Leslie Walford, Professor Ross Steel, Marita Blood, Skye McLeod (Leckie), Justin Miller, Lucy Turnbull, Naomi Parish, Brooke Tabberer, Karin Upton Baker, Melissa Hoyer, Jill Waddy, Mandy Foley, and Margaret and Gough Whitlam, to name a few.

I know this gadfly business must sound superficial, but as someone who documents Australian cultural change, I find it fascinating. The main thing is not to get caught up in it and to realise that most of these events are little more than product promotional events. The number of 'gift bags at the door' I have been given is simply ridiculous. Once, Mark and I were given gold Nokia mobile phones.

For a couple of years or so, I was also part of the 'food and wine mafia' but, like the social scene, have preferred to retreat into anonymity. Age shall not weary me, but the years do tend to condemn as the guest lists get younger and younger, signifying the changing of the guard. There was a time when I regularly wrote about food, wine and lifestyle for several leading magazines. In 1989 Sharyn Storrier-Lyneham, then editor of *Vogue Entertaining & Travel*, encouraged me to write about food and notably published a wacky back-page piece I'd written about cooking an entire meal in a dishwasher.

The whimsical dishwasher story eventually reached the producers of the ABC television program *The 7.30 Report* and presenter Justin Murphy came to my home to film a demonstration, It became a hilarious segment where I explained how I 'invented' the technique when my gas was disconnected and had a couple of chums over for dinner. I carefully demonstrated how to prepare and cook a delicious and nutritious three-course meal - all at once. The first course was green prawns with snow peas in a teaspoon of Thai fish sauce and a few crumpled kaffir lime leaves. The main course was snapper with chilli, red onion rings and coconut milk. Dessert was chopped banana with shredded coconut, sultanas, chopped almonds and a healthy splash of that liquor someone left at your place, probably Bailey's Irish Cream or Kahlua. All three dishes were safely cooked and wrapped in tin foil. And all cooked at the same high temperature and at the same time. Obviously, dishwashing powder was not recommended. For years I was asked, "Are you the bloke who cooked the meal in the dishwasher?".

I contributed off and on to Australian *Vogue's* various magazines for several years, including a ridiculous stint for USA *Conde Nast Traveler* where I did an annual review of Sydney restaurants. It was 'ridiculous' because they gave me an open budget for hatted restaurants like Tetsuya's, which was way out of my own budget. It was all the more 'ridiculous' because the reviews of the top ten Sydney restaurants were limited to a tiny paragraph on each establishment.

When ex-*Vogue* editor, the ever-stylish Karin Upton-Baker became editor of *Harpers Bazaar* magazine in 1990, I was invited to contribute to their food and wine pages. I enjoyed this challenge and wrote regular articles on food history and cuisine cultural change. I wrote on everything from asparagus to cabbage, and caviar to cocktails. I recall one article detailing what bottles were lurking at the very rear of our liquor cabinet, including mysterious bottles of

Midori, Jagermeister and Kahlua, which I never would have bought in a pink fit. Obviously freebies from some promotional event.

Thanks to magazines, I feasted on many memorable meals. Internet 'influencers' now do the job, but in the seventies and eighties, the public relations companies seemed to have endless promotional budgets, and they splashed out - French champagne, caviar, lobster - you name it they had it. One of the most memorable meals was served at Tony's Bon Gout, the Elizabeth Street, Sydney, restaurant operated by Tony and Gay Bilson from 1972. It was an invitation-only lunch for forty of Leo Schofield's friends to celebrate Leo's fortieth birthday (the year was 1975). There were forty courses! It was my first degustation and my first mouthful of delights, including truffle and stuffed zucchini flowers. (I was ill for two days as the pollen-laden flowers sent my allergy off the Richter scale.) The wonderful thing about Tony's Bon Gout was that on a normal day, you could get a main course for $9.50.

Food writer with benefits.

Although I find cuisine fascinating and have been spoilt rotten, I am far from a food snob. I prefer simple, tasty and healthy food. I am more inclined to cook than eat out. For those who care, I nominate the following Sydney establishments as my historical favourites. (I know some readers will nod their heads in agreement.) Most closed their kitchens ages ago: The Minerva (under the Hellenic Club), Illiad (Liverpool Street), Mario's (Stanley Street), Little Snail (Bondi), Malaya (when it was near Central Railway); Paddington favourites Patricks, The Hungry Horse, Lucio's and Bon Ricardo; Pappagallo and the Bayswater Brasserie (Kings Cross); Pier (Rose Bay), and, dare I say it, Johnny Walker's Steak Cave. It still makes me laugh when I think back about takeaway food in the fifties and how I was sent to the local Chinese restaurant with two saucepans - Tupperware was not introduced until the early sixties. Although I now live in Potts Point much of my youth was spent in Kings Cross. It was at the Cross I had my first espresso and schnitzel, both at Sweetheart on Darlinghurst Road. I felt very grown-up.

I also wrote for *BRW* magazine when it had a lifestyle section, contributing some strange articles, including a three-page article on getting my eyes laser-corrected. My favourite magazine was always *The Bulletin,* and I was fortunate to become an irregular contributor when Kathy Bail was assistant editor to Garry Linnell. I enjoyed the opportunity to prepare lengthy researched articles and especially one on its history celebrating the magazine's centenary. Writing for the same magazine as Henry Lawson and A. B. Paterson was thrilling. Over the years, I have contributed to many newspapers, magazines, books, and radio and television programs. I enjoy the solace of research and writing.

By situation or circumstance, I have been fortunate to have met many (in)famous people. Fame doesn't mean a great deal to me. Probably because of my time interviewing everyday people for my folklore collection, I know that so-called 'ordinary people' can also have fascinating stories to tell. Famous people can also be dull as dishwater, engrossed with their inflated importance and fame.

Through music and parties, and chance, I met many artists. Robert Rosen, the photographer, hosted a small dinner party where Boy George and Peter 'Marilyn' Robinson dominated the quirky conversation. Both artists were on tour and had been getting a bit of stick from the media. They were in a reflective mood, and it was interesting to get inside the conversation of Boy George, a singer I have always admired for his voice and persistent eccentricity. Jimmy Somerville was another singer I admired vocally. His soulful countertenor falsetto vocals in the Communards, Bronski Beat and Fine Young Cannibals always impressed. I also loved his opening appearance in Sally Potter's 1992 film *Orlando* where his voice soars over the lake. I signed Jimmy to Festival Records as an independent and found him an endearing character—likewise, another Festival

Jimmy, the indigenous country singer Jimmy Little. Jimmy Little popped in regularly to Festival to see if there were any royalties. It was a real pleasure when Brendon Gallagher of Karma Country approached me about producing a Jimmy Little tribute album. The 1999 *'Messenger'* album won an ARIA award and notched up solid royalties for the Little family. Olivia Newton-John was another Festival Records artist. When film director, Stephen Elliott, asked me if I'd like to handle the music licensing for his 2011 film, *A Few Best Men*, I jumped at the opportunity to reacquaint myself with her. Olivia was a dream to work with and allowed me to explore some new ideas in taking early Australian hits like *'The Pushbike Song'* and *'The Nips Are Getting Bigger'*, recording Olivia's vocals and then getting contemporary remixes. The soundtrack, released through Universal Music, was exciting but a commercial fizzer. Two of my favourite star friendships came with two New Yorkers, both singers of old jazz songs. Blossom Dearie, the consummate baby-voice singer and pianist, was a joy, and we always caught up when I visited New York, or when she toured Australia. I eventually became her record label distributor for Australia, but her friendship and music were far more important than the monetary return. Steve Ross and I have been friends since his first visit to Australia in the late seventies. A born-again Noel Coward mixed with Gershwin and Astaire, Steve has a huge song repertoire and delightful patter to bring them alive. One night, at my home, he played for three hours, including a bracket with Margret RoadKnight, one of my favourite Australian bluesy singers. Michael Nyman was another favourite musician, especially for his soundtracks for several Peter Greenaway films including *'The Cook, The Thief, The Wife and the Lover'*, *'Zed and Two Noughts'* and *'The Draughtsman's Contract'*. My record company distributed all his soundtracks, including Jane Campion's *'The Piano'*, and I persuaded Musica Viva to bring Michael and his band out for performances. The tour coincided with Michael's birthday and we had a rousing dinner celebration at the Sydney Opera House. Michael convinced me to sing some bush songs - and loved them.

As the distributor for Peter Gabriel's Real World Records for over a decade I was fortunate to meet many of my world music heroes, particularly Shiela Chandra, Geoffrey Oryema, U. Srinivas, Afro Celt Sound System and the great Nusrat Fatah Ali Khan. Nusrat, one of my all-time favourite singers, certainly the world's greatest exponent of qawwali, is still a frequent visitor to my playlist.

AFTER LEAVING HANSEN RUBENSOHN MCCANN & Erickson, I received a telephone call from the CEO of John Clemenger Advertising, who asked whether I would be interested in a position with one of their clients, Harry M. Miller Attractions. I was ready for a new challenge but hadn't thought about theatre, although I had been helping Nimrod Theatre with its marketing. I agreed to an interview and duly arrived at Miller's Haymarket office at 6.30 pm on a Monday night. I was ushered into Mr Miller's office, where a full argument was in session. There were shouts, harrumphs and protestations. I assumed they were discussing *Jesus Christ Superstar*, which had just been launched at the nearby Capitol Theatre. Harry indicated that I should join the arguing circle, so I timidly took a seat as the argument moved on. In attendance were in-house producers John Young, Freddie Gibson and Stefan Haig, finance director Richard East and head of publicity, Patti Mostyn. I hadn't a clue what they were discussing, and as Patti sent me a reassuring smile, Harry turned to me and asked what I thought. I blurted out that I would never offer an opinion until I knew all the details. This was the right answer. After the meeting, Harry had me stay back for a few questions - where did I live, did I like the theatre, and would I mind having an intelligence test?

I thought - what! An intelligence test? "Okay," I muttered as Harry handed me a card with a woman's name and telephone number. I did the test and passed. It wasn't much of a test, and I suspect Harry was bonking this girl, and it was all a bit of a joke. Whatever the case, I got the job. I spent two very exciting years as the marketing and advertising manager for the Harry M. Miller group, which included the theatrical productions, Hepburn Spa Water and the Simmental

Artificial Insemination Program for cattle. Talk about diversity. It was a huge challenge but one I relished. I had a staff of one - I appointed a young man named Ian Enright as my assistant. He was the brother of playwright Nick Enright. We worked like crazies to ensure all the print, radio and television advertisements were absolutely correct, including the continuing changes in show times. It was a nightmare as new sessions were added, some were cancelled, etc. We continued to stage the cash cow *Jesus Christ Superstar* during my watch. We also presented a mixed bag, including The National Ballet de Senegal, pianist comedian Victor Borge, farces including *No Sex Please We're British* (starring Eric Sykes and Jimmy Edwards), *On The Buses* (with Reg Varney,) and a string of variety concerts billed as *Sunday Night At The Opera House*. I was the assistant producer (to John Young) on the Sydney Opera House concerts and our brief was to provide programs that would appeal to family audiences, especially people who would never usually go to anything called an opera house. The concerts, I think we did six or eight weeks of them, were truly awful and completely sold out. We had club variety artists, old radio stars, magicians, hypnotists, novelty acts, jugglers and anything else we thought might appeal to the bedraggled masses. It was all about 'bums on seats'.

Harry knew a lot about 'bums on seats', and one of the keys to his outstanding success as an entrepreneur was his insistence on 'party bookings'. He employed an army of telephone bookers who seemingly rang every business in New South Wales, offering group discounts and specials to their social clubs. The call centre was controlled by Patricia Boggs, who also coordinated with several bus companies to transport the audiences from all over the city and state. Party bookings were the lifeblood of long-running shows like *Jesus Christ Superstar* and *The Rocky Horror Picture Show*. Pat managed The Metro and, later, the Capitol Theatre box office.

Harry got the rights to *The Rocky Horror Picture Show,* but there wasn't an available theatre, so Harry did what Harry did - he found one. The New Art Cinema on Glebe Point Road proved to be ideal. I remember going with Harry, Patti and Freddie Gibson (later to become manager of the Theatre Royal) to look at the theatre. Built in 1937 as the Astor, it had several name changes, including its last, The Valhalla. It had just the right amount of grunge, however, backstage the mechanics needed to be completely redone. The show opened in April 1974 and ran through until October 1975. Jim Sharman directed, Brian Thomson designed, and Reg Livermore was the prancing, dancing Dr Frank-N-Furter. Arthur Dignam was the first narrator. The show was a huge hoot and success, and established itself with a cult following. The film of the show came out in 1975.

When we were preparing the investor's brochure for the stage show of *The Rocky Horror Picture Show* I asked Harry if I could invest. I had a few dollars, mainly from ABC radio scripts, and I loved the idea of working on marketing and owning a slice. Harry's reaction wasn't quite what I expected. He point-blank refused my $5000, saying, probably screaming, that it was his policy that staff not invest in any of his shows. This was probably because the investor's contracts favoured the producer, Harry, and not the investors. I stood my ground, and Harry reluctantly took my money. For me, it was a matter of principle and a creative challenge. After Harry signed the Glebe lease,; Harry, stage director Jim Sharman, stage designer Brian Thompson, Patti Mostyn, and I inspected the theatre. It was in terrible shape, and Jim and Brian declared it "perfect." Producing a stage show in a new venue, especially a radical show like *Rocky Horror Picture Show*, was a gamble and one Harry was up for; besides, the rent was cheap. The show was a huge hit and returned my modest investment handsomely. I waved the first investment cheque in Harry's face.

I enjoyed working for Harry M. Miller Attractions. Harry was an inspiration with bounding energy, humour and style. He knew no timetable and would regularly send Gary, his driver and 'go fetch man', to collect me at 7.30 am on a Sunday 'for a meeting'. Meetings in the office on George Street near the Capitol Theatre regularly ran into the night and ended with the team marching over to watch the second half of *Jesus Christ Superstar* and overhear the departing audience comments. I grew to hate the songs but not the spectacle.

One of my stranger jobs was to promote and market bull's sperm. Harry's then-wife, Wendy, was a noted veterinarian, and they had the license for an artificial insemination program for Simmental cattle. I could never quite get over the image of the gorgeous Wendy Miller's arm up a cow's arse. They had a cattle stud at Manilla, near Tamworth, and I always thought Wendy preferred the country life over the city madness.

My office at Harry M Miller was chaotic, and everything was on a deadline. I had to originate everything from poster artwork, radio scripts and crazy promotions to last-minute changes in press advertisements - shows cancelled, extra shows etc. - and I certainly learnt about multi-tasking and double if not triple-checking procedures. I thrived on the pressure and still tend to set often seemingly impossible goalposts. My main ally at the office was Patti Mostyn, head of publicity and general balm to Harry's often irrational behaviour. Patti also worked under extraordinary pressure to create publicity out of virtually nothing. She was a magician of publicity of the old school where endless telephone calls, lunches and countless dinners resulted in front-page news, radio support and television coverage. Patti knew all the tricks and invented new ones. The media feared and loved her because she never gave up on a story, never suffered fools and knew all the right people. We worked well as a team; to this day, decades later, I still count her as a friend. Her late husband, Eric Robinson, owned Jands, the sound and stage company, and together Patti and Eric were a formidable pair over a dinner table.

Patti and I did some hazardous things in the name of promotion. We once had the almost-forgotten television and radio star David Cassidy on tour. When Harry announced he had signed Cassidy for a national tour, we both dropped our jaws in horror because he hadn't had a hit for years. We protested, but it was too late - the deal had been done. Worse still, Harry had booked Randwick Racecourse as the Sydney venue. We had images of fifty hardcore fans and us standing, cheering the near-forgotten singer. Patti went into overdrive to create excitement about the tour, including a major newspaper contest for 300 'lucky fans' to win a signed poster of the star. One night, over a couple of bottles of Chardonnay, we locked ourselves in the office and started signing 'With love and affection, David Cassidy'. We were hysterical with laughter because none of the signatures was the same. We didn't dare tell Cassidy or his management. The tour was a shocking flop and signalled the downturn for Harry M. Miller Attractions. The next disaster came with the scandal over Computicket, an event and theatre booking service, which eventually saw Harry sentenced to a few years in the slammer. Like many, I thought it a very unfair judgement and, in retrospect considering all the money market manipulation engineered by wanker bankers, his crime was minimal.

One of the last things I did with Harry was to try and help him get Patrick White's novel *Voss* produced as a feature film. Harry always wanted to be considered a 'serious producer', and he dreamt of a knighthood for his services to the high arts. He wanted to stage serious plays, present opera and ballet, and make Patrick White's novel into a great Australian film. I had done some work with Royce Smeal Film Productions and knew brothers Jim and Hal McElroy, who had worked on Peter Weir's first feature, *The Cars That Ate Paris*, and I thought them the ideal production partners. Harry arranged a meeting - another 7.30 am Sunday morning affair - at Harry's house, which was almost next door to Patrick White's old home, facing Centennial Park. Harry, the McElroy brothers, and I sat there waiting for Patti Mostyn, who had agreed to collect the great British film director, Joseph Losey, who had arrived the previous day. We waited, drank more coffee and waited some more. It was very unlikely for Patti not to be punctual or in contact. I could see danger signs and suggested I telephone Patti about the delay. The telephone rang and a very sheepish Patti answered - "Ouch! Don't tell Mr Miller, but I think Joseph Losey is dead in the hotel." The two of them had spent the night attacking bottles of vodka and were near dead but, thankfully, breathing. It was not a successful meeting, and the film director looked like a stunned mullet as vodka and perspiration rolled off his ashen face. The film never eventuated.

My time with Harry Miller was a real-life lesson. I framed one of the very first memos he sent me, a list of six essential lessons in theatre marketing.

- 1. What is it?
- 2. Where is it?
- 3. What date and time?
- 4. What will it be like?
- 5. How much does it cost?
- 6. Why the hell should I go?

The memo is now in my manuscript collection at the National Library of Australia.

PATTI and I left Harry M Miller Attractions before Computicket imploded. Harry had already started to wind down his theatrical productions, although he was trying to take *Jesus Christ Superstar* on the road and to the big clubs. 'See Jesus Christ at your local RSL'. Patti and I discussed setting up a business together, but it didn't happen. Harry agreed to contract us when he had 'something', and we did some work for a few other promoters, namely Garry Van Egmond, who had set up as a producer, and Robert Raymond, who brought us in to handle two large tours, Frank Sinatra and The Supremes. Patti and I could see that there was no consistency in work, and we let it slide.

13

GETTING INSIDE THE MUSIC

Early photographs of me tackling the concertina.

This is as good a time as any to explain my love of the concertina. The instrument was invented by Sir Charles Wheatstone in 1824 and was originally designed to perform classical and parlour music. It eventually became a folk instrument, especially in England and then America, New Zealand, South Africa and Australia where pioneers needed something light, inexpensive and portable. It faded out of popularity in the 1920s, probably related to the increasing presence of radio and the gramophone. In the 1960s, it became associated with the revival of interest in folk music. I first heard the instrument played by Mike Ball, an English singer who lived in Sydney in the 1960s and 70s. Mike played the chromatic 48-key English concertina rather than the so-called Anglo-German push-and-pull concertina favoured by most folk performers. I was determined to play the English model despite its frustratingly difficult fingering and when Mike Eves, a longtime friend, became a Scientologist, I bought his treasured Lachenal rosewood nickel-ended concertina. I had listened to this lovely instrument for about ten years and couldn't believe my luck in becoming its new owner. It took me a long time, nearly three decades before I got my head around the system. I took it away with me when I did my extended field collecting trip in the early seventies and taught myself the elements of music theory thinking this would allow me to master the instrument. I did learn about what musicians call 'the dots' but my playing was awful and I was never game to play it in public. Many years later, about twenty-five years ago, my determination button kicked in and I bought a couple of tuition books and decided to have another go. Seduced by eBay, I bought two more concertinas, a Wheatstone English and a Lachenal Edeophone, a superior instrument with ebony raised ends. As a singer I had been spoilt by having a series of incredibly talented instrumentalists and, as the main singer, playing an instrument was never on my list of priorities. Learning words to new songs took most of my music time. Musicians will nod when I say the only way to learn an instrument is to be born a child prodigy or practise, practise, practise. I played for an hour every day practising scales, improving my sight reading, and torturing my partner, neighbours and dog. After about five years I was still terrified of playing in public and, frankly, with good reason. I was note-reading and had very little musicality.

How could a larrikin resist a shirt that says 'hooligan'?

One day, totally frustrated, I picked the instrument up and started to play by ear and, to my surprise, I was making more musical sense. I put the music books away and spent a year training my ear. It was up and down the scales then playing some elementary bush dance tunes and then accompanying my songs. It was all starting to make sense. My fellow Larrikin members, obviously sympathetic to my determination, joined in whenever I played in public but, truthfully, this tended to put me off as I found it too hard to contain the music in my head. I then started to record myself singing and playing - mainly so I could listen to what I was doing wrong. It sounded okay. After I disbanded the last incarnation of The Larrikins, I started to do some duo shows with Marcus Holden and also some solo shows where I played a few songs.

With longtime musical partner Marcus Holden at the National Folk Festival, Canberra, 2012. Photograph Ian Fisk.

Bit by bit, it came together, my nerves subsided, and the accompaniment sounded pretty decent. I can now 'play' the concertina and love it. My style is slightly eccentric but it certainly works in accompanying my interpretations of bush songs, ballads, sea songs and the occasional dance tune. One regret is that my hands are developing Dupuytren syndrome which turns the hand into a claw. I am hoping the constant wriggling of my fingers will ward off this crippling disease which appears to be common in Celtic and Nordic people. (In 2023 I had the finger surgically corrected.)

Channelling 'Banjo' Paterson as I sing his classic 'A Bushman's Song'.

I have had several concertinas, mostly bought on the Internet or rescued from junk shops. My prized instrument is an Anglo-German, push-and-pull type made by J. Stanley in Bathurst in the 1880s. Stanley was Australia's only colonial concertina maker.

John Stanley first came to my notice when I found advertisements in The *Bulletin Magazine* for 'The Concertina Doctor'. He claimed his instruments were loud and ideal for dance accompaniment. He also did repairs in his Bathurst shop. Apart from the volume, his concertinas were very distinctive, with intricate fretwork on both ends and with the name of the purchaser and his own 'J. Stanley,

Bathurst'. I only know of two remaining instruments, and in 2020, I contacted the Museum of Australia asking if they would be interested in adding it to the national collection. They declined, seeing no value in such a simple object. I have always felt this museum was a dud and a lost opportunity for us to develop a Smithsonian-type collection.

Both my godsons, Emyrs and Jasper, are musical. Emyrs has a natural talent for piano, especially improvisational music. Many years ago I bought him Keith Jarrett's *'Koln Concert'* recordings. I doubt he needed inspiration for his music has always sounded individualistic and spacey in a Jarrett-styled way. Jasper tinkled a bit with the keys and also, with his father's urging, played a bit of acoustic guitar. In 2019, Jasper expressed an interest in the concertina. At twenty-one, he had already been to several music festivals, including folk festivals. He also liked the *Pirates of the Caribbean* films and thought some "pirate tunes" would be good to play. I gave him an English concertina and some basic lessons. He was like a dog with a bone and wouldn't leave it alone. This is the best way to learn any instrument. Leave it accessible and pick it up whenever you feel in the mood. He was and remains tenacious. The rather complex theme of *Pirates of the Caribbean* was ticked off in a couple of weeks and then a few Celtic tunes. At Christmas 2020, with my urging, his parents bought him a Lachenal Edeophone with metal ends, a top instrument that, has encouraged him to continue his musical journey. He is now a far better player than I ever will be.

Captured with rust at Tim Duggan and Ben McGregor Urquhart's Gundagai wedding. Photograph Ben McGregor Urquhart. Jasper Penfold Low and concertina. Photograph Rebel Penfold Russell.

I also play the jaw harp, sometimes called the jew's harp. It is a simple, underestimated little instrument capable of some very interesting sounds. The jaw harp is played by plucking a metal tong and using the mouth as an echo chamber cavity to produce sound. It can sound like a didjeridoo, a galloping horse or, best of all, as a means of playing a tune. If you accidentally hit a tooth, you'll never do it again. The first tune I learnt was the *'St Patrick's Day'* reel. If nothing else, it is a musical curiosity that deserves to live on. Kids are always fascinated by it. I also learnt mouth music or diddling, mouthing tunes using dah dah dah sort of language. It sounds weird but it works and was certainly part of many old-time bush repertoires. In 2021 I discovered a whole new world of jaw harps and the realisation that the ones I had been playing were totally out of tune. I bought two jaw harps from Russia and one from Ukraine. What a difference. These are tuned and produce a beautiful sound. I am still plucking them. I gave Jasper two jaw harps, and he worked them out perfectly. Last Xmas I gave him tin whistles.

I like performing for kids, especially the younger ones and have done hundreds of children's concerts. The younger children are completely accepting and, of course, listen. Older kids, and I mean twelve onwards, tend to become embarrassed and fidgety at the thought of learning or, God forbid, someone singing. I have a repertoire for these occasions and include several songs I collected like '*The Old Macquarie*', '*The Wonderful Crocodile*' and '*Three Men Went A-Hunting*'. I have also learnt that singing unaccompanied usually works better as getting the storyline over and the children to join in is easier. I believe too many present-day children's songs are simply rock or pop song formats with repeat choruses and actions. They lack fantasy. I work best solo when giving kids' concerts. In 2019, I was on tour with Max Cullen. We were in Oberon to present *Dead Men Talking*, and the local school requested a performance. I thought Max could talk about what it was like to be an actor—wrong idea. Max started talking to these toddlers about how he puts himself in a sad mood... by relating a story about his dog and, somehow or other, the story got out

Mentoring young children is always a treat.

of hand, and he started to talk about children being on a train to a concentration camp in WW2 and how Jews were going to be gassed. I had no idea where it was going or how to stop it. The kids were looking at us not having a clue what he was talking about. It just got weirder and weirder until I stepped up and said, "Time for a happy song".

Being on stage is hard to describe. It is both challenging and invigorating. Be it singing solo or with a band, or acting, one has to be part ham. You can be good or bad and, sometimes, rotten. Of course, performing is a discipline, and the more you do it, the better you usually are.

After establishing The Larrikins as a performance group in late 1968 I was becoming stronger as a singer. I never had tickets on myself as a singer - but am a reasonably good storyteller. Running a folk club, as I did when I started the Edinburgh Castle Folk Club in Sydney in 1970, was a good opportunity to calm my nerves. The Edinburgh Castle was a very successful Saturday club attracting about one hundred people to listen to traditional singers.

As a jack-of-all-trades, time is a factor in my life, always has been, and I'll probably jump into my grave trying to get projects done. When you are on the stage, you know if the performance is good, and this also spurs you on to be better. If you start with a mistake, a lost line, or a wrong key, you can be thrown off and it often means all downhill from there. Thankfully, I am resilient and 'tenderised' and have learnt to be steady rather than rush. Taking a step back and gaining breath control is vital to a good performance. With singing, I can go into a phase where the story of the song engrosses me; the tune is secondary, and, hopefully, if the ducks are lined up, I can pass this special feeling onto the audience. Sharing a story song can be magical, and it has little to do with the size of the audience, place or whatever. It has to do with producing a special magic where the story and song are shared. I guess this is what envelops me in folk songs. It's not about musical ornamentation or beauty of voice for I possess neither. It is about communication. Often I think about how I received the song. If it is something that I had been given, possibly recorded for my oral history folklore collection, there is a special bond. In acting, something that came to me late in life, it became apparent that being in costume and make-up allows a creative bridge to be established between the stage and the audience. Watching Max Cullen and countless actors in countless plays, I learnt skills that were not natural. Breathing, pausing, facial expressions, walking, standing, etc, are all important tools. I consider neither acting nor singing my 'day job'; they are simply something I do as part of what I do in my life's journey.

You know you've made it when you're squeezed in between Bogan Bingo and Eric Bogle.

14

COLLECTING STORIES & TELLING YARNS

When I started recording oral histories in the sixties the term 'oral history' had not come into vogue. I did 'recorded interviews'. Today, oral history is almost an industry and its massive results are evident in our most respected libraries. My main interest, like earlier folklore collectors, was in recording songs. I also wanted to record everyday speech and the stories behind the songs. When John Meredith and others started collecting, the raw tape was expensive, and I assume this was the main reason he and others refrained from recording very little speech. Or maybe it was the impatience of recording the items and moving on to the next contributor?

One certainly gets the impression they were working against a ticking clock. I now realise that since I started seriously collecting at the beginning of the seventies, I was one of the last to be able to record people who had been born in the nineteenth century. The majority of my informants were aged between 70 and 100, except for Jacob Lollbach who was a sprightly 102 when I recorded him.

Listening to the tapes now, in the 21st century, I can see how these recordings are of interest to linguists, especially since the subjects were ordinary Australians. Many of the people I recorded, like Joe

Watson of Caringbah, NSW, had been born in Australia, particularly the bush, but sounded Irish. Their accents reflected Australia's Irishness of their childhood, and, of course, the fact they hadn't been influenced, like later Australians, by waves of popular entertainment, particularly American television programs. Sadly, we have lost thousands, probably hundreds of thousands, of words and expressions that were used in the 19th century. Such is the march of time and language.

Undertaking field collecting was a challenge and a bit like assembling a jigsaw puzzle. Apart from the 1950s Australian collections, I was aware of the work of American collectors, John and Alan Lomax, in recording cowboy songs and so-called negro work songs, George Korson's work with coal miners, and also of Cecil Sharp's survey of Anglo-American ballads collected in the Appalachian mountains, and more specialist collectors like Gershon Legman and Randolph Snow's work in collecting erotica and bawdry. I bought books on folklore, song and mythology.

Unconsciously I was assembling the basis of a substantial folklore reference library, something which, like any collecting project, became an expensive and seductive pastime. I still hunt for books but now do it online, particularly through Abebooks.com and other specialist secondhand mail-order catalogues. I don't buy so many nowadays as I have run out of bookshelf space. (I am probably also running out of space in my brain!) I also find the Gutenberg Project, digitally scanned out-of-copyright books, a literary godsend. A handful of books became my bibles: Archie Green's 'Only A Miner', A. L. Lloyd's 'Folksong of England', Peter Kennedy's 'Folk Songs of England, Ireland and Scotland', Bronson's 'Child Ballads' series, Cecil Sharp's 'English Folksongs from the Southern Appalachians', Colm O'Lochlainn's 'Irish Street Ballads', 'Gershon Legman's various books on bawdry, Alan Dundes' American folklore collections, and the mighty Funk and Wagner *Dictionary of Folklore and Mythology*. I could also add books from Roy Palmer, Kenny Goldstein, Steve Roud, Hugh Anderson, Archie Green, D. K. Wilgus, Tristan Coffey and many others.

My bookshelves also hold early Australian songsters, poetry

books, observations on being Australian, books and folios on Australian folk music, indexes and, of course, books that I have written or contributed to in some way or another.

It was chiefly through books that I developed my approach to recording interviews. I already had quite a lot of ABC radio experience and knew my way around a microphone, and that also certainly helped on the technical side. The ABC enthusiastically endorsed my idea to undertake a detailed collecting project in 1971, lent me a professional Nagra tape recorder, and gave me a large box of blank tapes, however, their main support was at a grassroots level. When I arrived at a destination I would usually head straight for the ABC studio and arrange an interview with a local announcer. I would explain that I was travelling around Australia looking to record "old songs, poems, stories and bush dance music." I never mentioned 'folk songs' as most singers wouldn't know one if they fell over one. They knew 'old songs' and, possibly, 'old bush songs'. I would also explain where I was staying - "I am in the camping ground down by the creek. Look for the kombi van with 'Australian Folklore Unit' on the side panel."

Accordionist and storyteller, Dave Matthias, Forbes, 1973.

People seemed to get what I was looking for and I would get a few people knocking on my door or calling the ABC studio with a message. A mobile telephone would have been very useful back then! Occasionally someone would tell me about, "An old fellow that plays a fiddle - he lives about 100 miles up the road." I would typically drive up the road to find he had passed away or moved. I was collecting randomly which, in retrospect, was not the best approach. Far better to stay in a community for a longer period, get to know the locals, talk, talk, talk. I was probably too impatient. I did stay in some areas longer than others, particularly Lithgow and the Hunter Valley districts.

My home on the road - Australian Folklore Unit

When I started collecting no one had specifically searched for industrial folk songs. The handful of earlier collectors, understandably, tended to follow A. B. 'Banjo' Paterson's lead and were primarily interested in songs about shearing, droving, bush life and the goldrush era. My stays in both Lithgow and the Hunter proved very fruitful, and when I eventually returned to Sydney, one of my first projects, which became Larrikin's first album, 'Man of the Earth', was based on material primarily collected in these two areas.

A typical recording session would go like this - after establishing that I would like to record someone and they were agreeable, arrangements had to be made as to a convenient time and place. I found early afternoons were usually best. People seemed more relaxed, and recording in their most familiar surroundings, like the living room or kitchen, was the most conducive. There were a few considerations on my part including access to power and avoiding noise like traffic, barking dogs, birds, children and chiming clocks. The Nagra came with a very heavy and large microphone which I either held in my hand or stood on the table between myself and the informant. Older people were generally unused to microphones and had a tendency to want to grab them, despite my saying it should be ignored.

I was always mindful that country folk tended to eat early, often around 6 pm so I would excuse myself around 4.30 pm. My early collecting coincided with a very popular weeknight television series called *Bellbird,* and many the time, concentrating on the recording volume and recording panels, I noticed my contributors getting extremely fidgety. Later on, it dawned on me - no one wanted to miss *Bellbird.*

It was not unusual for my contributors to invite me to lunch or dinner and with the recording machine switched off, they sang me ditties or told stories that I would have preferred to have had on tape. Often these pieces are rarely as good as the first impromptu rendition. On a few occasions, I was given songs or poems in pubs but hotels are difficult places to control and bringing out a large recording machine was a cue to clam up (or ham it up!) I usually had a notepad. Once again, a mobile phone would have been a godsend.

Joe Watson, Caringbah, a treasure-trove of songs and poems.

Joe Watson was undoubtedly my favourite contributor and certainly the most surprising. Joe's son, a chemist on Sydney's North Shore, had written to me suggesting I might like to record his father about his days as a 'picture showman'. Joe was 92 when I first recorded him at his home on Caringbah Road, Caringbah. He lived a couple of doors from one of his daughters in a typical suburban Shire house. Joe had snow-white hair and a genial glint in his eyes. He spoke in a lilting Irish-Australian accent despite being born in Australia. He was a natural storyteller. I was fascinated with his life - he had moved from country butcher to showman and then country publican and by the fact that, at the time, he was the longest continual member of the Australian Labor Party.

I had come to record his life as a travelling picture showman so that's where we started. Joe was in partnership with a man named Paddy Doolin and the two of them spent several years travelling the east coast states of Australia with a variety show centred around the magic lantern. Paddy must have been the senior member of the duo because Joe told me that eventually, he had bought "about half a dozen houses within three miles of the Melbourne GPO". Joe eventually bought a hotel in Boorowa saying "I kept the pub in Boorowa - because it wouldn't keep me".

Boorowa first settled, in the 1820s, is in the southwest slopes of New South Wales, near the large commercial centre of Young. Joe explained there was always friendly competition between the two, especially since Boorowa was the older settlement. "We used to say, 'Boorowa was Boorowa when Young was a pup, and Boorowa will be Boorowa when Young is buggered up."

I asked Joe to describe a typical magic lantern night. "Oh, we used to charge a shilling and there would be a white sheet for a screen and we had all sorts of slides including some that you could wiggle to get optical effects. The slides were usually in series - the castles of Europe, the Royal Family, travel stories and things like that. Paddy would stand near the screen and I would work the magic lantern and announce the program. Paddy would take over, telling stories about each slide and then singing a song, accompanying himself on the Anglo-German concertina. At this stage, Joe stunned me by saying Paddy was completely blind. "Oh, he was a marvellous singer and musician, he knew hundreds of songs and monologues."

As a folklore collector, I was secretly lamenting that Paddy Doolin was no longer alive. My head was spinning at the thought of him dying and taking all those songs to his grave. I asked Joe if there were any Australian slides and he told me about a series on the Kelly

Gang. My immediate response was to ask if Paddy had sung a song about the bushrangers. Joe set his head back and in a slightly faux Irish voice recited 'Oh Paddy dear and did you hear, the news that's going 'round, On the head of bold Ned Kelly, they've placed five thousand pounds." My remorse at not having Doolin there must have intensified as I muttered something like, "You wouldn't happen to know the tune Paddy sang?" Joe looked at me, his eyes twinkling, as he sang all sixteen verses of the ballad. I was staggered, speechless, as this was the most complete version of the song ever recorded in the oral tradition. Joe must have sensed my excitement and added, "it's a good one isn't it!"

It turned out Joe knew a lot of songs and recitations but dismissed his singing as "Oh, these were well known in the bush, and I'm no great singer." The truth was that Joe was an extraordinary traditional performer. He had his songs and poems directly from Paddy Doolin and also songs and ditties he had heard in shearing camps and in the hotel business. He had a keen ear for a tune and was a masterful storyteller. It seemed to me that every time we talked about any subject, he had a song or poem - including horse racing, politics, boxing, shearing, droving and even the Chinese on the goldfields.

Cyril Duncan was in his late seventies when I recorded him. My collector mate, Bob Michell, and Brisbane singer, Stan Arthur, had taken down a few songs from him in the sixties and, with Bob's blessing, I went to interview Mr Duncan. I assumed Cyril had probably given Bob and Stan his full repertoire but, as it turned out, they hadn't scraped the surface.

I had been travelling Queensland in my Australian Folklore Unit kombi van and turned up unannounced on a Saturday morning at Cyril's Brisbane home. I introduced myself and explained I knew he had given some songs to Bob and Stan and asked if I could interview him, and did he possibly know any more songs? He looked at me and said a defiant "No, I don't know any more songs." then after we chattered awhile he asked if I was living in the van. "Yes, been travelling recording people's life stories." He then eyeballed me and said, "Do you drink?" At first, I thought he'd found God but after I nodded my head, in what was a mixture of confusion and embarrassment, he said, "I suppose you'd like a baked dinner?" I nodded again. "Well, come tomorrow at 5 pm - and bring some XXXX beer."

Cyril Duncan inherited a repertoire of traditional songs from his bullock-driving father. Brisbane, 1973.

Dinner with Cyril, his wife and his son was a cracker. He didn't waste any time in opening the first bottle, and the second. We talked about his songs and I sensed there was a problem. After the third bottle, and these were the large long-neck bottles, he said he was cranky because "They misquoted me in one of the songs published in the *Penguin Book of Australian Folk Songs.*" It was the classic ballad '*My Name Is Edward Kelly*', an extraordinary ballad, sung in the first person, telling of the bushranger's life. Apparently, the collectors had written a line 'We rob the banks, and shoot the traps, and quickly run away, " when Cyril had actually sung 'We rob the banks, and shoot the traps, and NEVER run away." With this off his chest and the power of alcohol, Cyril seemed a different person. He looked at me and asked if I'd brought my recording machine. "Yes, sure I have," I replied. "Go get it, and we'll put the right version on tape." The eventual recording, which is in my National Library of Australia Collection, is very emotional, and Cyril is clearly concentrating. He emphasises certain sections by occasionally breaking into a spoken line, and when he had sung the ballad, he went straight into a ditty, he claimed he hadn't sung for over twenty-five years, a ditty his bullock-driver father sang.

Farewell Dan and Edward Kelly,

Farewell Byrnes and Steve Hart too,

Those that blame you are not many,

Those who blame you are but few.

Thirty policemen did besiege you
In a manner, I am told,
Dirty policemen did outdo you,
For a paltry sum of gold.

Farewell Dan and Edward Kelly,
Farewell Byrnes and Steve Hart too,
Dirty policemen did outdo you,
For a paltry sum of gold.

Despite denying he knew any more songs than the half dozen previously recorded, Cyril went on to sing around fifty songs and ditties that evening. We were pretty drunk by the end, but he kept coming up with new ones. After singing his versions of *'The Banks of the Condamine'* and *'Bullocky-O'*, when I must have intimated I was familiar with them, he slammed his fist on the table. He said, "Here's one you bloody-well won't know," and proceeded to sing a rare English song *'The Parson and the Clerk'*. He sang songs about Lord Nelson at Trafalgar Bay, boxing songs, comic and music hall ditties and bush songs learned from his father. One comic song, *'A Long Time Ago On The Logan'*, celebrated a picnic race day conducted by the local Aboriginal tribe. Cyril explained that *cobbles* = carpet snake, *Yurragangs* = native dog, *Booribi* = native bear, *Nulla* = weapon, *Churrongs* = eels. I was always reluctant to sing the song until the local Beaudesert indigenous community asked me for permission to play the song in their museum. I readily agreed and then I asked their permission for me to sing it.

Oh, a long time ago on the Logan
There were blacks of all sizes and sorts
A meeting was held at Beaudesert
For the purpose of having some sports
First prize was a lovely fat booribi
Of cobbles, the number was six
Second and third, no difference.

Two iguana's half dead with the ticks
Chorus
There were nullas, carbuckers and cobbles
Iguanas and yurragangs too
Nullas and spears and burraguns
All thrown by that famous old Blow

Now Blow being the best at the throwing
And Andrews the best at the fight
Old Slab sent down for three bottles
For the purpose of keeping things quiet

Now Billy and Bobby got rowing
When there's drink how those old darkies will
Old Charlie near split his sides laughing
When Bobby upset Old King Bill.

Now Blow received many a present
And of churrongs he had quite a sack
The only one there seemed to grumble
Was that quarrelsome Nevertire Jack

Charlie Lollbach and his 102 year old father, Jacob, Grafton 1973

Another surprise was that when collecting in Grafton, I recorded Charlie Lollbach playing bush dance tunes on his button accordion. After the recording, he casually mentioned I should record his father. Mr Lollbach senior was 102 and knocked out a fine version of the bush classic, 'The Old Bark Hut,' and some bush poems.

The irrepressible story-teller and singer, Jack Pobar, Toowoomba, 1973

Jack Pobar was another Queensland find. He was a self-styled 'swagman' who knew all the classic poetry and song. He had also written quite a few poems. He was a bent old man with enormous mutton-chop sideburns. When I knocked on his door, I heard some shuffling, but he didn't answer, so I knocked three times again. Still, the door remained shut, but, like an echo, three knocks came from the other side. Eventually, he opened the door, welcomed me in and for three days we chattered and did recordings. He was a 'talking machine' and every story ended with a song or poem. Jack had a twinkle in his eye. He even claimed to have met Banjo Paterson.

Also from Queensland was Herb Green. Herb had worked with horses all his life including many years as a stable 'boy' at the Doomben racetrack. His speech was affected by his life at the stables, and he spoke, recited and sang like a race broadcaster. Herb had an interesting repertoire including a song about the champion horse, 'Mussellman', and another about the tragic death of the jockey Willy Stone. He also had a terrific song and poem about the Depression. In 2020 a journo mate of mine, Alan Howe, writing about COVID hard times, printed the words to the poem in *The Weekend Australian's* 'Cut & Paste' column. Herb would have been thrilled.

On one of the drives north, I had a letter from an elderly man who said he knew a shearing song that he felt was "worthy of recording." Edward Gilmer sang me the only recorded version of what has become known as 'The Limejuice Tub', a song about 'new chum' shearers and the ships they came out on which were colloquially called 'lime juice tubs' - because of the daily ration of lime juice to ward off scurvy. He had learnt it in the 1920s when he was shearing in the Riverina. Interestingly, the only other full version, a composite version "half-remembered" by the English folksinger A. L. Lloyd, who also recalled it from the same area and timeframe. Mr Gilmer's version is no doubt the original. It has a great line: 'The great jumbucks are shorn by the great humbugs'

Shanty singer Jimmy Cargill, Randwick, NSW, 1973.

Back in Sydney, I had a lead to record a man in Randwick. Jimmy Cargill had heard me interviewed on the ABC and wrote saying he knew a song I might be interested in. Jimmy lived in a boarding house on Avoca Street and his song was the wonderfully evocative 'Gumtree Canoe'. It is unusual for singers like Jimmy to only know one song, and, as it turned out, he knew dozens. Originally from Scotland, he had worked in the North Sea and migrated to Australia in the 1930s. He had a strong voice and knew lots of sea songs and shanties. As I was packing up, I casually asked if he knew any bawdy sea songs. He nodded, got up, closed the window, and proceeded to sing me a song called 'The Maids of Australia'. I was expecting something salacious but got an erotic song which is possibly the first song about a sexual encounter between an indigenous girl and a settler. It is not bawdy. An extraordinary find. I should add that Jim also told me how he was the one who discovered the Japanese mini-submarine trapped in the net across Sydney Harbour during WW2. I have the whole story in my NLA collection, including where he proudly says, "And the Government sent me fifty pounds!".

Mrs Susan Colley (holding baby), singer and concertina player, Bathurst. 1973.

Susan Colley was a resident of the Bathurst Home for the Aged when I went to record her. She was 92 and looked a bit like Mary Poppins. Mrs Colley played an anglo German concertina and sang sentimental ballads, Salvation Army songs and many bush songs. Her memory was slipping, but the tape recording showcased her strong voice, playing and stories. My heart took a beat every time she said "I didn't think anyone cared, I didn't think anyone remembered...." She loved sharing her music.

Sally Sloane was Australia's most important repository of

traditional songs. Pioneer collector John Meredith had taped her extensively in the 1950s, and since I had made Sally's acquaintance at the Bush Music Club, I also wanted to tape her repertoire, especially her background to the songs. She was a marvellous storyteller. I took a bit of stick from Meredith over my move to record her, but Sally encouraged me, and the recordings are an important study of the tradition.

In 2012 I produced one of the most important recordings I have ever created. It was titled 'The Australian Bush Orchestra' and I selected a team of musicians (led by Marcus Holden, Garry Steel, Mark Oats, Clare O'Meara and Ian 'The Pump' McIntosh) to interpret a particular sound I had in my head for what I felt was old-time bush dance music and associated colonial music. It wasn't the thump-thump of the broomstick lagerphone and tea-chest bush bass and was a more refined, tempered sound. I selected some bush dance favourites of reels, polkas, mazurkas and waltzes but also colonial quadrilles and polkas I had found in the NLA sheet music collection.

How could I not bring to life 'The Bulletin Polka', 'Pioneer Polka', 'Bottle-O Schottische', 'The Catadon' or 'The Colonial Polka'? To show the continuity of the tradition I used actuality segments from my recordings of Sally Sloane, Susan Colley and Jimmy Cargill to introduce the tracks - it worked a charm. Originally issued by ABC

Music, the recording has been recently reissued digitally by Rouseabout Records.

I could write a book about my escapades recording oral histories, especially songs. I feel very privileged to have had the experience of interviewing so many people. A handful of people collected before me, notably John Meredith, Norm O'Connor, Mary-Jean Officer, John Manifold, Ron Edwards and Bob Michell. Others came after, including Chris Sullivan, Barry McDonald, Mark Schuster, Dave de Hugard, and Peter Ellis, just to name a handful. The most significant collector over the past years has been Rob Willis who has industriously recorded thousands of wonderful stories.

Tracking the progress of songs down through history fascinates me. There are songs about nearly every aspect of Australia's history. As a cultural historian, I like to explain how I use songs as signposts to our history. TROVE, the National Library of Australia's world-class digitisation program has allowed collectors like myself to dig deep in search of songs. A keyword search for 'Sydney Exhibition 1879' produced a song describing the various exhibitors, a search for 'station cook' unearthed the original 1870s complete version of a song known as *'The Shearer's Hardships'* and so on. When I was writing my book on the Australian gold rush, *The World Turned Upside Down*, I found many unknown songs from the 1850s and 60s, especially songs from the NSW goldrush. I persuaded a young Sydney old-timey banjo player and singer, Luke Webb, to join me and record some of the songs for a CD of the same name. The banjo, so important to the sound of the minstrel troupes, provided just the right sound for songs from the 1850s.

In 2005, Graham Seal, Australia's first professor of folklore (Curtin University) and I collaborated to co-author the centenary edition of A . B. Paterson's 1905 *Old Bush Songs*. To my mind, Paterson was the first to actively 'collect' the bush songs. Soon after the success of *The Man From Snowy River and Other Collected Verse,* Paterson advertised that he wanted to receive the words of any old shearing, droving, fossicker, bushranging and overlander songs remembered by readers. He collected over one hundred and in the introduction to his 1905 *'Old*

Bush Songs', explained, 'There are many Australians who will be reminded by these songs of the life of the shearing sheds, the roar of the diggings townships, and the campfires of the overlanders. The diggings are all deep sinking now, the shearing is done by contract, and the cattle are sent by rail to market, while newspapers travel all over Australia, so there will be no more bush ballads composed and sung, as these were composed and sung, as records of the early days of the nation. In their very roughness, in their absolute lack of any mention of home ties or of domestic affections, they proclaim their genuineness'.

In our updated edition for ABC Books, Graham and I wanted to show evidence of the songs and their journey to the twenty-first century. We included several new additions to the collection, something I suspect 'Banjo' would have approved. Most importantly, the book showed that the old bush songs had a life of their own and, in some ways, Paterson's suggestion that there would be no new bush songs was incorrect.

Of course, recording oral histories was not just about songs and over the years, I taped the life stories of people I thought should be recorded. For example, Margaret Fulton and Joan Campbell, two household names in gastronomy's history, gave their insights into how Australian cuisine developed. Wendy Lowenstein and Shirley Andrews discussed their roles in the early folk song and dance movements. Sydney songwriter and busker John Dengate talked about songwriting and, in particular, his interest in Australian bawdy songs and poetry. Thankfully, the National Library of Australia has made many of my early oral histories available online.

15

GETTING RIPER NOT OLDER

Growing old is not for the faint-hearted. I don't like to say I am growing older and jokingly say I am getting riper. Ageing is both mental and physical, and both need regular exercise. I've always been an active person, although, as years pass, the body machine starts to get hiccups despite the mind's determination never to give up. I have not been the world's best sleeper for the past twenty-five years and often find myself going over the words of songs - completely pointless. Six hours a night is an okay average. Exercise is a pain in more ways than one. I try not to eat too much and, as my friends will attest, I am a healthy cook ladling out the lentils, pulses, lean meats, and salads and avoiding the creams, fats and anything with nasty additives. I enjoy booze, but my days of wild boozing have passed. A few glasses of good wine, the occasional beer and even less occasional spirit suffices. At least I never smoked tobacco.

Being born on January 3rd, I have never regarded my birthday as a reason for celebration. Most folks have been worn down with Christmas and New Year to be bothered with more celebration so early in the new year. Despite my cynicism, my fortieth, fiftieth, sixtieth and seventieth were all memorable events. Lord knows how I will cope mentally with eighty.

Turning forty in the times of AIDS seemed an achievement. The first cases were reported in 1981, and by my fortieth, in 1984, I had already started to lose friends to the disease. The last time I looked, the worldwide total of deaths from AIDS reached 32.3 million. As a comparison, as I write this in 2024, the total number of deaths from COVID-19 is 6.86 million. A sobering comparison.

My fortieth was a surprise party put together by my sister Zandra, partner Mark Cavanagh, and longtime friends Paul and Sandra Ferman. I have forgotten the pretext as to why I was being driven past the airport, past Brighton-le-Sands, past Pasadena Street, where I had grown up - until we pulled into the car park at the Ramsgate Botany Bay swimming enclosure. The life-saving clubhouse, a one-room wooden building, sprung to life with "Surprise!" as I looked in to see about fifty faces of myself. Every guest was wearing a mask made with a photograph of my face. It was hilarious and, in a way, rather spooky. The evening had been well-orchestrated, commencing with a sit-down Australian-themed dinner with guests from across my life. No detail of naffness was spared. Paul Ferman, a member of the Food & Wine Society, had even decanted 'good stuff' into Porphyry Pearl and Ben Ean bottles. As the meal neared the end, I heard someone shout, "food fight" and lamingtons and pavlova went flying. My sister's mother-in-law, Kitty Stanton, a granddame in her nineties, was one of the first to throw and closely followed by a fistful from food writer Leo Schofield. The food was flying everywhere and sticking to the guests and walls of the clubhouse. Amidst the carnage, I was 'kidnapped' by a group of strangers who tied me to a chair and made me sit in the middle of the room as guests lined up to throw cream cakes into my face. This might seem a rather odd entertainment, but at the time, I rarely ate dairy, especially cream and my tormentors claimed they were responding on behalf of "the waiters of Sydney" who had been subjected to my protestations of "No cream, please." It was all good fun until I explained I was wearing contact lens and had cream in my eyes and couldn't see. The 'strangers' turned out to be the wonderful Legs On The Wall acrobatic theatre that had been formed that year.

My fiftieth was a much more civilised event. Staged in Robert and Lisa Bleakley's private apartment at the Verona Cinema, Paddington, it was a surprisingly 'grown up' affair. I felt very loved. For my sixtieth, an event which, at the time, seemed impossible, Mark and I decided to escape to join friends in Rio de Janeiro. Apart from the wonder of New Year's Eve on Copacabana Beach (with over a million others dressed all in white), the highlight of the visit was a two-day walking tour of Oscar Niemeyer architecture.

If sixty seemed ancient, then seventy seemed ridiculous; however, the party, devised, nit-picked and executed by Mark and my 'faux sister', Rebel Penfold Russell, was a triumph. Rebel's Palm Beach house skirting the Hawkesbury and the ocean looked beautiful beyond belief and set up as a glamorous 'sunset club'. The guest list was equally glam. The inimitable Paul Capsis serenaded the guests, music bounced off the palm trees, kookaburras and magpies sang, and I had a smile as wide as the Harbour Bridge. I can't even imagine what hitting my next milestone will bring - probably a wheelchair, a thermos of tea and a good book!

I have often suspected I have tendencies towards being a hypochondriac. I put myself through agony at the slightest hint of a blemish, secretly thinking 'skin cancer'; when I puff after walking up four stairways, I listen for my pounding heartbeat; getting out of bed at 2 am to have a pee, I return thinking about prostate cancer. Don't even get me started on colon cancer, and when I have my three-year check-up, I go into surgery, determined the beast has finally got me. In his late forties, my doctor says he hopes he has 'my test numbers' when he's my age.

My biggest fear is losing my sight, and, unfortunately, it is more realistic than inner fear. In my early years, I was diagnosed as having 'odd eyes', and, later in life, in my late thirties, I noticed my eyes were slightly crossed whenever I was excessively tired. As I got older, the situation worsened. It never worried me because it really didn't affect my actual eyesight. I had laser surgery in the late eighties, I know the date because I was a regular contributor to *BRW Magazine* at the time and wrote a three-page article on what it was like having someone poke around in your eye. My eye surgeon, Dr John Elder, duplicated thousands of the articles and gave them to new patients. The laser surgery had corrected my vision and negated wearing glasses, but the crossed eyes were another story altogether. By 2004 the crossing had accelerated, and I knew I had problems whenever I gave a talk and scanned the room with "Any questions?". When I spotted a questioner, I would point and say "Yes" but my eyes, apparently, looked in the other direction. It was totally confusing for the audience. At a private screening of a documentary produced by Rebel Penfold-Russell, a man approached me and asked what was wrong with my eyes. I was used to this question from young children but never from an adult. He could see I was taken aback and introduced himself as an ophthalmologist and said that he'd like to fix my eyes at no charge. He was a senior eye surgeon at Concord Hospital. I did a few tests to see if I was a likely candidate, and then, two weeks out from the operation, he asked if I would mind if he brought his students in to watch the procedure. Three things worried me, the suggestion that he planned to operate on one eye and come back to correct the other in six months, the fact the operation would be at Concord Hospital, a place I remember with sad memories of my father, and the thought of a mob of trainee doctors watching my surgeon's every move. I decided to pass on his offer. Some month's later my optometrist referred me to Dr Donaldson, a Macquarie Street specialist, who, after examining my eyes, said he'd be happy to operate as long as I would be "happy with at least ninety-five per cent correction". He also said he'd do both eyes at once. The operation was done at his Epping medical centre. After three hours, most of which was taken up with waiting between general anaesthetic and the second part of the procedure, where I needed to be awake, went like a breeze. Ninety-nine per cent correction. I admit it was a trifle strange to have someone sewing up your eye muscles while awake, even if there was no feeling.

As I aged, sorry, ripened, and jumped the seventy sentry post, my eyes weakened and, unfortunately, I developed cataracts and hereditary glaucoma. In 2017, I had a cataract operation on my right eye, and as I write this, in 2024, I have had no less than five operations on that eye. I can barely see out of it because of the scarred tissue. My surgeon, Dr Tania Trinh, did her best to save the sight in my right eye, but I suspect we reached the end of the road because each successive operation accelerates the optical nerve, and this worsens glaucoma. I remind myself of my father's stoicism and can hear him say, "I once complained of bad eyes until I met a man with no eyes at all." I can't imagine life without sight, but I am not at that point yet. I have daily eye drops to maintain pressure and thankfully, the left eye is healthy and functioning fine. Reading and typing all day is probably not the best medicine. My positive side assures me if anything horrid happens, at least it will allow me to concentrate on my concertina playing by busking at Circular Quay!

Over the years, I have written many songs and arranged more traditional songs than I can remember. I think my first composition, way back in the early 70s, was an amateurish parody on the woes of ABC funding. I sang it at the Sydney Town Hall at a Save Our ABC Rally. One afternoon at Donald Horne's Woollahra residence, he reminded me I had also sung at the very first public meeting calling for an Australian Republic. I sang Henry Lawson's *'Freedom on the Wallaby'* with its ringing perceptive last verse:

> So we must fly a rebel flag as others have before us
> And we must sing a rebel song and join in rebel chorus
> We'll make the tyrants feel the sting
> Of those that they would throttle
> They'll never say the fault is ours
> If blood should stain the wattle.

A republican Australian makes so much sense to me and I was disappointed with the last attempt, which arch-conservative John Howard sideswiped. Monarchies are anachronisms but, then, so was Howard's view of Australia. Sure, Elizabeth 2 was an outstanding

Queen, but she should not have been our head of state, and, as time has shown, the whole idea of a royal family is ludicrous. Their recent history is farcical and downright embarrassing. Sydney songwriter and parodist John Dengate summed it up in his song *'Royalty Shock'*

> Elizabeth, Elizabeth 2, what's a poor monarch to do?
> Fuckwits and phalluses people your palaces,
> Royalty, royalty shock.
> Republican ceilidhs erupt when the dailies,
> Go royalty, royalty shock.

Colloquial phrases like 'fit for a king' are nothing more than an insult to the rest of us, implying we are subjects and thereby second class. I also believe when an Australian republic is finally agreed upon, and I hope it is in my lifetime, it will provide Australia with a new opportunity to reinvent itself, provide a new enthusiasm, and make us feel more Australian.

I admired Donald Horne in so many ways. He was erudite, modest, grounded politically, and always up for a chat. He also wrote *'The Lucky Country'*, a book that profoundly impacted my generation. Donald's wife, Myfanwy, was also great company and possessed more than the average quota of brain cells. We both served as Directors on the Geraldine Pascal Foundation Board of Governors.

Professor Russel Ward, one of Australia's greatest historians, was my other literary influence. Russel was a firebrand and had a real interest in Australian folk songs. His book *'The Australian Legend'* inspired me to script one of my earliest ABC radio series, which I also called *The Australian Legend*. Russel wrote the preface to my book *'The Balls of Bob Menzies'*. And, whilst I am dropping names of political thought, it would be remiss of me not to salute Gough and Margaret Whitlam. I knew Gough through Andrew Whitlam and the three of us regularly caught up over lunch, usually at Machiavelli's Restaurant in Sydney, where Gough, always first to arrive, would sit directly under the enormous photograph of himself. He was larger than life, enjoyed a joke, and was ever ready to talk about himself and, at the restaurant table, to receive salutations from his 'subjects'. Margaret and I also served on the Geraldine Pascal Foundation Board.

IN 1988 A JOURNALIST MATE, Peter Logue, suggested to Prime Minister Bob Hawke that I would be the right person to organise the entertainment for the first State Dinner at the new Parliament House in July of that year. It was a reception for the Irish Prime Minister, Charles Haughey. When Hawke visited Ireland, Haughey had arranged a hooley - with a traditional band and dancers - and Hawke wanted Australia to reciprocate.

In his welcome speech, PM Hawke commented, "In literature and the arts, in education, in the law, in sports, throughout Australia's history and contemporary Australian society, our proud Irish streak is clear to see from Charles Gavan Duffy to Ned Kelly, from the Wild Colonial Boy to Clancy of the Overflow, from C. J. Dennis to Tom Keneally and from Bill O'Reilly to Sidney Nolan."

It was a grand dinner. As the compere, I introduced musical segments featuring Eric Bogle's Band and The Larrikins. The songs and music were a terrific success, but the party had hardly started. As tables were being cleared, Senator John Button and Speaker Leo McLeay, ably encouraged by the rebels of the Canberra Press Gallery led by Peter Logue, announced, "A few of us are retiring to Leo's office - as Speaker he has the largest office and biggest liquor cabinet." And so began a very late night of singing and drinking led by Bob Hawke (and Hazel) and most of his cabinet. Even Paul Keating breezed through, but the music was a far cry from Mahler, and he didn't stay even when a rowdy *'Solidarity Forever'* raised the new building's roof. We finally wound up around 3 am on a very memorable night.

In January 2018, Sydney art gallery dealer and long-time friend Tim Olsen invited me to perform at a private lunch to honour his father, John Olsen's 90th birthday. Tim prefers to say he 'won me in a raffle', which is partly true. Sandra Ferman, an indefatigable supporter of the arts, asked me if I would donate some prizes for the annual Contemporary Art Benefactor's Dinner for the Art Gallery of

NSW. I handed over books, CDs and a redeemable coupon entitling the purchaser to a 'private talk, performance or whatever' by yours truly. Tim snapped it up with his dad's birthday in mind. The lunch, staged in the Olsen Gallery, was a wonderful celebration of one of Australia's greatest artists. Saskia Havekes of Grandaflora provided spectacular table flowers - a procession of strawberry gum nuts - and Lucio Galletto, of Italian restaurant Lucio's, arranged the wine and food - all under instruction from John. After the entree, I celebrated John's love of the outback with thirty minutes of song and yarns. Tim had told me John loved bush ballads; however, I was surprised when he boisterously joined in on Banjo Paterson's *'A Bushman's Song'*, encouraging guests to join in the chorus. Louise Olsen, John's daughter, explained the song was one of his favourites and the family had often sung it at parties. Next up, Barry Humphries read an original (hilariously funny) galloping poem on how he met John in the fifties when they were members of the Sydney Push. Humphries, the master of witty doggerel, was in a wonderfully wicked mood. Speeches and laughter followed. The guest list was distinguished. Lucy Turnbull, Garry Sheard, Tim Storrier, Edmund Campion, Jill Dupleix and Terry Durack, art critic John McDonald and more painters than you could poke a brush at. John called me over and demanded I sing at his 100th. I took the opportunity to ask him if he had in fact, written the bawdy song *'Vincent Van Gogh'* - he had, and, to prove it, sang it for me. Some of the verses ran:

> Feeling quite randy, can't tell you why,
> Let's go to the brothel, just you and I,
> Arrived at the brothel, randy and gay,
> Turning to Vincent, said, "It's your turn to pay".
> Up comes the madam, "Well, what's for you, dears?'
> And turning to Vincent, said 'What funny ears!'
> Well, roses are red, boys, to Vincent van Gogh,
> He ran all the way home, to cut off his ear off.
> Well, it fair turned me off, boys, it fair turned me off,
> I'll go no more a-whoring, with Vincent van Gogh.

The 'art crowd' (I've always wanted to use that expression) usually enjoy that I sing at the drop of a hat (or the downing of a shiraz), especially over a dinner table. This is my favourite stage and often my most appreciative audience. Enjoying a good meal, wine, and song is a magic formula, even better if the table talk is lively. Kerrie Lester, a great friend, was a regular Sunday lunch pal, and we talked about everything from art to music, puppy dog's tails, to wanker art events. She was refreshingly brutal and sadly missed.

The late gallery owner, Ray Hughes, was a consummate lunch host, and thankfully, I was on his coveted invitation list. His Thursday long lunches at the gallery were legendary, with about thirty-five guests seated around the long rectangle table with Ray, complete with his trademark colourful tie and pocket handkerchief, surrounded by art (and smoke from his endless cigarettes) and a generous spread (both on his belly and the table). The guest list, always eclectic, surveyed politicians, artists, critics, celebrities and the occasional 'ring in' potential client. The talk was of politics (Ray was a lifetime Labor supporter), art and who's up who. Inevitably, I would be called upon to sing a song, tell a yarn or recite. It was great fun, and I miss the man and his naughty sense of humour.

IN 2016, at a memorable long lunch for about twenty-five arts and whatever guests, Ray was in his element, boisterously entertaining his audience, when he accidentally knocked his red wine over a guest who stood up and shouted, "Look what you've done to my suit- that's $20 dry cleaning!". Ray wickedly threw the rest of his wine over the suit and said, "Make it $50."

Mucking up at Margaret Olle's 85th birthday lunch, 2008

I am a great believer in giving back to the community. When I had businesses in Paddington, I became the President of the Chamber of Commerce, although I preferred to call it the Chamber of Horrors. I loved Paddington's history and especially the heritage of the retail strip, one of the last remaining Victorian strip shopping centres. I was President for a decade, and I fought against brand-name stores obtaining shop leases. I knew businesses operated from a head office usually had no real interest in the community. One of our major problems was the ridiculous fact that one side of Oxford Street was controlled by Woollahra Council, the other by South Sydney. This meant very little was done as the Liberal-controlled Woollahra wouldn't talk turkey with the Labor-controlled South Sydney. Frustrated, I went to NSW Planning, then under Bob Carr, and we set up an independent control body. Our other big achievement was establishing the Paddington Restoration Program to raise funds and convince property owners to subscribe to a colour-coordinated heritage renewal plan to bring together the historic above-awning facades. After I left Paddington, the street became dominated by brand names and, true to my prediction, imploded and eventually became a retail wasteland.

Year's later, as a resident of Potts Point, I was elected Chairman of the Kings Cross Chamber and was party to it reinventing itself as the Potts Point Partnership. We staged two highly successful festivals, including the 2012 Kings Cross Festival, which attracted thousands to hear artists like Renee Geyer, Jeff Duff and a terrific bluegrass band called The Pigs. I also started a Facebook page for the community called Potts Point & Kings Cross Life and, in 2015, merged it with Carrington Brigham's Potts Pointers. Today we are co-administrators and have over 17,500 members. I sometimes say, "I feel like I have the keys to the asylum." Managing a large community group, especially in a precinct like inner East Sydney, which is both diverse and perverse, can be a challenge, especially if you correctly balance the heritage issues with the community needs. A case in point is the upgrade of Macleay Street, Potts Point. The street has a marvellous history of dining, nightclubs and bars, but the years have carried scars, and the street needed a spruce up. In 2018 I started the ball rolling by presenting a case to the Lord Mayor, Clover Moore, for an upgrade program saluting heritage yet being practical with continuous footpaths, new landscaping and widened footways. After lengthy community consultation, this program commenced in 2020 and was completed in 2022.

In 2023, Dr Peter Sheridan, author of two books on the area's Art Deco and modernist architecture, asked me if I'd help establish a community group to protect local architecture. We wrangled in a few friends and established the Potts Point Preservation Group. Our intention is to have the small, approximately one-mile peninsula encompassing Potts Point, Kings Cross and Elizabeth Bay as a unique heritage area. In doing so, we hope to preserve the rapidly disappearing social and built fabric of one of Australia's most unique areas. We have already started our campaign and have the support of our local member for Sydney, Alex Greenwich, and the Member for Wentworth, Allegra Spender. Watch this space!

I have always been capable of multitasking. My recording company work is easy; I sing or act when able, history projects roll in and on, and, as those who know me will testify, I am always working on a book. In 2010 I was asked to present a program for the Sydney Festival's 'Sydney Talks' series at the Seymour Centre. I had already been gathering photographs and clippings on the precincts of the 2011 postcode - Woolloomooloo, Rushcutters Bay, Elizabeth Bay, Potts Point and Kings Cross. The two talks were a sell-out and I immediately began working the material into a book I hoped to publish in 2011, the postcode and the year coinciding. As it unfolded, I realised I had more stories than I envisaged and the book, The Good Old Bad Old Days, wasn't published until 2016. I also decided to self-publish, something I am naturally wary about as it means a lot of extra work and storing copies of the book. I designed the book using Adobe InDesign, a nifty but somewhat challenging book formatting app. It allowed me to type directly into the page, manipulate images, etc., and I learned a lot about Photoshop and Adobe. The main problem was that Adobe continually updated and changed the work system, which drove me nuts. I managed to produce a fairly attractive and effective paperback book, printed 1500 copies in China and eventually received the stock after a lot of customs and delivery issues. To date, I have sold around 1300 copies, which is pretty decent considering I didn't use a distributor, reasoning that most sales would be local. The local Potts Point Bookshop sold a lot, and so did the State Library Bookshop however, like most of my recent publications, I sold the majority through book launches, events and by giving talks. If nothing else, it is a fascinating ramble through my local area especially of the architecture, social history and characters.

I didn't renew my Adobe contract and jumped to Vellum, a very straightforward and visually attractive app produced by the people who set up Pixar. I wrote and designed this book on Vellum and couldn't be happier. The great thing about apps like Vellum is that, when completed, the PDFs can be given to the publisher or printer and are ready to roll. And that's exactly what I did with *Dead & Buried: A curious history of Sydney's earliest burial grounds*. Self-published in 2022, it has nearly sold its first (and only) print run of 1200 copies. It was my 'covid project', and, to my surprise, very well received by the cemetery and family history mob. I also used Vellum to compile a book, 'Gone With The Wine', for Rebel Penfold Russell on the life of her mother, Rada Russell.

I doubt if I will ever self-publish again, other than digitally, as it is simply too hard and, as mentioned, I have limited storage space. I consider myself extremely lucky to have had so many books commercially published.

Reading has always been part of my life, and despite my often ridiculous schedule, I try to make time for books. I don't consider my history, folklore and music reading part of my *real* reading time, for I prefer fiction to fact, as this allows me to switch off. I love a good novel and usually go through the Man Booker list each year, discarding those that don't grab me in the first 20 pages. When I find a writer who thrills, I usually read the complete body of work with relish. Such has been the case with Gore Vidal, Bruce Chatwin, John Boyne, James Hamilton-Paterson, E. L. Doctorow, Philip Roth, Mordecai Richler, F. Scott Fitzgerald, Ernest Hemingway, Michael Connolly, Charles Dickens and, dare I say it, not surprisingly, Henry Lawson.

A few years ago, I thought I would try recorded books, a genre that I was familiar with since Larrikin distributed over 5500 titles, including EMI's Listen for Pleasure range and Harper Collins Audio. I always thought the public underrated these recordings as they are mostly well-recorded, feature some of the world's great voices, and, of course, are wonderful to listen to, especially if one does long drives. I had listened to a few recorded books, and since I was planning some overseas travel, I thought I'd tackle two books forever on my list: '*Moby Dick*' and James Joyce's '*Finnegan's Wake*'. I completed the four readings of '*Moby Dick*' but only managed half of the daunting '*Finnegan's Wake*'.

Jumping a decade or two, I started to read novels on my iPad. I found it convenient but somewhat lacking. I was somewhat of a pioneer in writing books for new technological devices, the iPad in particular. I was certainly the first author in Australia to produce an enhanced e-book. ABC/Harper Collins published the print edition of *Australia: its Folks Songs and Bush Ballads* in 2010. I suggested they consider releasing an e-book version that offered readers videos and sound recordings for each song. Like all contemporary publishers, they were keen to be seen as producers of electronic books, and mine offered an opportunity to test the market. It was published with a whimper. The three-volume ebook series looks great, the large format musical notation effective, and it includes recordings of traditional versions of the songs from the National Library of Australia oral history & folklore collection. It must have been an expensive learning curve for Harper Collins because getting the news out about its availability was nigh impossible. Besides, millions of ebooks are cast into the market every year. Most float silently to the bottom. I have recently secured the rights to reissue the three ebooks on my own imprint, Bodgie Books.

16

REAL MUSIC IN A SEA OF SHIT

I never held ambitions to be a businessman and certainly never imagined myself as proprietor of a music shop. I knew I didn't want to stay working in advertising and my sideways stint at Harry M Miller Attractions, although extremely challenging and successful, had steered me to a certain independence. When Harry closed up shop I opened my own. The idea was to rent a small office and offer myself as a freelance marketing person in tandem with Patti Mostyn handling publicity.

In 1973 I leased a shop at 38A Oxford Street, Paddington. It had two small rooms which I intended for my office and, when I could afford it, a secretarial assistant. As usual, my brain was working overtime encouraging me to do too much at once. I had already started my journey with the ABC and had several radio programs to my credit, including Australia's first series of what became known as 'world music'. I remember signing the lease on the shop and thinking about how would I be able to afford the weekly rent which, in today's money, was probably peanuts. I was already importing LPs for my radio programs so, in what I considered a brave move, I wrote to my main suppliers, Topic Records in London, Ocora at Radio France and

Folkways in New York, and asked them if I could buy wholesale in quantities of 25 LPs or more. They all agreed and I made the decision to turn the front room of the tiny shop into a record bar. I had no racks or money to build them, so I simply put a sign on the window 'Folkways Music', and stacked the boxes on the floor. It didn't take long for specialist record hunters to sniff me out. It was a madcap year as I also used the tiny shop as the headquarters of the Port Jackson Folk Festival, for which I was program director.

In 1974, Patti and I worked on two major tours for the 27-year-old producer, Robert Raymond: The Supremes and Frank Sinatra's last tour. 'Cranky' Frankie was not as cranky as the media made out and Patti certainly scored the headlines, despite the media turning on the singer and declaring a black ban. With Sinatra holed up in Sydney's Boulevard Hotel, Bob Hawke, then head of the ACTU, was called in to arbitrate. That same year I also did some work for Leo Schofield's advertising agency, Schofield, Sherborn & Baker. One of the projects involved coordinating a television commercial featuring around 100 showbiz personalities fronted by Danny Kaye. We hired a sound stage at the Sydney Showground and the commercial centred around Kaye as an ambassador for UNICEF. My cast of volunteer celebrities were keen to meet the American star. I had grown up listening to *'Tubby the Tuba'* and Kaye's elastic-voiced wacky humour. It didn't take long for Kaye to disappoint just about everyone on that stage - the celebrities, crew, advertising agency and me. He was simply the most disagreeable person imaginable and obviously did not want to be there. A great disappointment and we couldn't wait to see the arse-end of the man.

THE SEVENTIES WAS a good time for independent record labels and my new label partners issued a steady supply of new releases. All three labels were quite large so I had hundreds of releases available and, of course, you couldn't buy these recordings anywhere else in Sydney. I was shipping the LPs by sea as air freight in those days was expensive.

I staggered the orders and gradually added new label partners. There was no time for freelance marketing jobs so I concentrated on developing the shop. It also became clear I had to move to larger premises. There was a three-storey terrace shop in the next block at 58 Oxford Street, Paddington, and I signed a lease and moved in. Timing is everything and it was time I established a record wholesaling business. I already had the distribution rights to half a dozen labels and the new premises allowed me to separate the Folkways retail from the wholesale division, which I named Larrikin Distribution. I had already founded the Larrikin record label in 1974 when I released *'Man of the Earth'* (songs of the Australian mining industry). The next twenty years saw me 'robbing Peter to pay Paul' - in this case the Folkways' cash cow to pay the money-devouring Larrikin label.

Browsing Folkways 58 Oxford Street, Paddington.

In the new store, I built record racks and bookshelves. It looked rustic but it worked fine. I opened seven days a week. When I started opening Sundays there was hardly another local shop open, however, I reasoned, music buyers like browsing and Sundays were a great browsing day. The shop was gaining some notoriety as a specialist shop where you could find the weird and wonderful. Blues, bluegrass, old-timey, English folk music, cajun, zydeco, Celtic music, singer-songwriters, documentary, sound effects, jazz, and music from just about every culture on the planet. Folkways also carried music books, particularly the 'how to play' books from Oak Publications and Mel Bay. I had also started to stock small musical instruments like harmonicas, tin whistles and ocarinas. Larrikin's distribution and labels were growing like topsy and once again space was becoming an issue.

The main strip of Paddington's Oxford strip was the place to be, despite its higher rents. More passing traffic equals more customers, or so I had heard. Paddington at the time was an eclectic mix of retail with Woolworths and lots of service shops. Eventually, this was all changed when the 'convenient' Edgecliff Centre and Westfield Bondi Junction opened. Paddington was also hippyish. The old terrace houses, some of the world's best organic architecture, were being renovated by creatives, and the old guard, especially the Greeks, Italians and Portuguese, were happy to sell their homes for ready cash. I would have liked to have bought there but had recently taken a $22,000 mortgage on my first apartment in Woollahra.

I found a recently vacated shop at 282 Oxford Street. It had been an antique shop and prior to that a succession of businesses including an ice cream factory, milliner, cake decorating supply company and a furniture store. It was owned by Mr Levi, a second-hand furniture dealer at Bondi Junction. I arranged to meet and tell him I would like to take the shop. Mr Levi was a very likeable man and, to my relief, agreed to lease the shop to me as long as he could keep his boat in the rear section. The building was multi-levelled and long. An attic, extensive first floor with outdoor area, large ground floor retail space and a rear level ideal for a warehouse. It even had a loading dock (with a boat in it!).

Moving a mountain of warehouse stock was a Herculean effort. With specially-constructed record and book racks, the new Folkways looked spectacular. It was exciting for the staff and customers. We had three decks to preview records (we were still in the LP era), a long shop counter with a display for our small instruments, plenty of wall space and a layout where recordings could be displayed in categories. We added more and more specialist categories, including some specific artist sections. The shop was always busy but weekends were chaotic and very exciting. I didn't work in the store during the week as I was inevitably upstairs running the label or standing on milk crates picking wholesale orders from the shelves. When I worked Saturdays I used to bet the staff I could sell anything! I would select the weirdest music - pygmy chants, Tibetan throat music, Greek rembetika, western swing, sean nos, rare blues (the scratchier the better), sea songs, high and lonesome bluegrass, Portuguese fados - you name it and I probably played it, and loud - and sold multiple copies. Some favourites sold hundreds - Peter Rowan, Nancy Griffiths, Alison Krauss, John Pizzarelli, Maddy Prior, Dick Gaughan, Christy Moore, Planxty, Solomon Burke, Irma Thomas and Kate Wolf all benefited from my over-enthusiastic Saturday programming.

Folkways Mark III, 272 Oxford Street, Paddington.

Being in the main strip put pressure on the shop to sell pop and other modern music, but I resisted. I did expand the shop's music to include an extensive range of classical and some 'modern' artists. How could I not carry Dire Straits, Tim Buckley, Jeff Buckley, Joni Mitchell, Mark Knofler, Talking Heads, Bruce Springsteen, and Bob Dylan? Being selective and, through careful buying, it developed a reputation for having 'intelligent' pop. Folkways also carried an extensive range of film and stage tracks, sound effects discs, audiophile recordings, music theatre, children's music and other specialist areas. What I refused to carry was mindless pop, MOR, dance music, metal and those dreadful compilations of hits.

The musical instrument section. Warren with store manager, Larry.

I started using the attic for music tuition and offered guitar, banjo and dulcimer lessons. John Morris, a talented guitar player, led the teaching and was part of Folkway's history for over a decade. The next step was for Folkways to become an authorised outlet for Australia's premier guitar maker, Maton. We also carried dulcimers, flutes, mandolins and banjos. At one stage we even had an agency for R. M. William's bush outfitters and Akubra hats!

By the eighties, business was booming, and I opened a branch on George street in the heart of the historic Rocks area of Sydney. It was a compact shop carrying bush music, indigenous releases and books aimed primarily at the tourist market. Later, when the show business record shop, Ava & Susan's, moved out of their Double Bay store, we moved a Folkways shop in. It was short-lived, and after two years, we realised Double Bay was not for us.

282 Oxford street, sandwiched between George Warnake's junk shop and Loyal Florist.

Folkway's biggest strength, apart from its wide range of music, was its mail-order business. I became the king of cut and paste and issued a regular catalogue with short reviews, photographs, album recommendations and artist stories. Most issues were about 20 plus pages and printed A4 and folded and stapled. They just squeezed into a standard envelope. Recipients, especially people in the country, told me the catalogues were 'devoured' and often passed on to family or friends interested in music. I should also say that during this time, especially when ABC FM was launched in 1980, I was a regular on the radio. 'Sunday Folk', first with Jack King and later with David Mulhallen, presented numerous programs that gave folk music a national audience. The mail-order business always astounded my fellow workers and me. Every morning, the mail would bring a pile of orders and cheques, and the staff would have to prepare and pack orders, do the banking and then arrange to mail orders. It was endless and a great contributor to the business success story.

With the move to Paddington central, I made the bold decision to use 'Real Music in a Sea of Shit' as a marketing line. What did it mean? I wanted to differentiate the shop from other record outlets, grab attention, and have something outrageous that suited Paddington's then-naughty reputation. The message was painted across the building awning and remained for a decade. I also featured the motto on our LP sleeves, carry bags, t-shirts, and Jacky Howe blue singlets (I still have one). I feared Woollahra Council would come down on me, but we never received a single complaint. The only awkward moment came when a nun from St Vincent's hospital purchased a record and suggested, "Maybe not the bag, Mother Superior might not understand."

Along the way, I teamed up with William 'Bill' O'Toole and established the Larrikin Booking Agency. We ran it successfully for a few years, representing musicians, bands, singers, jugglers, dancers and some quite weird (and wonderful) acts. There was even a Chinese juggler who balanced massive plant urns and walked on eggs. Bill had started the band, Sirocco, which had released several albums with Larrikin and ABC Music. Bill went on to become an internationally recognised guru in the world of event management.

Folkways had many regulars. Brett Whitely came nearly every week and bought recordings of world music. Gallery owner and jazz aficionado Kym Bonython was a regular, and artists Luke Sciberras, Keith Looby, Alex Trumpf, John Firth-Smith (a keen banjo player), and Gunter Christmann (a jaw harp player), were also regulars.

When he lived in Sydney, David Bowie came often and included a photograph of the Folkway's neon sign in his *Black Book*.

The folkways neon sign

David Gulpilil was a regular, and we would often sit on the back balcony, eat fish and chips and make music.

Visiting international artists were often sighted - everyone from Divine to Sylvester, B. B. King to Barry Manilow. And, of course, there were always Australian artists flicking through the racks, some looking for their own recordings and others for inspiration. It was not unusual for visitors from interstate or the country regions to buy $500 worth of records and books in a single visit.

Jazz became a major part of the Folkways story. It was the only store where you could see the entire ASV, Blue Note, Black & Blue, Prestige, Atlantic, ECM, Telarc, and Concord Jazz catalogues. We carried every form of jazz from early blues to vocal, traditional to Avant-Garde. Blues collectors were the most determined, and whenever I received a shipment of rare labels like Biograph, the word would get around, and the recordings would sell like hotcakes. It helped I liked the music and encouraged the staff to play them in the shop. I like most music, and the shop, in some ways, because I was the ultimate buyer, reflected my wide interest in music. Today, I am just as likely to listen to an early blues singer or a Nordic jazz musician in preference to the ordinariness of so-called 'popular music'.

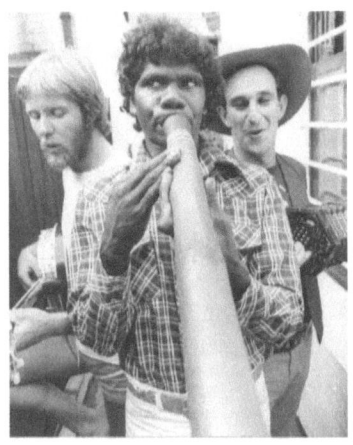

Folkways manager, Denis Greer, David Gulpilil and Warren Fahey

Guarding the doorway at Folkways 282 Oxford Street, Paddington.

. . .

I SUSPECT I had a popular music bypass at an early age.

A younger version of me when Folkways was at 58 Oxford Street, Paddington. ABC TV 1976

After a couple of year's paying rent to Mr Levi he came to me and said, "I have a plan. I want you to buy the building". I laughed and thought - if you only knew how my record label business is burning money. I guess he could read my face and said, "I'm serious. My two sons are looked after and I'd like to help you. When I was young someone did me a favour and I am now offering you a favour." I continued to laugh but he was determined. "You have a flat in Woollahra. Sell it and give me the money as a deposit and I will lend you the money to buy the building." I admit I'm not the smartest business brain on the block but I realised he was genuine and then he hit me with an offer I couldn't refuse - "Buy the building for $150,000 as long as I can keep my boat there." I was flabbergasted and nodded in shock. This was a silly price for prime real estate in the seventies.

ABC TV interview 1976

Victoria Cobden presented me with this old Jacky Howe singlet in 2015.

Folkways became increasingly famous for its extensive catalogue holding. Thousands of records, and some of the strangest in the history of recorded music. I lost count of the number of humpback whale song albums I sold. I was never surprised by customer enquiries. One man, a veteran showground carney who owned a steam-operated merry-go-round, would eagerly buy any calliope recording I could find. Early country music collectors would seek out the rarest of recordings, and the same for blues and jazz collectors. Because I distributed the Folkways USA label, I also carried such marvels at John Cage's first music, an album titled 'Sounds of the Vortex' (yes, the throat voice box), Dr Martin Luther King's fiery speeches and collections of beat poets including Ginsberg, Kerouac, Burroughs and Ferlinghetti. In 2022, the ABC television *Rage* program screened a 20-minute documentary they had made with me (in Folkways shop mark II) in the nineteen-seventies. I shuddered. I looked and spoke like a right prat.

In 1991, I sold the building for $1.35 million and also decided to sell Folkways. Twenty years is long enough to own any business, by my reckoning.

IN 1992 I sold Folkways Music to customers, Keith Chee and Jon Foo. They were also friends. They ran the shop for a further 16 years. By 2009, the record business had changed dramatically, and the shop closed its doors for the last time.

Richard Jinman, writing in the *Sydney Morning Herald*, lamented its closure, 'For almost four decades, Folkways was a musical landmark: a reliable source of folk, world music and other esoteric sounds. It also encouraged thousands of people to make their own music.'

Jon and Keith invited me to the 'wake'. It was a sad occasion but, to my mind, one of their own design. Folkway's charm was its determination to restrict what it sold to 'real music', and it hadn't been long under the new ownership when dance music and 'latest hits' replaced the best of blues, jazz and world music in the stand at the front of the store. U2, 20 Mega Dance Hits and Elton John replaced Ma Rainey, the Chieftains and Alison Krauss. The old

Larrikin warehouse at the rear of the building became a Scandinavian furniture store, and the musical instruments disappeared completely. This was indeed the day the music died. Folkways lost focus and its valued custom.

Richard Jinman also pointed to another side of the old store's success story. 'Selling an estimated 75,000 harmonicas, 50,000 tin whistles and 5000 jaw harps during its first 20 years of operation'. We also had plectrums, strings for all fretted instruments and an instrument repair service. For a few years, we even had a Ticketek agency, but we tired of the associated bookkeeping and systems rigamarole - and ridiculous questions from people wanting tickets to sporting events and the like. The shop also carried many music and folklore books, many imported and some from local publishers. 'How to Play' music books were extremely popular.

Over the years, I have been asked to nominate my top ten all-time recording favourites. It's an impossible ask for someone who has been exposed to so much music. I could possibly draw up a list of my top ten blues, bluegrass, folk, jazz, classical, cajan, tex-mex, Celtic, songwriters, instrumental players, hokum, gospel (yes, even God had a few good tunes) and, then, a top ten for every country or culture on earth. I dislike musical pigeonholing and, as we know, the world's musical taste has dramatically changed and improved, especially since access to music on the Internet. It is still unthinkable to me that I can dial up a Bandcamp or Spotify playlist of, say, world music songs collected by Alan Lomax or a tribute album of Ewan MacColl songs.

I am going out on a limb here and nominating ten albums I would take when marooned on a desert island, or should that be when isolating against the COVID virus? *Joy of Living* (a compilation of Ewan MacColl Songs featuring artists from across the worlds of pop and folk including David Gray, Rufus Wainwright, Christy Moore and Eliza Carthy), 'Andy Irvine & Paul Brady' (self-titled 1975 album of total brilliance), *'Peter Rowan'* (self-titled first solo album of one of my all-time favourite 'high and lonesome' singers, and this album also features the tex-mex accordion king, Flaco Jimenez), *'Anthology of*

American Folk Music' (Harry Smith's eccentric 1956 compile of blues, jazz, honky tonk, gospel and everything else fine... it's an unholy mess of an album and every track on the 2CD set is a reminder of how music is created.) *'Song For Everyone'* (Indian 10-string double violin player, L. Shankar brings east to west and heads north with Jan Garbarek, Zakir Hussain and Trilok Gurtu), *'Kind of Blue'* (Miles Davis gave us the greatest jazz album of all time), *'Music for 18 Musicians'* (I bet you didn't see that one coming.) Steve Reich's minimalistic Balinese gamelan-inspired album, ideal for the introspective times), *'The Gathering'* (Celtic classical ensemble led by Martin Hayes, the 'Miles Davis of the fiddle'), *'Arbos'* (another one you didn't see coming) - Estonian contemporary classical composer, Arvo Part, with a symphony of brass), *'Blonde on Blonde'* (yes, surprise! I could have picked several Bob Dylan albums but this would remind me of his brilliant difference), and, finally, *'Rogue's Gallery'* (a very weird collection of pirate ballads, sea songs and chanteys featuring an even weirder group of artists including Lou Reed, Louden Wainwright III, Richard Thompson, Nick Cave, Bryan Ferry, Bill Frisell, Sting, Rufus Wainwright & Kate McGarrigle, Martin Carthy, Eliza Carthy, Bono, Lucinda Williams).

I recall being interviewed by ABC radio's wonderful Margaret Throsby. I listed entirely different desert island discs and, in 2021, another completely different list in an extended interview with the Music Show's Andrew Ford.

People still ask why I sold such a successful and inspirational business like Folkways. The easy answer is that I needed the money to sustain the record label and distribution company. In 1991, with the money from the sale of the building, I bought Avan-Gard Music, an independent record distributor owned by Judy and Ali Knoll, and financed the demanding growth of the combined label and distribution company. Ali was a long-time associate and friend and owned a warehouse at 70 Wilson Street, Newtown. Sadly, Ali had a stroke and didn't live to see the new entity grow. I moved Larrikin into his building, employed his wife, Judy, to run the extensive classical side of the business and redesigned the company as Larrikin

Entertainment, incorporating the labels, distribution and music publishing. A new chapter had begun. Larrikin was to become Australia's largest, most diverse, independent record label and music distribution company. It was certainly the only one that started with a few boxes of LPs on the floor of a tiny shop.

By the end of 1993, Larrikin had outgrown the Newtown building, and GM Geoff Weule found new premises at an industrial park on Botany Road, Rosebery. It was a huge, modern warehouse with enough office space to accommodate the rapidly expanding staff. At one stage, we had over 40 people on the payroll, plus agents in each State. I sold Folkways Music that same year to fund Larrikin's growth. All fairly daunting for a business that never intended to be a business.

Through Larrikin, I met some of 'the *least* influential people in the music business' - well, that's how we often jokingly described ourselves. In truth, independent labels and distributors played a pivotal role in making music accessible. We met every January at the Midem music market, in Cannes, France, and swapped stories, signed label representation and export deals and generally had fun. Barry Poss of Sugar Hill went on to produce a series of award-winning bluegrass albums with Dolly Parton, Bill Nowlin, Ken Irwin and Marion Leighton, three college student founders of Rounder Records, created one of the largest independent labels in the world attracting artists such as Alison Krauss, Harry Chapin, Mary Chapin Carpenter, Robert Plant, to name a handful. I started representing Rounder when it had five LPs and continued to represent the label for over twenty-five years. Another of my long-standing relationships was with Topic Records, probably the oldest surviving record label in the world. I commenced importing Topic in 1973 when I established Folkways. At the time, it was operated by the intriguingly named Worker's Music Association. Specialising in folk music, under Tony Engle, the label notched up an impressive catalogue led by Martin Carthy, Eliza Carthy, The Watersons, Ewan MacColl and A. L. Lloyd. Rod Buckle of Sonet UK was another mate and like-minded soul, as were Bruce Kaplan of Flying Fish Records, Richard Nevins and

Michael Collins of Shanachie, Canada's Bernie Finklestein of True North Records, Gilles Fruchaux and Francois Dacla of EPM Buda and Amelia Haygood of the classical label, Delos. Interestingly, these label owners were roughly the same age - we were the first baby boomers born of the sixties folk revival.

17

LARRIKINS & ROUSEABOUTS

I have three words of advice for anyone thinking of starting a record label. Get Over It. A few years ago I started to tally up the number of albums I had been responsible for as either producer, label owner, compiler or artist. It was heading towards 1000, the majority of these being Australian recordings. Apart from my own labels, I produced quite a few albums for other labels, including EMI Australia, Universal Music, and BMG and some for international labels like Rounder, M7, Topic and Arc. Most of these international releases were project albums or compilations.

Three of my notable early Australian projects included the landmark *'Glenrowen to the Gulf'* by The Wild Colonial Boys (EMI), *'Euabalong Ball'*, the first (and disastrous) attempt to record an instrumental album of bush dance music (EMI) and *'The Day The Pub Burned Down'* with the great Declan Affley (M7 Records). I also produced projects for the majors, including working with Bill Robertson on a 10 LP set of Peter Dawson (EMI), then *'Australia: Its Land, Its People'* (2 LP sets vol 1 & 2 for EMI), and preparing notes for the 5 CD box sets of Slim Dusty (EMI) and Eric Bogle (BMG). I had a close association with EMI Australia and made the first two albums of my group, The Larrikins, for them in the late sixties, *'Navvy on the*

Line' (Australian railway songs) and 'Limejuice & Vinegar' (Australian maritime songs). I worked with EMI producer Eric Dunne and A&R with Geoff Weule and Bill Robertson. Geoff was to play an important role in my later business life as General Manager of Larrikin Entertainment.

I established Larrikin Records as a label in 1974, a year after I had set up Folkways Music, and this was followed by associate labels, defined by the type of music I was issuing. Jarrah Hill was an ambient/fusion label obviously inspired by Windham Hill Records, an American label that mainly released ambient guitar music. Jarrah Hill released a wide range of music from aspirational to experimental. Knot Records issued rock as did an earlier joint venture label, Green Records, owned by Roger Grierson and Stuart Coupe and released on Larrikin. Roger tells me the label's name was inspired by a conversation about Graham Greene. Green Records was a major statement in the 80s, issuing Dave Studdert, Tactics, Do-Re-Me, Allniters, Spy V Spy, Thought Criminals, Naughty Rhythms and North 2 Alaskans. Grierson, a Thought Criminals' musician, ran the Larrikin warehouse from 1978 to 80. Green was a musically brave label but the sales were not there to make it tick. Roger went off to have a stellar career in music publishing and, eventually, was appointed Chairman of the Festival Mushroom Group. Stuart, a respected music journalist, started Laughing Clown Records.

It was through the Larrikin label I released the bulk of my releases. The first album, carrying the number LRF001 (the F standing for full price) was 'Man of the Earth', a collection of Australian coal and gold mining songs I had collected in my fieldwork. I arranged a bunch of musicians, including Andy Saunders, Tony Suttor, Phyl Lobl, Dave de Hugard and Mike Jackson, allocated songs to them and booked a couple of recording sessions at Supreme Sound Studios, Paddington. I had no inkling Larrikin would become a continuing label. I simply wanted to get the music available. If anyone ever doubted my intention, I would refer them to the releases that immediately followed, five recordings of Papua New Guinea traditional music and LRF007, an album called 'Bush

Traditions', which offered recordings from my fieldwork and where the average age of the singers was around 80. Oddly enough, *'Bush Traditions'* sold enough to cover its production.

Noted musicologist and *Sydney Morning Herald* classical music reviewer Professor Roger Covell pointed to *'Bush Traditions'* cultural importance and the beauty of its simplicity. For the next twenty years, Larrikin released a steady flow of albums, including the first commercial recordings of The Bushwackers, Robyn Archer, Redeem, and so many other Australian artists. Some, like Redgum's debut *'If You Don't Fight, You Lose'*, proved big sellers (it sold nearly 10,000 in 1978) and Mike and Michelle Jackson's *'Bananas in Pyjamas'* (which received a gold disc from the ABC). For every record that did okay, a dozen scraped through on the bones of their behinds. This was fine by me. All I wanted was for the records to cover their cost. I was never interested in the race to find the 'big seller'. Case in point, I released *'A Night in an Australian Rainforest'* (nature sounds), *"Queensland Rainforest Indigenous Song Poetry',"* The Lyrebirds of Tidbinbilla' and even a digital recording of the *'Complete Bird Life of Antarctica'*, which was mainly albatross squawks. Talk about being bird-brained.

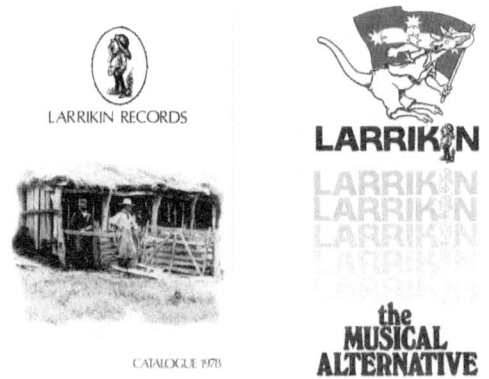

Two Larrikin Record catalogues 1977 and 1984

Because of my interest in folk music, the Larrikin label automatically had a reputation for releasing folk music but, in truth, it was a small part of the label's output. If anything the label's three most active areas were jazz, indigenous music and singer-songwriters. The label's main claim to fame would be diversity and endurance. There were so many firsts, including the first available commercially released didgeridoo song cycle (Wandjuk Marika 1976), the first album of feminist/lesbian songs (Robyn Archer's *'The Ladies Choice'*) and the first collection of Australian industrial folksong (*'Man of the Earth'*).

Adding to the label's image confusion, most of my recordings with The Larrikins were issued by ABC Music and not on the Larrikin label. These included *'Billy of Tea'*, *'The Larrikin Sessions'*, *'A Larrikin History of Australia'*, and, in 2012, the ten-CD set *'Australian Folk Song & Bush Verse'*. The latter was a mammoth effort where I set out to record well over 250 songs arranged in themed discs, each with detailed booklets. It allowed me to explore and record, for posterity, many previously unavailable songs and ballads. Some, especially in the *'Rare Convict Broadside Ballads'*, required the fitting of either traditional or original tunes, a skill I seem to be well-versed in providing. There was even an album of Australian *'Songs of Romance'*, albeit some were slightly bawdy. The albums were co-produced by Marcus Holden and featured Garry Steel, Clare O'Meara, Mark Oats and a few guest artists. The series was an ARIA award finalist and sold enough to cover my costs in producing the master tapes and the ABCs production. Rouseabout Records digitally reissued the complete set in 2023.

I look back on Larrikin's output and shudder and mutter, "What was I thinking?". Had I not pursued the record label releasing endless recordings I would have been a wealthy man. So what! Wealth was never an ambition. I believe in 'cultural karma' - put it out there and rewards will come. I used to look at others in the music industry and be taken aback by their obsession with making money which, usually, translated into releasing crap music, especially television-advertised '20 greatest hits'. In 2015 I was the recipient of the Australian Sound Recording Association's Lifetime Achievement Award - that's the sort of reward that gladdens my heart.

I have worked with Eric Bogle for nearly 50 years.

Eric Bogle's recordings became the mainstay of the label's catalogue of singer-songwriters. It is hard to believe Eric wrote his epic 'And The Band Played Waltzing Matilda' in 1971. The song became an international hit along with 'Green Fields of France' and his first Larrikin album, 'Now I'm Easy', originally released privately by Richard Collins, eventually reached Gold, a rarity for Larrikin. The label went on to release a continuous flow of Eric's albums. Rouseabout continues to represent Eric's catalogue, now over twenty-five titles, and after forty years we must be the oldest continuing music relationship in Australia.

By the late seventies, Larrikin was finding its future and, in 1975, formed a relationship with the Sydney Festival, then under the direction of Stephen Hall, later to be nicknamed 'Festival' Hall. Stephen and I put our heads together, and the Larrikin Folklife Festival was born for the second Sydney Festival. I ran the festival for a decade. Firstly, in the Sydney Opera House Concert Hall (yikes, what were we thinking?), then at the Verbrugghen Hall at the Conservatorium of Music, and then at the Regent Theatre. The idea was ten concerts each night for ten days straight. Programming was a mix of Australian and International artists. The ABC joined to record most concerts for 'Sunday Folk'. It was exhausting work and I am not too sure how I managed to succeed. Experience at Harry M Miller Attractions definitely helped. I virtually had no support other than my Folkways and Larrikin staff and David Burwood at the Sydney Festival office. I am an old hand now at producing festivals and events but ten nights of large concerts was a challenge. On the bright side, we had some spectacular concert performances. Internationally the festival showcased some extraordinary talent including British folksingers Shirley Collins, Peter Bellamy, High-Level Ranters, Roy Harris, Lou Killen, Robin Williamson of the Incredible String Band; guitarists Stefan Grossman, Bert Jansch, John Renbourn, Ton Van Berg, Duck Baker and Ginger Baker; Christine Lavin, Gove Shrivenor, Johnny Shines, bluesmen Johnny Shines and John Hammond; jazz legend Little Brother Montgomery; old-timey artists Mike Seeger, Hazel Dickens, Gove Schrivenor, Alice Gerrard, Bill Clifton and the first artist I ever toured Australia, Jody Stecher. The festival also allowed me to present two traditional singers, the border shepherd and ballad singer Willie Scott and, probably our biggest success, the Irish sean nos singer, Joe Heaney, who packed the Concert Hall.

The program for the 1978 Larrikin Festival of Folklife.

Australian artists were primarily drawn from the Larrikin family and included Jeannie Lewis, Margret RoadKnight, Eric Bogle, Jim Jarvis, Cathie O'Sullivan, Keith Garvie, The Larrikins, Bernard Bolan, and The Bushwackers, to name but a handful. Many of the Australian concerts thematically celebrated the bush, city living, indigenous music, and even one memorable one of yarn telling, bush poetry, and bird imitations! With news of the closing of The Regent Theatre, we drew the final curtains on the festival.

In 2016, to mark the fortieth year of the Sydney Festival, the festival director, Lieven Bertels invited me to create a stage show for the Famous Spiegeltent. Titled '40 Ways to Love Your City' the show featured Mic Conway, Christa Hughes, Marcus Holden and a cast of musicians. I had come full circle with the festival.

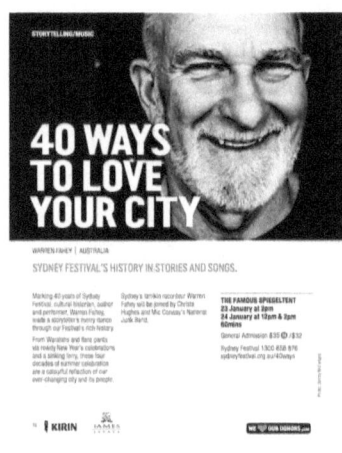

2016 Sydney Festival '40 Ways to Love Your City'

Also coming full circle was an invitation in 2022 from the incoming festival director, Olivia Ansell, to recreate a month of Sundays during which I recreated the Sydney Domain's Speaker's Corner at the festival's club.

Writing songs and getting them out to listeners is always a challenge and frustration shared by writers, singers, publishers and record labels. Once again, Larrikin's idea of success was to sell enough to recoup the outlay in manufacturing and marketing and, looking back, I suspect fifty per cent worked. This, of course, is not a reflection on the songs because so many variables jump up as roadblocks. Radio airplay was always the main obstacle for independent labels like Larrikin. I gave up on commercial radio very early on when I realised the hard fact that they were not at all interested in music. How silly of me to think radio stations would actually like music. Getting music reviews and articles in the popular press was also a challenge as we needed to push aside the big promo budgets of the major companies. Thankfully, there were reviewers interested in music and our labels in particular. Larrikin employed a publicist and had a succession of dedicated publicists, including Rob

Miller, Kay Blackman and Morag White, who understood what was needed and appreciated my instructions of 'don't knock on doors - knock them down'.

Larrikin's brigade of singer-songwriters included John Summers, Phyl Lobl, Bernard Bolan, Bob Hudson, Casey Chambers & The Dead Ringers, Mark Pengilly, Robyn Archer, Kev Carmody, John Ewbank, Doug Ashdown and Anne Infante, to name a handful. We were also releasing some great Australian blues but it was our jazz releases that attracted a following: Johnny Nicol, Marie Wilson, Christine Sullivan, Noel Crow, Dick Hughes, Bob Bertles, Brian Browne, Serge Ermoll, Kerrie Biddell, Chris Duffy, Bruce Cale, Marie Montgomery, Charlie Munro and Onaje.

In 1977 I teamed up with country music historian Eric Watson, and we launched a new label division for Australian country music. We released around 25 albums, including the double historic collection *'Country Music in Australia'*. We also championed Reg Poole, a singing farmer and legendary singer. Later, I released the recordings of legends Chad Morgan and Reg Lindsay - two originals and all-around good blokes. I see the history of Australian country music intertwined with the history of early Australian radio and the gramophone industry. In some ways, I accept responsibility for keeping the flame alive by reissuing the vintage material. In 2012 I produced a two-CD compilation titled *'Down the Overlander Trail'* for ABC Music, where I tracked the pioneer artists including Art Leonard, Smoky Dawson, Buddy Williams, Smilin' Billy Blinkhorn, Bob Dyer, Shirley Thoms, Tim McNamara, The McKean Sisters and, of course, Reg Lindsay, Chad Morgan and Slim Dusty.

Larrikin was probably so closely associated with folk music because I was actively performing with my group, The Larrikins, and also regularly on ABC radio. Oddly, as mentioned, most of my own recordings came out on the ABC Music label and not Larrikin. The Larrikin key folk performers were Sirocco, Cathie O'Sullivan, The Bushwackers, Dave de Hugard and Gary Shearston. Our compilations were another side of the label story. *'On The Steps of the Dole Office Door'* and *'Game As Ned Kelly'*, conceived by Graham Seal, were timeless. If you wanted shearing songs, bushranger ballads, union songs, convict ballads, etc., you automatically turned to the Larrikin catalogue. Ditto indigenous recordings, where the Larrikin catalogue offered more than one hundred releases.

I liked releasing series, figuring that if you find an audience for a particular field of music, you could build up a market for similar music. I had already issued some theatre music with the wonderfully eccentric Denis Watkin's musical *'Dingo Girl'*, and his co-write with Nick Enright 'The Venetian Twins', plus two recordings with songstress Geraldine Turner. The latter earned my favourite album title *'Torch Songs and Some Not So Torturous'* (1985). Mind you, I could probably add my title for Renee Geyer's Paul Kelly-produced album *'Difficult Woman'*. Renee, she of the melting voice and difficult reputation, wanted to call her Paul Kelly-produced album 'Winter, Summer, Fall & Spring', and I baulked, suggesting *'Difficult Woman'* as a far more suitable title. It has recently been released on vinyl.

With the success of Eric Bogle's albums, we also did a deal whereby Larrikin strengthened its fledgling music publishing business, Larrikin Music. However, it didn't take long to realise that it was extremely difficult for a small publisher to collect income from overseas releases, especially from independent labels. In the late seventies, Eric achieved considerable success with a number one in the Irish charts (The Furies) and an increasing number of cover versions of his songs. In the days before email, it was nigh impossible to do the accounting and collection. Norm Lurie, the newly appointed MD of the international music publishing company, Music Sales International, introduced me to its owner, Bob Wise. I liked Bob and his approach to music publishing (he also owned Oak Publications), and I especially liked him when he offered to purchase Larrikin Music. Long story short, Bob and Norm wanted to use the purchase of Larrikin Music to build their Australian publishing arm. After due diligence, it was obvious that apart from Eric Bogle, Mike Jackson, Bernard Bolan and a few other writers, there wasn't much value, but they bought it and relieved me of a headache. Then, a few years late, they gave me a far bigger headache when I found out they were taking legal action against Men At Work and their label, EMI, for infringement of copyright in using a sample from the children's rhyme 'Kookaburra Sits On The Old Gumtree'. Ouch! I knew this was not going to end happily.

The Kookaburra saga continued for several years, and, as I have often said, the only people who made money from the legal stoush were the lawyers. It was all very unfortunate. After buying Larrikin Music, Music Sales bought the rights of 'Kookaburra Sits in the Old Gum Tree' for around $5000 from the State Library of South Australia, who had been left the song in the will of its creator, Marion Sinclair. They put the song out for tender and Music Sales were the successful bidder. Most people were shocked and assumed the innocent children's rhyme was traditional and in the public domain. It wasn't, and Music Sales had every right in the world to buy it and add it to the Larrikin Music catalogue. After the song was used in a question on the ABC television music quiz *Spicks & Specks* the legal battle commenced. I was asked to be an 'expert witness' for both sides of the argument but declined, believing it was inappropriate.

After the verdict, in favour of Music Sales International, I went public on ABC radio and on my website, explaining that I believed the entire affair to be unnecessary and painful. Considering the song's iconic status, I even suggested that Music Sales gift the song to the Australian people through the National Film and Sound Archive. They could have made such an arrangement through the Cultural Gift Program and received, at least, their original purchase of the song rights and their reputation. I was concerned that Australian children were deprived of a simple nursery-style song long held to be traditional. If a music publisher could sue and win a case against Men At Work what chance would a school or performer have in using it?

However, I often explained that I would never have sued Men At Work, that I had worked with Colin Hay, and that I sold the publishing company years before the court action, but I couldn't win. I received death threats and vile abuse and was continually linked to the case by ill-informed media stories. Thankfully, many Australian performers came to my rescue to explain the facts, but because of my association with the word 'larrikin' through my record label, music distribution company and performance persona, I was damned. Google 'larrikin', and there I am. I still get the occasional online abuse and patiently explain my innocence.

In 2010 I was awarded Australia's major prize for lifetime achievement in music. The Don Banks Music Award (established in 1984), administered by the Australia Council for the Arts, is a true honour and had previously been given to 'serious' music people, classical and jazz composers, conductors and performers. I was thrilled to be the one to break the musical mould and pleased to say that subsequent recipients included non-classical artists Archie Roach and David Bridie. My award was presented on the main Budawang stage at the National Folk Festival, which was quite an event. The Minister for the Arts, Peter Garrett, made the presentation, and later, we burned the midnight oil celebrating.

Midnight Oil's and then Minister for the Arts, Peter Garrett, at the national Folk Festival 2010.

Gongs are definitely very nice, and the Don Banks Music Award was the only one to come with a big fat cheque; however, the others are equally appreciated as they recognise I have done something positive with my life.

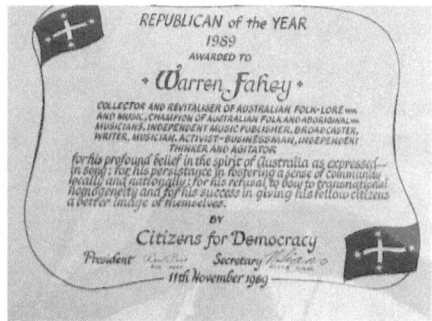

Republican of the Year waiting for the Republic!

My first award, in 1984, was the Advance Australia Award, a government recognition for exporting music and culture, then came Republican of the Year in 1989, then the Order of Australia AM in 1997 "In recognition of service to Australian music and Australian folklore, particularly as a record producer, broadcaster, author, folklore collector and performer". 2000 Australian Music Industry Person of the Year. 2001 Prime Minister's Centenary Medal for services to the Australian music industry. In 2004, the Judith Hosier Award: Bush Laureate Golden Gumleaf Award for lifetime achievement in bush balladry. And, in 2015, the Australasian Sound Recording Association Lifetime Achievement Award. There were also a few lifetime membership awards: Folk Federation of NSW, Potts Point Partnership and patronage of Heritage and Arts, South Australia. Thanks, folks.

In late 1995 I sold Larrikin Records, once again reckoning twenty years was enough time to own any business. I also wanted out of the financial stress. After buying Avan-Gard Music in 1991 and moving into their Newtown warehouse, and, after a year of running out of room, we relocated the entire operation to an industrial business complex, Harcourt Business Park, on Botany Road, Rosebery. It was large, secure, and had a large warehouse and office suitable for the rapidly growing company. By late 1994, we had a staff of around forty, including interstate sales offices. Forty people, plus all our agents, relying on me for wages and well-being was stressful. The company was going gangbusters; we'd even had a mega hit selling over 100,000 copies of the soundtrack of Michael Nyman's 'The Piano'. All the money I had received from selling the Paddington building and the Folkways Music business went gurgling into the record company. Larrikin was distributing some of the world's greatest independent record labels, and our warehouse stock sheets showed over fifty thousand titles. We were sitting on warehouse stock of over four million dollars at cost. Annual sales topped nearly sixteen million, however, at any one time, perennial late-paying customers also owed us around three million dollars. We had far too many customers, and sadly, too many went broke on us. Brashs, the largest chain in Australia, closed shop, Edels went down and so did dozens of small retailers. We all had to pay our suppliers, label partners and company obligations. It was hard and stressful and I wanted out. I also wanted the bank off my home mortgage. In looking around for a likely buyer, there weren't a lot of choices.

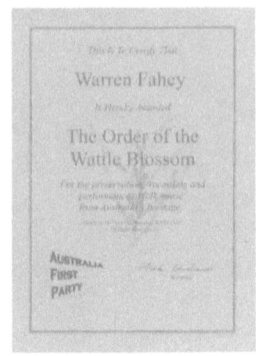

Another award for the shelf. What'll I do with it?

Festival Records, owned by News Ltd, offered a fabulous history and, at the time, felt the heat from the dog-eat-dog multinational companies who continued to yap at their heels and take their label partners. Most of these labels sold to majors on an international basis, and Festival suffered through no fault of their own. Buying Larrikin made sense because it represented over 120 quality labels, which could immediately help Festival's sales figures. Geoff Weule made the initial approach to writing to Festival. Lachlan Murdoch and Festival's Chairman, Alan Hely, signed off on the deal and in October 1995, the company merged with the Festival Mushroom Group. In agreeing to the buyout, Festival also wanted my key staff and me, so we went from working for Larrikin on Friday to working for Larrikin *at* Festival on Monday. I was still the MD of my own company and freed from the stress of ownership. Yippee. I was also relieved to have found employment for a dozen of my trusty staff, including Larrikin's General Manager, Geoff Weule.

I loved Festival although there were obvious inherited problems. It had far too many staff. I was shocked to find it had a carpentry department and its own canteen. The staff were loyal, and many had been with the company through thick and thin. These were thin times, and the future didn't look too solid as the industry was changing rapidly as it came to terms with technological change. I was also shocked to discover I was the only person with an email account in the company. Festival's business practises were old school, including all international business being conducted via fax. Under Alan Hely, recently appointed MD and longtime staff member, Bill Eeg worked with company public officer Bill Hoey. My old surfing mate from school, Anthony Givney, was the finance manager.

After six months, I was summoned into News Ltd's head office to meet with Lachlan Murdoch, who wanted to know what I thought of Festival's operation. "In need of oxygen," was my response "and some serious redirection," Murdoch instructed Hely to appoint me deputy group MD. Alan gave his Chairman's office to Bill Eeg, and I took Bill's MD office with its notorious red light over the door - a leftover from the Jim White era. When the red light was on, no one dared knock on the door, not even if the company scored a number one record! In joining Festival, I embraced its history and staff but was also party to some serious business rationalisation. It employed more people than multinationals WEA and BMG and needed a haircut.

It also needed to modernise. I always arrived at the Pyrmont office early, around 7.45 am, but Bill Eeg always beat me. I didn't realise his main aim was to get to the fax room and take all the faxes. Later in the morning, we would get a folder with our faxes and occasional messages scribbled on them from Bill. It was his way of staying in touch. He and I were the only ones with keys to the fax room. It was ridiculous, and one day, I exploded and told him the company had to get News Ltd to set up an email service immediately.

Alan Hely was preparing to retire, and unbeknown to Bill Eeg (but certainly known by me since I had recommended him to

Lachlan Murdoch), Roger Grierson was about to be appointed Chairman. Bill made a quick exit along with a parade of staff. 1998 was the time for the old guard to be changed. I think Roger was an inspired choice to shake up the company. He had worked for me (and, I suspect, at the same time, himself) at Larrikin; we had a label with Stuart Coupe; he was rock-connected, a performer and, above all, a rebel. He and I were a good team and had a lot of laughs as we set to remake the company. At one stage, we discussed employing a skateboarder to zip up and down the corridors. When asked why? We answered, "To shake the bloody place up." Festival had also commenced the takeover of Mushroom Records. Twenty-three-year-old James Murdoch, the youngest Murdoch son, effectively became the boss of the Festival Mushroom Group. We were happy with that as James, a savvy operator, owned the punk music label, Rawkus, lived in New York, and let us have full reign.

After a year, Roger and I chatted, and he asked if I was happy. I was happy, but he knew I had taken on a lot more of the dull side of management than I wanted. I was head of sales, and marketing, overseeing A&R and music publishing and running Festival and Larrikin's labels. He knew me well and suggested we bring in Jeremy Fabyini as MD - and he could do all the stuff I wanted to escape from, especially the all-important financial management. Good idea. I willingly found a new office upstairs with my own boardroom! I could devise new CDs, sign artists and do the company projects I enjoyed here. I didn't need a red light over the door.

Festival Records had a reputation for being a 'family'. It was a strange family and, I suppose, by progression, Rupert Murdoch was the grandfather. Murdoch senior only visited the building once while I was in management. He met with Chairman Roger Grierson, Jeremy Fabyini and me to 'see how we were going'. His arrival at the reception was a great start when the receptionist, who had been briefed, didn't recognise him and asked who he was and who he wanted to see! He took it with good humour. The meeting went fine except for a lengthy hijacking when R.M. had to take an important call (from News Ltd investor Prince Al Waleed bin Talal.) It was more about Rupert endorsing the move to have his son, James, oversee the company.

The rest of Festival's family, including the distant Mushroom members mostly based in Melbourne, were staffers who had been with the company for what seemed like centuries. All good people, but there was a dearth of talent and a sense of desperation. Chart positions were few, the catalogue was tired, enthusiasm was hard to muster, and the former oil company building was not conducive to efficient or effective work. I arranged for interior decorator Brian Kiernan to refresh the reception and boardroom, making cosmetic changes but at least a brighter change. I loved that the company had its offices, studio, music publishing and warehouse all under the same roof. At one stage, it even had its own factory to pump out vinyl records by the millions. It had a history in an industry with small regard for history.

I was busy. I arranged the reissue of the remastered Sherbet catalogue, signed country artist Adam Brand, produced several new Larrikin titles and set about reissuing the historic Spin catalogue of early Australian rock and roll in collaboration with Festival's sound engineer Warren Barnett. Festival had also built itself by working with collaborators, often seen as estranged members of the family, and I wanted to bring them back into the fold. I fostered better relations with key allies, including Col Joye at ATA, and producers Martin Erdman, Brendan Gallagher and Garth Porter. Making the wheels of the music industry turn is a people business.

I had been appointed to the Australian Record Industry Association (ARIA) Board in 1984 to represent independent record labels. Prior to this, ARIA had been a tightly-held 'boy's club'. I remained on the board up until 1994 and then, occasionally thereafter, joined representing Festival Mushroom. I have to say that, recent history aside, I always found Sony's Denis Handlin and the rest of the board extremely supportive of my independent spirit. It's certainly a brain-stretcher to ask, 'where are they all now?' It was encouraging to see Natalie Waller, Head of ABC Music & Events, elected Chair of ARIA.

Back at Pyrmont, I started the wheels rolling for Festival's 50th-anniversary celebrations with a focus retrospective exhibition at the Powerhouse Museum curated by Peter Cox. 'Spinning Around', named after Kylie Minogue's hit song, was a spectacular success. It was fun hunting the building for treasures, and we found long-lost boxes of artist contracts, old posters, catalogues and some oddities to tell the company's illustrious history. Even newbie Larrikin got a head's up in the exhibition.

For a couple of years I sat on the News Ltd synergy board, which represented management of the various News Ltd companies, including News Digital, Harper Collins Publishers, Foxtel and Festival Mushroom Group. If nothing else, the experience showed me just how big and disjointed major corporations can be.

The gang of four, James, Roger, Jeremy and myself, redesigned the company dramatically. The record industry was changing at one hundred miles an hour, and being independent; we had to change quickly. A decision was made to trim the catalogues and concentrate on developing Australian artists. Considering my history in producing Australian music, I couldn't argue against this. On the dark side, it meant saying goodbye to Festival and Larrikin's label partners, most of whom went back twenty-five years or more. These were hard decisions. Labels felt deserted - where could they go? Some, like Prestige Fantasy, had an impressive history with well over five million local sales on the Creedence Clearwater Revival catalogue alone. We had to say farewell to some of the world's most respected labels like Rounder, Virgin Venture, World Circuit, Arc, Saydisc, Real World, Pointblank, Topic, Telarc, Concord and Shanachie. Our catalogue shrunk, and a new distribution deal established with Sony BMG saw our warehouse close. Even the canteen and legendary recording studio shut shop.

The gamble paid off, and in 2002, Festival Mushroom had Australia's highest-selling single and a string of album hits. Overheads were also considerably lower.

I spent nearly six years with Festival. They were good years and challenging. Lots of nice people and memories but I was growing bored of predictability, tired of nine-to-five, typically eight-to-seven, and, besides, I knew I had a few more challenges left in me. Roger ambushed me one day and asked if I wanted to escape. Saying I could stay as long as I wanted, but if I wanted to jump, he'd make it very easy with a year's salary. I didn't have to think twice. The biggest pay-off came when I realised News Ltd, in taking over Larrikin Entertainment Pty Ltd, had also taken over my superannuation dating back to when Noah was in the Ark. For the first time, I had decent money in the bank and no mortgage.

The first thing I did when I left Festival was worry about what I'd do with my time. I was fifty-five and reasoned too young to sit and stare at the television. I took a small Paddington office and started receiving emails from many of the record labels I had represented at Festival. I had no intention of establishing another Larrikin Distribution, but here I was back representing Rounder, Topic, Shanachie and a dozen other labels. I called the new company Planet Distribution and decided to do it differently - no warehouse and, apart from my assistant, no staff. I did a distribution and warehouse deal with Sebastian Chase of MGM, and we were away. A year later, Shanachie USA suggested I create Shanachie Australia and go on their payroll. So, Planet became Shanachie Australia and all distributed through MGM. I realised I was trapped again. After a year, I told Richard Nevins, co-owner of Shanachie, I didn't want to be 'employed', and Shanachie returned to being Planet Distribution. I was getting giddy. To add to my life, I started a new record company, Undercover Music Australia, with Nick and Tony Wales as partners. We also put this through MGM. In 2004 I sold Planet Distribution to MGM for peanuts. It still operates successfully and offers an impressive catalogue of imported distributed labels.

Undercover Music still operates, has nearly 200 albums in its catalogue, and in 2023 celebrated its twenty-first anniversary. Managed by our 'staff of one', Stuart McCarthy, it does an outstanding job releasing and marketing what I describe as 'intelligent' music. We don't chase big-budget pop, preferring to issue indigenous, folk, songwriters and project albums. Many of Larrikin's artists are now represented by Undercover's Rouseabout Records, a label I devised and executive produce. Recordings include the extensive Robyn Archer and Eric Bogle catalogues, John Munro, Buddy Knox, CODA, Gary Shearston and Russell Morris. It has also allowed me to indulge in historical reissues, including several recent productions devised by Michael Alexandratos, a gifted young musicologist specialising in vinyl heritage compilations. Some of his releases are fascinating, like the one showing the misappropriation of Aboriginality in popular music and the vintage Hawaiian compilations. Rouseabout is a purposely low-key label of love and quality. Mind you, I'm still not sure if anyone cares!

A BUSINESS that makes nothing but money is a poor business.

18

IS IT THAT TIME, ALREADY?

As I write this, I am in my late seventies, hurtling towards a birthdate clash I can't avoid. Thankfully, I am relatively healthy, financially secure and surrounded by people I love and who love me. They say genes are everything and, thankfully, the Fahey and Phillips are relatively long-livers. Having seen my three-score-and-ten in the rear vision mirror, I am now looking at my own mortality and determined to continue living with hope and happiness as long as possible. It is daunting to think my next milestone will be eighty.

I run to a timetable. I am more fowl than owl. I wake with the birds and prefer to hit the sack no later than 11 pm, earlier if I wish. I can't say I get tired, but evenings are generally a wasted opportunity. Apart from dinners with friends, a show or film night, I do not work in the evening. Reading is enjoyable but I am prone to nodding off. I don't nap during the day, although I hear it's recommended. My day is for work. If you could call my folklore research, writing, speaking or performing 'work'.

I enjoy cooking and sharing food. Scraping, chopping and even washing up is enjoyable. I am a decent cook, although Mark always accuses me of making things up when I should, possibly, refer to the occasional recipe. I make labneh nearly every week. I soak and prepare lentils for curries and boil up rice puddings, and our refrigerator is usually bulging. Occasionally I will bake what I call 'healthy' biscuits. Food for me has always been a joy. Memo to self: I think some of my clothes have been shrinking lately!

ONE OF THE drawbacks of aging is the continuing loss of friends. It often feels like hardly a month passes without someone or other checking out. I get sad rather than depressed and then bolster myself by check-listing why I liked their company and why we remained connected for so long. Although social media has a dark and often insanely irresponsible side, it has been wonderful for reconnecting with old friends. I have always travelled in wide circles, and receiving the 'do you remember when…' messages is heartening. We have one life, and we should celebrate it.

Ageing also slows the body and changes us in so many ways, and in writing this memoir, going back into my own 'time machine', I am brutally aware that life is wonderful and, as they say, 'it is whatever you make of it.' Of course, sometimes, the process can be tricky. One of my oldest friends is experiencing creeping dementia. He is not ready to pack up and shuffle off, he happens to be exactly my age, but the memory loss is a reality. I stepped up to become his Enduring Guardian and Power of Attorney a few years back. It is a responsibility that assures him that he will complete his life cycle knowing all will be well. That's what friends are for.

2020, the year of COVID, was a year of fear and determination. I feared for the world as millions died of the virus. I feared for America as the madness of Donald Trump accelerated, especially post-election. I feared for Australia as the worst bushfires in my history ripped across the land. Floods came next, then a plague of mice. I feared for all those people living with fear. Early on in the year, as COVID alarms were ringing, I became determined to turn what was to be the strangest of years into a year of productivity. During the isolation period, I set out to video myself singing a song a day and posting it to my Facebook page. I saw it as an opportunity to document some of my favourite songs and poems and also a challenge to improve my concertina playing as accompaniment. I eventually stopped at 85 songs, considering my personal challenge achieved. I subsequently added them all (and more) to my website. Mid-year, I accepted an invitation to host one of the Home-baked Concertina programs in a series of six. I also sang a song in this series. The 2021 Sydney Folk Festival was scheduled to take place in August; however, like many musical events, it was cancelled and replaced by a Zoom festival. I did a 30-minute bracket in the opening concert and a two-hour workshop the next day. It was peculiar performing to a hidden audience, but it worked.

My biggest challenge of the year came when I successfully gained a City of Sydney Creative Fellowship. Knowing so many artists had seen their bookings blown away, the City offered a series of grants for innovative programs. Mine was a series of twelve short video programs on 'curious aspects of Sydney's history'. It must have read like an 'offer too good to refuse,' and I successfully bagged a $15,000 grant. The Vine Foundation also contributed an additional $8,000 to make the program viable. I called it *The Sydney Dozen*, but later, as I started to edit, I realised *Sydney Stories with Warren Fahey* would have more traction. The Folk Federation of NSW acted as the auspice organisation for the grants. The National Film & Sound Archive became my collaboration partner offering film footage and digital release on their YouTube channel. The twelve stories examine Sydney's curious history, including programs on the Domain, Convicts, Kings Cross, Larrikins, Early Burial Grounds, Social Life, Chinese, Sydney Royal Easter Show, Youth Tribes and Sydney Harbour. It's a very mixed bunch. The talented video creator Mic Gruchy, my collaborator on the 2010 Biennale of Sydney multi-screen installation *'Damned Souls & Turning Wheels'*, came in as editor. I am still shaking my head trying to work out how I made twelve fifteen-minute films for $23,000, which is less than $2,000 a film. After paying film and music rights, recording studio work and Mic's final edits, there wasn't a great deal over to cover my creative work, including research, scripting and preparing running production guides, but, at the back of my skull, I figured the cultural karma would be sufficient return. Maybe the satisfaction of completing another project was return enough. https://www.nfsa.gov.au/tags/sydney-stories

In 2021 the cultural karma did pay off when, COVID housebound, I devised a new series of videos. *Outback Stories* celebrates the pioneering spirit of the men and women of the outback, especially in the nineteenth and early twentieth centuries. I tend to go at new projects like a 'bull in a china shop' - do the research, write the first draft of scripts, scratch my head, and think about how best to make the dream a reality. In this case, I had an advantage. Christo Reid, the great-grandson of Sidney Reid, who married one of Sidney Kidman's daughters, offered me the use of the family's 16mm films. Kidman had bought a camera and film, handed it to his son-in-law (also a director of the Kidman firm), and said, "Film me and the outback." The pair took an extended tour of Kidman's rural NSW and Queensland properties. The film footage became the nucleus of the video project. The next step was to take my begging bowl to the National Film and Sound Archive so I could plunder their collection. This would be a far more expensive series than *Sydney Stories* because there was so much archive film to access. I sent a proposal to 'Twiggy' Forrest thinking this was a natural sponsorship from R.M. Williams. I received a 'thanks but no thanks' reply. I do not give up lightly, so I sent the proposal in several other directions. Driz-a-bone - ideal, but short of marketing dollars at the time of my approach. Then a friend-of-a-friend, familiar with my approach to history and storytelling, suggested he knew someone who knew Gina Rinehart.

Long story short, Mrs R is Chair of S. Kidman & Co, a lover of bush poetry and a woman of considerable means. S. Kidman & Co became the sponsor of *Outback Stories*. There was only one proviso - that I make one of the films be about her great-grandfather, James Nicholas and another about Sidney Kidman. I had never heard of Nicholas, but after digging through TROVE, I realised this was a terrific story, and the man was a major figure in the story of Cobb & Co. My gal pal and cultural hero, Rebel Penfold Russell, also returned to help fund the project through Rebel Films and The Vine Foundation, a family philanthropic fund. I was off and running. Once again, I collaborated with the hugely talented Mic Gruchy and Marcus Holden and, between the three of us, delivered a series of films that, I believe, salute the outback and its pioneers. I am fond of saying, 'It doesn't matter if your family came out on the First Fleet or a leaky boat last week, this modern country was built in the outback, and we should always celebrate its heritage'.

Promotional flyer for the 2023 stage show.

Where to next? Although I am continually juggling projects, I am never too sure what the future holds. I believe I still have a few tricks up my sleeve. In 2023 I joined the renowned British singer Martyn Wyndham-Read, and Clare O'Meara for a season of performances of Martyn's stage show *I Don't Go Shearing Now*. It's a celebration of the shearing songs, poems and stories of the golden age of wool. It was enjoyable to share the stage with Martyn again. We toured NSW's 'sheep country' (Dalton, Goulburn, Carcoar, Braidwood and Gunning). Also, we performed three shows at the National Folk

Festival - an appropriate place, as I always refer to Canberra as 'a good sheep station ruined!'

WRITING KEEPS ME BUSY. A friend, another author, Tim Duggan, interviewed me in March 2023 for his next book on maintaining creativity as you age. Hmm, interesting subject, and I sprouted forth on how I remain focussed in a world of distraction. I am usually at my desk by 8.30 am and still tapping away at 6 pm. I am conscious of not allowing myself to sit for long periods and make sure I stand, twirl and take the dog for a walk. Cooking is another distraction. My penchant for undertaking several projects simultaneously ensures my mind doesn't get too comfortable.

Some projects nag me, and others frustrate me because they depend on other people's decision-making. For example, I have a book I commenced four years ago, *A Hop, a Skip and a Jump' - a compendium of Australian childhood amusements'* and, as I write this, it is sitting on my computer staring at me. This memoir jumped the queue, and I now need to revisit the children's book manuscript and do something with it. This is how I work - on several projects until one of them pushes the others aside.

I've also got a couple of other books churning in my mind's eye. Hopefully, there are still a few people out there who'd like to hear some old bush songs, concertina tunes, yarns, and recitations to remind them about who we are and the tracks we have travelled as a nation. And, of course, I can always smell the sea's salt and hear the sirens calling me to travel.

IT'S A CRAZY LARRIKIN LIFE, alright!

ABOUT THE AUTHOR

Warren Fahey has been a voice on ABC radio for over fifty-five years. In 1968, he began regularly reviewing books on music and folklore and presented Australia's first radio series on world music. He went on to script several major series exploring Australian stories and folksong, including *The Australian Legend*, *While the Billy Boils* and *The Songs That Made Australia*. With the launch of ABCFM, he became a regular on *Sunday Folk*. ABC Music and ABC Books went on to release his catalogue of records and books. For the past twenty-five years, he has contributed as 'the expert 'talking head' when the ABC can't find an expert!' - discussing everything from the history of the bush biscuit to Australian slanguage, convict stories to tales about maritime mysteries.

The ABC partnered with Warren's music company, Larrikin Records, for a decade in presenting the annual Sydney Festival Larrikin Folklife Concert Series, broadcasting the recordings on ABCFM. His Folkways Music stores were legendary for their specialist catalogue of recordings, music books and musical instruments.

Considered one of Australia's foremost cultural historians, he has been honoured with the Order of Australia, Advance Australia Award, Judith Hosier Golden Gumleaf Award for lifetime services to the bush ballad, The Australasian Sound Recording Association's Lifetime Achievement Award, the Prime Minister's Centenary Medal and, in 2010, Australia's highest award for lifetime achievement in music, The Don Banks Music Award.

Author of over thirty books and producer of over 800 Australian recordings, he is a sometimes actor, singer, filmmaker and heritage events producer.

ALSO BY WARREN FAHEY

Dead & Buried. The curious history of Sydney's earliest burial grounds'. Print & Kindle eBook.

All At Sea - *Australian Maritime Traditions*, Bodgie Books. Kindle. eBook

The Good Old Bad Old Days - *a curious history of Woolloomooloo, Potts Point, Kings Cross, Elizabeth & Rushcutters Bay*, Bodgie Books. Print & Kindle eBook

The World Turned Upside-down - *a history of the Australian Gold Rush*, Bodgie Books. Kindle eBook

Australia: Its Folksongs & Bush Ballads, ABC Books

Australia: Its Folksongs & Bush Ballads, ABC/Harper Collins. three-volume eBook.

Sing Us Anothery, Dirty As Buggery. - *Australian bawdry*, Bodgie Books. Kindle eBook

Manar: a Potts Point local history, Bodgie Books. Print & Apple/Kindle eBook.

Old Bush Songs - *the centenary edition* (with Graham Seal), ABC Books.

Classic Bush Yarns, Harper Collins. Print & Kindle eBook

Great Aussie Yarns, A&R Harper Collins.

The Big Fat Book of Aussie Jokes: Australian humour at work in the 21st Century, Harper Collins. Print & Kindle eBook

Ratbags & Rabble-rousers - *Australian political parody and satire in the 20th century*, Currency Press.

Diggers' Songs - *the songs Australian diggers sang in eleven wars from the Maori Wars to the Gulf War*, Australian Military History Press

When Mabel Laid The Table - *the folklore of eating and drinking in Australia from colonial days to takeaways*, ABC Books

The Balls of Bob Menzies - *Australian political folklore from Federation onwards*, A&R Harper Collins.

The Songs That Made Australia - *107 bush songs*, A&R

Australian Folksong Guide - *the bush band*, CBC

Eureka. - *the social history of Australia as seen through song*, Omnibus Press.

Pint Pot & Billy. *A selection of Australian songs*, William Collins

Joe Watson - his life and times, Folklore Associates

Folklore of the Australian Wedding, Bodgie Books. Kindle eBook.

While The Billy Boils. *Australian history (with accompanying 16 tape set)*, ABC Books

Tucker Track: *the curious history of Australian food*, ABC Books.

Contributor. Oxford Companion to Australian Folklore, Oxford University Press

Contributor. The Stockman, Kevin Weldon Publishing

Contributor. The Companion to Australian Music, Currency Press

Contributor. Missing in Action, MUP

Contributor. Australian Almanac 1989/1991/1992, Angus & Robertson/HC

Contributor. Verandah Music, Curtin University

Contributor. Folklore Essays (edited Graham Seal/Jennifer Gall) 2010 Curtin University Press

Over the years, ABC Music, Larrikin Records and Rouseabout Records have issued Warren Fahey's extensive catalogue of recordings. They are all up on Spotify, iTunes and whatever the latest digital platform is this week.

www.ingramcontent.com/pod-product-compliance
Lightning Source LLC
Chambersburg PA
CBHW022049290426
44109CB00014B/1034